Jump In!

Mark
Burnett

Jump In!

Even If
You Don't Know
How to Swim

BALLANTINE BOOKS
NEW YORK

Published in the United States by Ballantine Books, an imprint of
The Random House Publishing Group, a division of
Random House, Inc., New York.

Ballantine and colophon are registered trademarks
of Random House, Inc.

Library of Congress Cataloging-in-Publication Data

Burnett, Mark (James Mark)
Jump in! : even if you don't know how to swim/Mark Burnett.—1st ed.
p.   cm.
ISBN 0-345-48098-8
1. Burnett, Mark (James Mark) 2. Television producers and directors—
Great Britain—Biography. I. Title.
PN1992.4.B89J8 2005
791.4502'092—dc22   [B]   2004062681

Printed in the United States of America

Ballantine Books website address: www.ballantinebooks.com

9 8 7 6 5 4 3 2 1

FIRST EDITION

Book design by Carole Lowenstein

For James and Cameron,
always remember in order to succeed
you must be willing to fail.
I hope you both always
"Jump In."

Acknowledgments

A big thank you to the show runners, producers, field producers, editors, assistant editors, loggers, casting associates, accountants, camera, sound, art department, unit and challenge teams on shows like *Eco-Challenge, Apprentice, Casino, Contender, Restaurant,* and *Survivor,* who number more than 1500. It is impossible to thank you all individually, but you know who you are.

I will confine my individual acknowledgments to those directly involved in the writing of this book.

I'd like to first thank Marty Dugard, with whom I worked on my previous three books, and who again played an enormous role in guiding me through this process. Other huge contributors were my "reality show" coordinator Kristen Parks who traveled the world with me, pushing me to write every day while on various locations, and my tireless office staff of Barbara Bellanca, Cecilia Le, and Renee De Los Santos who worked the long hours necessary to keep my world running smoothly and get the details of this book pushed through.

I would also like to thank Rachael Harrell, Diane Winkler, Casey Capshaw, Michaela Starr, Kevin Gilbert, and Sue Guercioni for their invaluable contributions, and also my book agent, Scott Waxman. This could not have been achieved without the tireless efforts of Nancy Miller and Dana Isaacson at Random House.

A special thank you to Conrad Riggs who has played a huge role in all of this, and has always been in the driver's seat of the innovative deal-making for Mark Burnett Productions.

Thanks to my parents for making me believe anything was possible and for always encouraging even my craziest of ideas. And lastly, thank you to my sons James and Cameron for being so willing to embrace the adventure and for never making me feel bad for the long absences when they were younger.

Contents

Introduction

Mark Burnett is many things to many people, but above all, he is a great visionary. Before Mark approached me to work with him and star in *The Apprentice,* many other television networks had likewise asked me to do a reality show. As good as they are at selling, I had absolutely no interest. But when Mark presented his concept to me, it was a combination of his idea, track record, and salesmanship that left no doubt in my mind—I would do *The Apprentice* with Mark Burnett.

Mark is a great leader as well as a visionary—an unbeatable combination for out-of-the-box success, which accounts for our over-the-top ratings for *The Apprentice.* Mark was able to describe an exciting, incredible, groundbreaking show to me because he could already see it happening. He convinced me to see it his way, and because of his vision we've got a huge hit on our hands. Working with Mark has been a great experience—not only because of the tremendous success *The Apprentice* has attained, but also because I truly enjoy working with people of great talent—and Mark tops that list. Few people realize the tremendous work and high levels of brainpower necessary to create a great, successful show, and the leadership required to make it happen.

I'm proud to call Mark Burnett a friend as well as a partner. He's a great example for people of all ages. When he told me my first book, *The Art of the Deal,* was instrumental in successfully turning his life around, it made me understand something else about Mark: He pays attention, learns, applies what he's learned, and moves forward with everything he's got. His innovations have changed the television industry for the better, and his vision, leadership, and humanitarian principles will continue to distinguish him for years to come.

The book you are about to read is more than a motivational business primer or a fast-moving adventure story—though it is certainly both of those things. Above all, this is the inspirational rags-to-riches story of an American immigrant. Arriving nearly penniless in the United States, Mark transformed hard work and an inspired vision into the realization of the American dream. Mark doesn't feel the need to overanalyze and micromanage everything he does. Instead, he continually moves forward, relying primarily on his instinct and energy. Now a major power broker in the entertainment industry, Mark truly jumps in (sometimes literally!) to each successive exciting venture with deep courage and great enthusiasm. Readers of this rousing book would be wise to follow this gifted man's example and jump in!

—DONALD J. TRUMP
November 13, 2004

Jump In!

Chapter One

Jump In

I pulled up to the guard gate at Universal Studios in my triple black 1969 Firebird convertible, living the Hollywood dream. I was on my way to meet with none other than Steven Spielberg. We had never met before, but I had dreamed of this day for years. Just getting this meeting had given me a temporary membership in Hollywood's Big Boy Club—with a heavy accent on "temporary." What I would do with that membership—whether I could turn it into an opportunity for greater success or whether I would fail to seize the moment—was up to me.

Now, my triple black Firebird is a car near and dear to my heart. I grew up in London, but the muscle car phenomenon is distinctly American, something I saw only in the movies—something I always wished I'd been a part of but had missed out on. In fact, the only truly selfish gift I had bought myself after the success of my television shows was the Firebird. Only eleven hundred of this particular model with black exterior, black interior, and a black convertible soft top (hence "triple black") were manufactured. I love this car. There's nothing like putting down its roof and getting behind that wheel. Of course, it's an old car, constantly "running a little hot." Despite knowing it was over ninety degrees that afternoon in the San Fernando Valley, I still decided to put the roof down and drive the Firebird to my meeting with Spielberg. It felt so good as it rumbled nicely along the beach road through Malibu

canyon and onto the 101 freeway, where the ocean breezes were replaced by the stifling heat of the Valley. As I drove toward Universal, the
engine temperature rose a little, but all seemed well until I got off the
exit and stopped at the first light. Once at a standstill, the engine
coughed a little, and as the temperature dial rose quickly into the red,
my anxiety rose with it. After what seemed like an eternity, the stoplight turned green. I breathed a sigh of relief as I drove on and the temperature dropped. This scenario repeated at each subsequent stoplight.
Finally, I reached the guard gate at Universal Studios and gave my name.

One guard punched it into the computer while another gave my car
the requisite security once-over. Well, actually it was twice over. He
loved the car and asked me a hundred and one questions about this
beautiful piece of "Americana," failing to notice how the idling became
more and more irregular as the engine temperature rose. I answered the
questions about the wheels, the engine, and the brakes, all the while
praying that the guard on the computer would hurry up before the
triple black overheated.

Then, well, the triple black died.

For two whole minutes I turned the key in the ignition and pumped
the gas, struggling to get it to start. Each time it would sputter and
cough I felt a twinge of joy. But that glimmer of hope would end with
the sound of silence as the engine died again. The line of cars at the
gate, which is always four or five long, now numbered so many that I
couldn't see its end when I turned back to look. The guard tried to be
polite, but I could tell by the pained smile on his face that he didn't
know quite what to do with me and my now-useless piece of Americana. So much for my Hollywood dream day.

It wasn't supposed to be this way. I was on my way to the most important meeting of my life. Things were supposed to go smoothly. But
then, my entire career has been built on making success out of
calamity—well, if not calamity, then at least chaos. Why should this
day be any different?

Why, you might ask, would Steven Spielberg want to meet with me? After all, I just make reality television, and he makes some of the most important films of our time. The meeting came out of a new show I was making with Spielberg's partner at DreamWorks Studios, Jeffrey Katzenberg. The show is called *The Contender*, and it's unlike anything I've ever done.

My television shows have always been about reality, but in a sort of parallel universe, a place where shipwrecking regular Americans on an island and forcing MBAs to coexist in a Manhattan loft actually seems normal. However, when filming is complete, the people in my shows return to their normal lives, stepping from my reality back into their reality. They may have changed as individuals as a result of their experience, but any greater ramifications to society are minimal. I hoped this was about to change. *The Contender* has the potential to revitalize a dying institution and give glory to a group of men who have labored in obscurity their whole lives. More than any of the other reality shows I've filmed, this show will blur that line between televised reality and the world itself.

And it had begun with a surprise phone call.

December 2003: Just after returning from Panama, where I'd been filming *Survivor: All-Stars*, I was collapsed from jet lag on my office couch, watching a rough cut of the show, when the phone rang. "It's Mark," I answered.

"Mark," said a calm voice, "this is Jeffrey Katzenberg."

I was floored. This was one of the biggest, most powerful names in Hollywood, responsible for Disney's great animation hits of the 1990s—*The Lion King, Beauty and the Beast*, and *The Little Mermaid*, to name just a few—before moving on and starting DreamWorks with Steven Spielberg and David Geffen, where he produced *Shrek* and *Shrek 2*, the biggest-grossing animated film franchise of all time. He repeated his animation genius with *Shark Tale*.

"I've got an idea I'd like to discuss with you," he said. "Is there a chance we can meet sometime soon?" Within minutes, I was on my way to his Burbank office.

At our meeting, Jeffrey was complimentary, saying he considered me the best nonfiction storyteller on television. Deeply flattered, I relaxed, comfortable that the meeting was going very well. Then he asked an odd question: "Do you like boxing?"

"I *love* boxing," I immediately replied.

I wasn't just saying that because I was talking to Jeffrey Katzenberg. Two of my cousins had fought at the national level in Britain when I was growing up. One of them, Jimmy, was a British schoolboy champion. The other, Alex, was another champion, and he boxed on television. My own dad had trained them. (Once when Jimmy broke my dad's ribs with a punch, Dad complimented him on his technique!) Furthermore, every man who gets accepted into my former British Army Parachute Regiment has to go through a series of tests, one of which is a form of boxing with no rounds, sixteen-ounce gloves, and no pauses—literally a nonstop battle. Because it's nonstop fighting with arms flailing it's called "milling," as in windmills. Anyone who has ever been in the Parachute Regiment knows what it's like to do milling, stepping into a circle of men to fight another man. Inside that circle, getting knocked down is not held against you. It is failing to get up and continue to fight that is considered dishonorable. The army wants to see who keeps getting up off the floor. The point is to show who has the guts to go behind enemy lines. There are boxers and there are fighters, and boxers may have the technical skill to win, but fighters will keep on keeping on, doing anything to win. Any man who goes behind enemy lines needs to be a fighter.

> Everyone gets knocked down. What's important is getting back up.

So I know something about stepping into the ring, feeling the crash of a fist on my face. These are the moments when the bullshit stops. I remember, as a kid, watching with my family the night Muhammad Ali fought England's Henry Cooper on television. (Everyone in the United Kingdom was on pins and needles about that fight, which ended with a rather controversial victory for Ali.) Later, when I moved to America, I watched the Sugar Ray Leonard–Roberto Duran fights, and then the Sugar Ray Leonard–Thomas Hearns battles. Back then, everyone knew about those boxing matches. They were marquee events. But these days, nobody can even name the current champ. Greedy promoters, charges of fight fixing, and boxers who are unable to capture the public's imagination have resulted in some people calling for the sport's banishment.

"I have many fond memories of boxing," I told Jeffrey. "But, truthfully, I no longer care about boxing. I don't think anyone does."

"Exactly," Jeffrey responded with enthusiasm. I had taken his bait. "That's the opportunity! What better business to be in than a business about a sport that, when done honestly and openly, had stars like Muhammad Ali—the most famous sporting icon on the planet? Or Sugar Ray Leonard? How could such greatness no longer be valid?

"The problem is obvious," he went on. "The public today thinks boxing is corrupt. So we remove the corruption by ensuring that the judges are unbiased and by treating the boxers fairly. We'll model their deals after the movie industry, where they pay only fifteen percent to their managers, not the sixty percent boxers now pay. We'll create a boxer's bill of rights to make sure they get treated fairly. Equally important, the public won't care about boxers they know nothing about: We'll build their characters, something *you* know how to do. Anyone who can create a television program where unknowns like Richard Hatch, Rupert Boneham, and Omarosa become household names should certainly be able to find great boxing characters who can make the public care again about the fights."

A lightbulb lit up above my head. The idea was raw, it was smart, and best of all, it was a chance to reinvent a sport I loved. Clearly, this new idea Jeffrey and I were discussing could do something special for boxing, and it would be a great long-term business.

"Let's partner on this," Jeffrey offered. I was in.

The Contender was born.

> ### If you don't come in on Saturday, don't bother coming in on Sunday.

Jeffrey then called a 7:30 Saturday morning meeting at his Malibu beach house. Workhorse Jeffrey's mantra goes like this: "If you don't come in on Saturday, don't bother coming in on Sunday." Cynthia, his assistant, often calls executives at 5:30 A.M. Right away they know it's Jeffrey on the line: No one else would dare call that early. Spending time with Jeffrey has made me more focused, and from him I have learned a great deal about the work ethic. Like Donald Trump, Jeffrey is inspirational. He jumps in and does it. He thrives on taking action and overcoming obstacles.

And what I like best about Jeffrey is that he never stops. After getting fired from Disney by Michael Eisner, Katzenberg got right to work to: (a) sue Disney for money owed him for his years of hard work and (b) start DreamWorks with Steven Spielberg and David Geffen. Could anything have been harder than convincing Spielberg (fresh off the enormous success of *Jurassic Park*) and Geffen (who just sold Geffen Records for a huge profit) to partner with him and form the first new major movie studio in fifty years? Only Jeffrey Katzenberg could pull off such a daredevil stunt.

He has an inclusive style whereby, when he calls a meeting, he wants everyone who has anything to do with the project to attend. That Saturday it meant me; my manager, Conrad Riggs; my co–executive producer, Bruce Beresford; and several lawyers and DreamWorks executives. Jeffrey arranged a catered breakfast in that beautiful setting overlooking the beach in Malibu. We discussed the legal issues, which network to pitch the show to, and the intricacies of boxing regulations, trying to figure exactly how the show would come together. "Okay, who's the Trump?" I finally said, meaning "who's the show's focal point?"

The question went unanswered, hanging over the meeting even after we moved on to other topics. After the meeting broke up, Jeffrey and I walked through his garden beside the Pacific Ocean. "Let's think about it," he said. "This show is about giving a fair chance to boxers who live on the mean streets, who have families to feed. . . . Who is the true embodiment of those ideals?"

We answered his question together: Rocky. The last time the world rallied around a boxing story was during the heyday of the *Rocky* films. Clearly, Sylvester Stallone's character Rocky was the embodiment of a "no-hoper" from the streets who became a world champion. Sly was the ideal figurehead for our new show. "Do you think we could at least get him to listen to our idea?" I naïvely asked Jeffrey, forgetting that he was the ultimate Hollywood insider.

He laughed. "You've got a lot to learn. Sly and I have been friends for twenty-five years. I'll set up a meeting."

Monday night found me in front of a beautiful Tuscan villa improbably set in Beverly Hills. Its front doors were at least twelve feet high, like the doors to a castle. As I approached, the doors opened. Standing there, larger than life, his enormous hand extended, was Sylvester Stallone himself. Having been a huge fan of the *Rocky* and *Rambo* movies, I would never forget this moment. "Hi, Mark," he said. "Come on in."

Even after the success of *Survivor* and *The Apprentice*, I was still a Hollywood outsider. I was still the kid from London's blue-collar East End who had struggled to build a career since the first day I arrived in America. But as I shook Sly's hand, suppressing a burst of euphoria, I thought, "I've met Stallone. I've made it!"

Waiting inside the great room of this Tuscan-style villa, its pastel walls lined with massive paintings depicting scenes of Roman life, were Jeffrey Katzenberg and Nancy Josephson, Stallone's agent from ICM, along with Jeff Wald, who formerly managed Crosby, Stills, and Nash and Mike Tyson. My best skills have always been telling stories and pitching ideas. And here I was with the guy who wrote *Rocky*, the most popular boxing movie in history, and I was pitching him an idea about making a boxing show, knowing he'd probably heard a million such pitches over the years.

To me, the most important part of *The Contender* was that people had to care about the boxers competing. That was also important to Stallone. (He later told me that the secret to *Rocky* was that the movie was really about Adrian, not Rocky Balboa.) This reaffirmed to me that we were on the right track.

Also, I emphasized that *The Contender* would look and feel like a feature film. I'm an enormous fan of epic films and am always delighted when people say that *Eco-Challenge* or *Survivor* or *The Apprentice* reminded them more of a feature film than a television show. My gut told me there was no way that a major movie star like Stallone, or, indeed, his experienced ICM agents, would have allowed him to host a reality show if it didn't have an epic quality.

Stallone made me feel totally at ease. He's a warmhearted man, down-to-earth despite all his success. Before I left that night, he even showed me around the house, displaying his collection of *Rocky* and *Rambo* memorabilia.

More important, he agreed to do the show.

We were off and running. Over the next couple of weeks Jeffrey and I tirelessly worked to prepare a TV network pitch. We needed a big budget. *The Contender* would need a kind of "movie quality" in order to give it that winning competitive edge. We had a great idea, a major movie star as a host, and Jeffrey and me at the helm. But this project needed something else.

We had to bring in the fight fans. We had to make it authentic. We needed to find a genuine world-champion boxer to cohost *The Contender* with Sly. Again, the choice was obvious. We wanted six-time world champion Sugar Ray Leonard, the man who beat Thomas Hearns, beat Marvin Hagler, and even made Roberto Duran quit (saying "*no mas*"—"no more" in Spanish—as he did so).

The clock was ticking, and we wanted to quickly take this idea to the four TV networks before someone could rip us off. (Ideas have a way of getting around Hollywood pretty quickly.) Talks continued until, two weeks later, we suddenly got word on a Monday evening in February that Ray had been approached by a competing show. If Ray signed somewhere else, it would be a major setback. Getting the best deal in Hollywood is all about leverage. That means being the first, the best, the *only*. With our last major element about to disappear, we needed to act fast. As I was wondering what the hell we should do, I got a call from Jeffrey. He wanted me to meet him at Sugar Ray's house in forty-five minutes.

Katzenberg had again gone into action.

I had dinner plans that night in Malibu with my girlfriend, Roma Downey, and her family, who were visiting her all the way from Ireland. As I drove to the restaurant, I wondered how the normally easygoing Roma would take my last-minute upheaval of our plans. Walking through the courtyard, I spotted my group sitting at a beautiful outside table. This tranquil setting was a million miles away from the world inside my brain. If we lost Ray to a competing show, it would be in the newspaper the next morning and would cost us all the leverage we currently had to get a big enough deal. The only hope I had of Roma understanding was that she knew this business. She had starred in *Touched by an Angel,* a major CBS series, for almost ten years and had successfully renegotiated her own deal. She had also produced a dozen TV movies and knew that deal leverage was everything. My hope was that her understanding of the business—plus the fact that she'd seen me working night and day with Jeffrey on this deal—would allow her to be cool about our changing plans.

I needn't have worried. She was sweetly supportive and sent me on my way with a hug for good luck. She simply said, "Go do it. Ray would be crazy not to place his bet on you and Jeffrey and Sly."

> Getting leverage means being the first, the best, the *only.*

It turned out that Sly, Jeffrey, Jeff Wald, and the team of lawyers had also broken their dinner plans. We arrived at Sugar Ray's house, interrupting his dinner, too. The last thing Sugar Ray's wife, Bernadette, wanted to see was all of us traipsing into her house as she was just about to put dinner on the table. But we all went downstairs and, four hours later, we had a deal. Our leverage remained intact.

> **The only thing you can be certain of in business is that problems you have not thought of are headed your way.**

What I have just described is the embodiment of a business philosophy that I simply call "Jump In." It's about taking action. Nothing will ever be perfect, and nothing can be totally planned. The best you can hope for is to be about half certain of your plan and know that you and the team you've assembled are willing to work hard enough to overcome the inevitable problems as they arrive. And arrive they will. The only thing you can be certain of in business is that the problems you have not thought of will eventually crop up—and always at the worst times. The best plan of attack is to know that you and your team have what it takes to fight hard, fight smart, and be brave when everything goes south. Being calm and action-oriented in the face of difficult problems isn't taught in any MBA program. Sure, they can teach you about economics, about balance sheets, and how to write business proposals. But they *do not* teach you that your most important asset is trusting your own intuition before plunging into an endeavor—and equally important, to keep trusting that intuition when the inevitable avalanche of problems piles on.

If you're passionate, committed, and willing to believe in yourself, anything is possible. It all starts when you take that half certainty, mix it with your intuition, and Jump In. Overanalyzing whether to start a business, and if you do start one, overanalyzing how to deal with time-sensitive problems, will be the beginning and the end! Jump In—even if you don't know how to swim!

It's never easy, as this book will
demonstrate. My story is as much
about failures and nearly catastrophic
moments as it is about success. But

Don't overanalyze.

that's okay, because only results count. It's like the time I was skydiving
and my parachute didn't open. Eventually, I found a way to release the
backup chute and float safely to the ground. My adventures in television and business aren't as life-and-death as that scenario, but they are

Embrace adversity,

then learn from it.

just as much about taking the plunge,
battling adversity, and ultimately finding a way to achieve success.

Where I am now may sound great
to you, but how I got here is a story of
nightmares and headaches and knots in
my stomach. But each of my setbacks made me that much stronger and
more capable of dealing with both business and life.

If I can do it, anyone can. Perhaps by looking closely at the success
that emerged from my failures, you too will be inspired to Jump In.
Try it.

This strategy, however, requires perseverance. The trick is to embrace adversity, then learn from it. Repeating mistakes is not part of any
business strategy.

In the abstract, this is easy. I have to admit I wasn't so keen on the
adversity I was embracing at the guard gate to Universal Studios that
spring morning as I went to my meeting with Steven Spielberg. My
muscle car simply would not restart. This was highly embarrassing. Finally, the Firebird's engine sputtered to life, and I began driving the half
mile across the lot to Spielberg's office.

My beloved triple black Firebird seemed to have developed a case
of flatulence. It backfired continually. As I made the journey past
soundstages, production bungalows, and sets, everyone stopped and
stared. Making matters worse, the car was barely running. I couldn't get
it to go faster than ten miles an hour. A line of cars was strung out behind me as if I were an automotive Pied Piper, impatiently enduring my

backfiring convertible, as they struggled to get to meetings of their own. The lighthearted confidence I'd felt when I initially pulled up at the guard gate was a distant memory. I had a hard time imagining the other members of the Big Boys Club similarly chugging across Universal Studios.

I practically *willed* the car across the lot. But then, just as the end was in sight and I could plainly see the adobe bungalows and gates to Steven Spielberg's Amblin compound, the engine died entirely.

My good luck: The final hundred yards to Amblin were downhill.

I put the car in neutral, released the brake, and rolled, not quite sure where I would end up. The Amblin guard was expecting me. Almost on cue, he opened the gates and pointed to a single parking space right in front of the studio, almost dead ahead. The only problem was that the road curved upward into the space. I would need some momentum to make it up the rise. If I didn't achieve enough speed, the car would be stranded in parking lot no-man's land, blocking everyone. I didn't enjoy the thought of getting out and pushing.

I leaned forward in my seat, as if that would make the Firebird go faster. I was gaining speed but couldn't tell if it was enough. As soon as I began heading uphill, the sensation of speed abruptly vanished, and it felt as if the car had stopped.

But it hadn't. My beloved black Firebird coasted straight into the space, coming to a halt at the exact moment I was perfectly parked. As I breathed an enormous sigh of relief, the security guard walked up and told me with a laugh, "I guess that was meant to be."

By the way, the meeting with Spielberg went great. It turned out Spielberg was a fan of both *Survivor* and *The Apprentice.* He'd never missed a single episode, and he considered it more filmmaking than reality TV. He told me he felt that I was ready for the "the next act of my career"—that I should make movies and that he hoped I'd make them with him and DreamWorks Studios. It would have been enough that Spielberg knew my name, but to have him offer to help me get into feature films was a dream come true.

And the Firebird? Well, after my meeting, it had cooled down enough to start up on the first try. The day had definitely improved. As I drove home to Malibu, I replayed the Spielberg meeting. Me, a working-class boy from London, actually having a one-on-one with the world's greatest filmmaker. It could only happen in America. My mind raced back twenty-two years.

On October 18, 1982, I had just stepped off a plane at Los Angeles International Airport with $600 in my pocket and no return ticket. I was a young, naïve British ex-commando in search of the American dream. Unable to find work and having no place to live, I took the first job that came along: as a nanny to the children of a wealthy and influential Beverly Hills family. Think that's funny? Well it was . . . and is— so much so that a year ago I successfully pitched the premise as a comedy called *Commando Nanny* to Peter Roth, president of Warner Bros. TV.

All this underscores the fact that if a working-class kid from London, who starts off as a nanny, can make it in the United States, anybody can. Let me tell you how it happened.

Chapter Two

The American Dream on a T-Shirt

I bade my parents farewell at Heathrow Airport in October 1982 and flew to Los Angeles, not even knowing what it was I *hoped* to find there. It was not my first big jump—indeed, my whole life to that point had been one headlong plunge after another—but fresh out of the military, twenty-two, and naïve to the ways of the world, with no college education, I had been literally a bus ride away from taking a factory job. In my pocket, folded inside my passport, was a telegram that had arrived earlier that morning from my mother's sister, Aunt Margaret. It read: "To a star, Hollywood ain't seen nothing yet. Good luck." The funny thing was, I had no idea that Hollywood was anywhere near Los Angeles. And anyway, what chance would an ex-paratrooper have to work in the entertainment business, let alone become well-known? I had smiled at the note and not given it a further thought. To be honest, I didn't even know who I was. Those were eleven very anxious hours spent in the air between London and Los Angeles.

Before leaving England, I had conceived a plan. I would stop briefly in Los Angeles, then continue on to Central America, where I had heard a former SAS (Special Air Service—Britain's equivalent of the Green Berets) operative could offer someone like me a good living as a "military adviser." Saving some money and smoothing my transition into civilian life, I would then move on to some other—I hoped—successful occupation.

An unlikely roadblock presented itself in the form of my mother, Jean. She was a poor Scottish immigrant who moved "south of the border" with my father Archie. Both were looking for a better life as factory workers in vibrant London. Mum labored in the battery compound next to the Ford Motors plant where Archie worked. She took the early shift while Archie worked the night shift so that between them, I, their only child, would be taken care of. I was showered with unconditional love. My mother had always encouraged me, telling me that although we were poor and she couldn't afford to give me an expensive education, I could achieve anything I wanted. When it came time to fly to America I hadn't wanted to scare my mother with plans about Central America. I had told her of a "security job" waiting for me in Los Angeles. She accepted this subterfuge without question, but when we were saying good-bye at Heathrow, she said, "I've got a bad feeling about that security job in Los Angeles. Maybe you should think it over before accepting it."

Your gut instinct is rarely wrong.

My mother's intuition had always influenced her, but she had never voiced concern during my previous years in the Parachute Regiment—a stint that included dangerous duty in Northern Ireland and combat in the Falkland Islands War. She always "knew" I'd be okay.

The chaotic scene at Heathrow mirrored my mother's discomforting words. Frantic people of every nationality surged around us, rushing to planes, tearfully saying farewell to loved ones, or just looking dismal and jet-lagged after some transoceanic journey. My father, taking the train in from London to meet us at the departure gate, had been delayed. So not only did I miss the chance to say farewell to my father, but I had to leave my beloved mother upset and alone in the turmoil of the airport. Looking at her standing alone, scanning the crowd to find my father in that enormous jumble of terminals, tore me apart. But Mum was more concerned about me. Wiping away her tears, she looked me directly in the eyes and asked me to reconsider my future.

Up to this point, she had supported every crazy thing I had ever done. I knew that what she was telling me came from a genuinely fearful intuition rather than her desire to see me remain in England. I inherited her deep trust in intuition (or "going with my gut," as I like to say), and had also felt concern about my secret plan to go to Central America. But I was so eager to come to the United States and chase the American dream that I had ignored that nagging inner voice. That voice has never once failed me—as long as I heeded it. I have sometimes been scared to listen to that voice, but I believe we all get in more trouble by not heeding our gut instincts.

I told my mother I would reconsider the security job. She knew I would. I would never, ever lie to my mother.

On the flight to America I pondered my future. What outcome did I want besides to be a huge success? What was my immediate goal? To find a job and a place to live. By the time I had landed and cleared customs, I'd made up my mind: My military days were over. I would stay in Los Angeles and make a new life there.

I have always been more comfortable with risk than with the easy life. My astrological sign is Cancer, the crab—often equated with the qualities of tenacity and never letting go. Mere tenacity can overcome enormous odds when combined with a healthy attitude toward failure. Failure is not fatal but merely a setback. I somehow knew that tenacity, combined with my desire to succeed, would eventually get me where I wanted in America.

My friend Nick was picking me up at the airport. He knew nothing of my Central American connection, just that I needed a place to stay for a few days. Therefore, he required no explanation for my ever-changing plans. He, too, had come from England and had gotten a job as a chauffeur. He liked the work, and he got to drive around in a Lamborghini.

Nick was delighted to hear I wanted to remain in L.A. and told me of a similar live-in job he had heard of through his boss, though as a nanny instead of a chauffeur. The position was in Beverly Hills, and the interview was that very night. Driving someone's kids to school and vacuuming the living room carpet didn't exactly constitute fame and fortune, but it was a start, supplying a place to live, a car to drive, food in my stomach, and a few dollars in my pocket. I've since realized that people striving to make it don't consider any task beneath them; they do whatever it takes. I'm still that way.

> **Consider no task beneath you. Do whatever it takes.**

I went into the nanny interview determined to land that job. Though never having been a nanny or even a babysitter, I envisioned the sorts of things a nanny was required to do. The wealthy couple interviewed me together at their enormous Beverly Hills mansion. I was nervous, but need creates performance and I rose to the task. I had an answer for every question. When they told me that a male nanny was somewhat unusual and made them a bit uncomfortable, I countered that having a former British paratrooper in the house was guaranteed security—like hiring a nanny and a body-guard at the same time. When they asked if I knew how to iron a proper crease into a dress shirt, I replied that I could iron more precisely than any dry cleaner—British army training, of course. When they asked if I could clean the house, I explained the concept of military white-glove inspections. Finally, as to the subject of references, I sealed the deal by giving them my army discharge papers showing exemplary service and my parents' phone number so they could check my upbringing. The next day they offered me the job. Let the record show that the first job I ever performed in America was unloading a dishwasher. It was the first time I'd even seen such a contraption.

During the next two years, I worked for three different families for whom, in addition to babysitting, my duties included helping with homework, running errands, driving two boys to and from school, and even coaching basketball. Well, the thing was, I'd never so much as dribbled a ball before coming to America. So it just may be that I looked a bit uncoordinated when I finally gave it a try. As I coached the boys one day, one of their dads pulled me aside. He was the actor James Caan. His son Scott (who would also go on to a successful acting career) was on my team. "Where you from?" Mr. Caan asked.

"London."

"You don't know what you're doing, do you?" he said bluntly.

"No."

"That's what I thought," he said. I was horrified. I had been uncovered as a fraud by a major movie star. I looked at Mr. Caan and nervously waited to be fired in front of all the kids. Instead, he laughed, slapped me on the back, and gave me pointers on what to do, before he walked off and let me coach.

Eventually I left the nanny profession and got a job working in the insurance company of Burt, my third and last nanny employer. I was in awe of Burt and curious about how he'd come so far in life. So one day I asked him, "How can I have what you have?"

Burt started by telling me that I was lucky to be an immigrant. I was starting at the bottom. I had no place to go but up. Second, not having a safety net in the form of parents or family would give me a better chance to be wealthy because I would never be expecting someone to bail me out. Third, being new to the country gave me a powerful naïveté that freed me from limited thinking and opened my mind to unconventional ways of doing business. "But to really get anywhere," Burt told me in all seriousness, "you've got to work for yourself, start small, and build."

Start small, and build.

I took Burt's words to heart. Two years later, I decided to rent a fence at Venice Beach—not the whole fence, actually, just a ten-foot section. I was going to sell T-shirts on the weekends (while working my insurance job during the week). My goal was to buy T-shirts with minor imperfections from a clothing factory for $2 per shirt, then sell them to the beach crowd for $18. My display rack was the fence. The guy I rented it from was a brash New Yorker named Howard Gabe. I was nervous that the whopping $1,500 a month I was paying him was too much. I didn't have much money, and blowing it on a fence seemed not only risky but rather dumb. Up until then I'd scrimped and saved, watching my money carefully. Giving it away to rent a fence made me suffer a few second thoughts, but I steeled myself and decided to Jump In.

I showed him a few shirts. "This is good stuff," he said curtly. "Good stuff always sells. How much you charging?"

"Eighteen dollars."

"What're you buying it for?"

"Two dollars."

"You're making sixteen dollars a shirt. You'll do fine. Believe me, you'll be glad you rented this fence."

I'd never worked as a salesman, never attended any kind of sales seminar, never read a book on sales techniques. My whole sales technique for those T-shirts was to stand back and hope passersby liked what they saw. Not much of a technique, really. Why wasn't I taking a more aggressive approach? Because I was scared of rejection and didn't perceive myself as a salesman. It's hard to believe, because now selling is what holds my business together, but back then I hadn't a clue that, deep within, I possessed this very important skill.

Do not fear rejection.

When the first Saturday of our fence lease came, I went to the beach early and hung shirts on the fence. Venice is a trendy, seedy, funky corner of the universe, where street people and movie stars rub shoulders. On a warm Saturday morning, when Los Angelenos head to the beach, Venice is where they go.

I knew I wouldn't lack for foot traffic. Still, I stood against the fence as the first wave of Saturday morning beachgoers wandered past. My mouth shut, I spoke only when spoken to, nodding politely at all who looked my way.

It was still early, and mostly only joggers and roller skaters were out. Standing there all alone in front of "my" fence, I wished the earth would swallow me whole.

I started to have sickening thoughts that nobody would be interested in buying my clothes and that the entire idea was stupid. It's so easy to have self-doubt, and that doubt only gets worse the longer you are alone and allow your inner voice to taunt you.

I was in one of those inner-voice daydreams when suddenly a young woman roller-skated over to look at the display. "How much?" she asked.

"Uh ... er ..." I stammered, embarrassed to tell her the price. I feared she would laugh in my face. "Eighteen dollars."

"Okay." She quickly pulled a $20 bill from her purse. I gave her the shirt and her change in a state of shock. As she skated away, another person arrived. Same thing. Suddenly I was holding $36. I was overjoyed, and my confidence grew.

My fears vanquished by success, I began chatting up everyone who passed by, calling out for people to step over and take a look at the shirts. When people asked the price, I no longer worried it would be too steep. As the afternoon wore on, Venice Beach became a mass of humanity. I was selling clothes faster than I could make change. I went home with almost $1,000 in cash. Later that afternoon, my fence landlord, Howard Gabe, came by. Howard watched as I frantically tried to simultaneously sell, accept money, put clothes in plastic bags, provide change, and focus on a growing line of customers. He helped me, all the while wearing a huge smile. I remember him saying, "Only in America, Mark. Only in America!"

Dealing with people at the street level was the best sales course I could have taken. Over the next two years I learned the art of selling on Venice Beach. The same strategies I used to sell those T-shirts apply to selling TV shows.

I learned how to turn a no into a yes. No doesn't means no. It is merely an objection to overcome. I also learned the importance of reading people. Customers buy from people they're com-

> No doesn't
> mean no.

fortable with, people they consider to be their friends. By adjusting my personality to mirror their own, I could win their confidence and broker a sale. Different personalities respond to different sales techniques, and I broke them into four groups: analytical, emotional, passive, and motivated. Analytical people are engineers, doctors, rocket scientists. These individuals are able to be convinced and sold by facts—not hyperbole. When selling something to an analytical person, I provide rational, practical, research-laden reasons for them to buy a product. They want to know how the shirt was made and whether the stitching will last. My delivery is no-nonsense, to the point, and devoid of emotion.

> Customers buy from
> people they are
> comfortable with,
> people they consider
> friends.

Conversely, emotional people respond to a delivery that drives to the core of their being. Facts make their eyes glaze over. They want to feel the fabric and enjoy the colors—it's not about the stitching. In theater, this would be called playing to the audience. In sales, it's giving the customers what they want emotionally. It's also just common sense.

The passive customer likes to be dominated. Passive people want to be taken by the hand and told what they like and dislike. They don't like to be bullied because that preys on the side of their personality that already imagines victimhood. If you overaggressively pressure them to buy, they rebel against you. Passive customers have to be dealt with sensitively.

Motivated (aggressive) customers, on the other hand, are leaders. They want the salesman to be passive. When that sort of situation arises, I put my ego in my pocket and let the customer be the boss. Did it feel insulting to have someone treat me like their servant? Yes, but I was looking to make a sale, not gain intellectual validation. These customers want to prove they are right. They're especially easy to sell to when they're with a group because they want to show how smart they are and what a great financial deal they're getting—even when they can't afford the product.

I made so much money selling T-shirts that I wanted to quit my insurance job. I was making more in a weekend on Venice Beach than in a month at the insurance office. Since Burt had gotten me the insurance job, I owed him the courtesy of asking his permission to leave. However, I was sheepish.

"I hope I haven't let you down by wanting to leave," I told him.

Far from it. Burt was ecstatic. I was making money selling shirts and I was my own boss. "I'm happy for you. You're on the right track, Mark," Burt told me. "Let me know if I can help you in any way." This reaction reminded me that Burt's way of being positive and seriously happy for the success of others was how I wanted to be. He's been my mentor ever since.

He was correct about me being on the right track. A year later I leveraged the money from T-shirt sales into a lucky real-estate deal where I made $75,000 in thirty days, then used that money to start my own marketing business. I nibbled at success over the next few years. My gut, however, told me there was something missing. I had a pleasant home, a nice car, my own office, and a sizeable bank account. I'd been able to fly home to the East End of London to visit often, looking the picture of affluence to my school friends. All the while I tried to ignore that nagging inner voice about something missing, but that voice would not shut up. What, then, was I searching for?

I got my answer at a dinner party. During the predinner discussions, I noticed that when I told people I was in

> Being creative may be a risky business, but nothing beats the rewards.

marketing, they got a bored look in their eyes. Meanwhile, I overheard another man answering the same question. His job, he told people casually, was movie producer. He had an office at Columbia Pictures. Now, it's important to note that this guy had never produced a movie, and I doubt he had much money to his name. In fact, I would learn later, guys like him got an office and a small stipend for "developing ideas." He may not actually have been producing, but day in and day out he was trying to be creative. And he was having an adventure.

People at that dinner party fell all over this guy. I was unbelievably jealous. What was it that caused this? It was Hollywood—exciting, glamorous, and the most creative place on earth.

That's what I was missing: creativity. On the surface, I was jealous of that producer because he was getting more attention. But underneath, I recognized an inner need to work on a product that would be enjoyed around the world. A product that would be seen over and over. I needed to take bigger risks. I needed to really Jump In. Somewhere deep within my paratrooper soul still beat the heart of an adventurer. I needed to bring it forth before it was too late. Shortly after the dinner party, inspired by that revelation, I changed my life in a most dynamic way.

Chapter Three

Suffering and Deprivation; Or How I Got My Start in TV

An Eskimo named Igjugardik said something profound: "All the true wisdom is to be found far from the dwellings of man, in the great solitudes, and can only be attained through suffering. Suffering and privation are the only things that can open the mind of man to that which is hidden from his fellows."

I lay in bed the morning of February 21, 1991, lingering over the *Los Angeles Times*. Catching my eye was a color photo of a canoe in a dark jungle river. The water was opaque, and it didn't take much imagination to realize that wasn't the ideal spot for a swim.

Always attracted to adventure and wild places, I focused on the article. In vivid prose, the writer detailed a French adventure competition known as the Raid Gauloises. The goal was for five-person teams to race nonstop over mountains, down rivers, and through jungles so snake-infested that teams carried their own supply of antivenin. Their modes of transportation were trekking, horseback, rafting, kayaking, white-water rafting, and even parachuting. The races lasted up to two weeks and covered several hundred miles. Teams carried all their own food, water, and gear. They slept just one hour each night.

This was the sign I was looking for. I was inspired: I decided on the spot to launch an expedition-length race of my own in the United States. I'd seen research showing that the three dominant themes of the

1990s would be the environment, extreme sports, and self-actualization through challenge. No other format combined all three like expedition racing. My race would be called *Eco-Challenge.*

As part of my strategy for launching *Eco-Challenge,* I would race in the Raid Gauloises. This would show me how my future participants actually felt while competing, and it would help me become a better race producer. The event changed locations each year and would be held that fall in the Arab country of Oman. I had roughly seven months to find a team, acquire financial sponsorship, and transform my body back into the hardened steel of a British paratrooper's.

That last bit would entail a total body makeover including weight training, dietary adjustments, running, kayaking, and rock climbing. I was ten years out of the parachute regiment and nowhere close to the superior fitness level I had once taken for granted. I knew it would be a huge risk to race, but my gut told me that this was the path to the future.

If for some bizarre reason you want to know what it feels like to have dreams ridiculed, you should have been in my shoes then. Even friends couldn't hide their smirks as I explained about expedition racing and *Eco-Challenge* and my grand plan to make it an international brand name. Because I was about to get married to my girlfriend, Dianne, some friends laughed that this was my "last big adventure" before settling down. (How wrong they were!) Some even told me that at thirty-two years old, I was suffering an early midlife crisis. Their perplexed response to me was that I was making great money in marketing. Why would I rock the boat?

Choose teammates who possess greater skills than you.

My naïveté shone bright like a beacon as I prepared to race. On the negative side, that dynamic led me to choose my teammates poorly—among them a stockbroker, an actor, and a personal trainer. They were good people and gym-fit, but lacked outdoor adventure skills. I had realized this when I selected them but thought these handicaps could be overcome if I shared my British army training with them. In actuality, I should have selected teammates with greater outdoor skills than I, not lesser.

I lined up a lucrative series of corporate sponsors to back my team and jump-start my *Eco-Challenge* corporation. I promised them media attention as a return on their investment. To fulfill that obligation I cold-called media outlets, pitching the story of my plucky team. Back then, I thought that was how it was done. Improbably, it worked. *Runner's World* agreed to do a feature story based solely on my exuberant pitch to their editor. I even requested a particular writer. Later, that writer told me he'd never heard of such a thing: Editors don't take cold-call pitches and *never* let subjects of such features choose their own writer. But I didn't know this rule, so my unbridled enthusiasm got it done. I didn't overanalyze. I jumped in!

Coupled with great enthusiasm, naïveté can be a strength.

On the strength of this first magazine piece and a subsequent news segment on CBS, a Los Angeles television station agreed to send a camera crew to Oman to film a one-hour special on our race. I convinced them to work with me in securing sponsors who would then both sponsor the team *and* buy commercials. They'd keep the money from the commercials, and I'd keep the team sponsorship. I—a total television novice—would be getting sponsorship dollars for a special being aired in the most influential media market in the world. And it had all been there for the asking. Again, my naïveté and Jump In philosophy had, against all odds, succeeded.

In that unlikely manner, I made my entrance into the television and sponsorship industries.

Our name was Team American Pride. In November, we flew to the medieval land of Oman. This tiny nation on the Arabian Sea featured daunting desert and mountain topography, blistering days and frigid nights, dead-end canyons, and riverbeds prone to flash floods.

My teammates and I were awed and more than a little intimidated by Oman, and by the wiry physiques of our fellow competitors. The pressures of being a first-time competitor and a first-time subject of a television show, and the first-time responsibility of satisfying sponsors weighed heavily on me in the days leading up to the race, but I was filled with optimism about the race. Team American Pride would be the surprise of the field. I was sure of it.

And we were. But it was not the sort of surprise I'd envisioned.

The purpose was to race nonstop across the mountains and deserts for almost four hundred miles, staying together as a team at all times. We rose at 3:30 race morning to prepare for the predawn start. The Raid would begin with twenty-some miles of horseback riding, then we would dismount and trek fifty miles through the Jebel Akdar mountain range. After that, we would kayak on the Arabian Sea, then another mountain trekking section, then a sixty-mile camel ride.

In what would be the first of many mistakes, we selected our horses poorly and immediately fell behind. Our horses were lame and stubborn. One nag refused to let us ride her; we had to drag her the entire distance of more than twenty miles. While the fastest teams took just three and a half hours to reach the waterfalls of Snake Canyon, the end of the horseback section, Team American Pride took twice as long.

After that less-than-auspicious start, we began the difficult roped ascent up through the waterfalls of Snake Canyon. Frigid water beat down on our heads. It was grueling, but we pushed on and made it through by dark.

We had finally gained some momentum, but then my teammate Owen refused to continue racing until we built a fire and dried our clothes. With time of the essence, I thought his request absurd. Owen and I argued. The night was cold and the sky filled with stars. Under normal circumstances, its beauty would have been dazzling. But I was bristling with rage, and I lost the argument.

We built a fire and waited until morning before continuing. Team American Pride had ceased to be a competitive squad.

Our entire race became a downward spiral from hope and optimism to miserable failure. Inexperience and mismatched personalities, combined with my own poor navigation, forced my team to fracture when things got tough. At one excruciating point, we were so low on water we had to take turns drinking the last sip from our canteen, swirling it around our mouths, then spitting it back into the canteen and passing it to the next teammate.

The sensation that my teammates and I were alone in the wilderness was overwhelming. We passed the next several days hearing only our footsteps, labored breathing, and assurances to each other that if we kept moving forward we would eventually emerge from the wilderness and reach the Arabian Sea, where our kayaks were waiting for the race's next leg.

One day, we came to the edge of a cliff. Looking down from above, I could see the ground one hundred meters below. The race organizers had affixed five ropes to the top of the cliff, one for each teammate. We would descend by rappelling, that is, clipping ourselves to the rope, stepping backward off the edge, and carefully lowering ourselves down the face—a thrilling task once one gets the hang of it. The potential for error is, however, great.

Don't waste time on overpreparation.

I set my pack on the ground and pulled out the proper equipment for a rappel. On my right hand I slipped a $40 calfskin rappelling glove. On top of my head I set a special helmet that I'd purchased for $100 at a gear store back home. Then I cinched the web climbing harness about my waist and thighs. A special titanium device known as a carabiner was next, clipped through the front of the harness and screwed securely shut so it wouldn't open during the descent. Then a second carabiner as a precautionary measure in case the first one failed. Next came another wonder of modern metallurgy known as a "figure-eight," through which the rope dangling over the edge of the cliff would be threaded to slow my descent.

I clipped the rope, the carabiners, and the figure-eight together in the proper configuration, and turned around to gingerly take the first step backward off the edge.

Out of nowhere, a little old man appeared. He was a local and couldn't have been a day under seventy. He wore the sheerest of fabrics over his tanned, leathery body, and no shoes. At first I thought he was crazy, because his smile was so broad as he walked briskly to the edge of the cliff. Clearly, he was about to commit suicide.

But then, keeping that same silly grin plastered to his face, that old man grabbed one of the secured ropes and leaped over the edge! He bounded down that treacherous face in mere seconds. Not walking carefully backward, with the best in modern climbing equipment, as we were about to do, not afraid to death of making a fatal mistake—but bounding in massive, joyous leaps. No technology. No gear. Just one barefoot, half-naked old man who had lived alongside this cliff his entire lifetime. I was blown away.

That just goes to show you that results are what's important in life. Not appearance. Not intention. Results. With all the modern technology my teammates and I possessed, none got down that cliff as gracefully as that tiny old man. I never forgot that moment, and whenever I feel I am wasting time overpreparing, I follow his example and Jump In.

The defining moment of the ordeal occurred during the kayaking leg. We were paddling parallel to the coast a mile offshore when a storm struck. The skies turned black, the ocean surface became a nauseating undulation of six-foot swells, and the wind raged so hard that salt spray cut like shards of glass as it slashed against our exposed faces. Navigation was nearly impossible. Though teams faced disqualification by being rescued, the air filled with rescue helicopters. Sharks circled. "The storm was huge," I wrote later in my journal. "To be honest, I think the only reason we got through it was because we were all so scared."

Not all of us got through it, though. When the storm was at its worst, Owen panicked. He abruptly announced that he wanted to quit, or at least rest on shore until the storm passed. The rest of our team told him he was crazy. As Southern Californians, our strong suit was ocean kayaking in big swells, and this critical juncture provided us with the ideal opportunity to make up distance between us and other teams. Furthermore, the beach was being pounded by huge breakers. We could very well die if we tried to paddle to shore for a rest. In kayaks bobbing like corks, in the middle of a storm, we argued again. I forbade Owen to go ashore.

In an act of mutiny, Owen paddled hard toward the shore. Since Raid rules dictate that all five members must travel and finish together or be disqualified, he was effectively terminating our months of training and hard work. After a moment of furious disillusionment, we did what we had to. We paddled on without him. Hours later, a rescue helicopter found Owen washed up on the beach, asleep and dazed. When asked if he knew our whereabouts, he shrugged and said he had no idea. It was assumed that we were lost at sea. When this news was radioed back to race organizer Gerard Fusil, one of the largest manhunts in Raid history began. No one had ever died during a Raid, and it seemed a cruel act of fate for the novice American team to be the first. A desperate Fusil himself set aloft in a search-and-rescue helicopter to look for us around where Owen had been found.

He didn't find us. We had paddled many miles to the south. Unbeknownst to us, we were the only team still out on the ocean. We spent the night with locals in a small fishing village. As we beached our kayaks, about a hundred children helped us pull the heavy kayaks the one hundred meters to get above the high tide line that would wash in later that evening. The local fishermen then ran their hands along our sleek craft, examining every aspect of their design. They had never before seen fiberglass boats.

An impromptu feast followed, as they shared their food with us and we spent a wonderful Arabic evening. We slept briefly, then put to sea at dawn and paddled on through the early morning light, not knowing that Raid organizers had canceled the kayaking section due to weather. When we arrived at Wadi Shab at noon, Fusil was so relieved, he celebrated. "The Americans have arrived! The Americans have arrived!" he cried joyfully.

There was no celebrating, however, when we confronted our renegade teammate. Now clean and shaved, he came out to greet us. Because of the storm's ferocity, and more important, because he wanted the publicity associated with an American team finishing the race, Fusil had decided to bend the rules and let him rejoin us so that our team could continue officially. The four of us remembered his selfishness and mutiny all too well. Looking our former teammate in the eye, we told him one by one that we wouldn't take him back. Then we shouldered our packs and continued the race, unofficially as an incomplete team of four.

A second team member withdrew as a result of an injury a few days later, but I continued the race with my two remaining teammates and a group of athletes whose teams had also splintered. In the end, we were a combined makeshift team of French, Japanese, and American; exhausted, smelly, hungry, and driven by the desire to finish what we had started.

After ten days, one hour, and fifteen minutes, we arrived at Checkpoint 22, which—due to the cancellation of the final camel leg on account of uncontrollable camels—had become the official finish line. With me were Susan and Norman, my surviving American Pride teammates. First we cried, and then we celebrated with cold French champagne, hot showers, and a good night's sleep.

Micromanage at your own peril.

Even as the sublime sensation of accomplishment washed over us, however, I began a mental survey of what I had done wrong. First, I'd chosen my team poorly. I needed professional adventurers. Second, I'd been a poor manager. I have a talent for outdoor adventure, but my strengths are coordination, macromanage-

ment, and deal making. There's no way I should have been the naviga-
tor, micromanaging every single moment of the race. Ideally, I should
have brought together an experienced team, then ceded control during
the race to an individual with better tactical and navigational skills.

My failure nagged at me. What would I tell the sponsors? How
would this affect *Eco-Challenge?* Before my plane home was halfway
over the Atlantic, I had my answers. I would learn from my failure to
keep my epic dream alive. That's the day I realized that *Eco-Challenge*
and the world of adventure was my destiny. No longer was I just an immigrant trying to scrape his way to the top. I had learned a hard, invaluable lesson and would not let my dream die. It had been imperative
that I finish the Raid as a means of establishing credibility.

Years later, my staff began calling me "the Method Producer" for
my need to personally prerace every early *Eco-Challenge* course to know
what competitors would experience. One young producer noted that
that would be like an actor getting shot before filming a gunshot scene
so he could better know the sensation.

What was I going to do now? Go back to the Raid—and win. The
1993 Raid was being held in Madagascar, a barren moonscape where
crocodiles filled the rivers and temperatures shattered the thermome-
ter. I had a year to assemble a crack team and increase my fitness to its
greatest level. Not only did I want to win the Raid for personal reasons,
I was going back with the intention of producing another television
show about my Raid experience. This time, however, I wanted the
Madagascar show to air to a bigger audience. I wanted everyone in
America to have a vicarious taste of expedition racing. Doing that
would make it easier to secure a national television deal for my own
Eco-Challenge when the time came. I thought ESPN would be the perfect outlet. The question remained how to get them on board.

Chapter Four

Madagascar

Failure: a unique opportunity to gather yourself, take a deep breath, and remind yourself that the past is the past. It's over. Learn and move on. Keep cool. No matter how bad things get, you must continue to make calm, levelheaded decisions. Giving in to panic-generated adrenaline and fear will turn a potential success into a failure every time. The final months before the 1993 Raid in Madagascar (also known as "the Red Island," for the color of its soils) were a case in point. From an emotional and physical standpoint, nothing was easy. My life seemed to be one massive, ongoing test.

From a business point of view, I was struggling to get my new *Eco-Challenge* venture off the ground, which was made all the more difficult because I was training several hours each day for the Madagascar Raid. Looking back on it, choosing to race in the Raid again was entirely selfish. I'd learned enough about the "business" of producing an adventure race in Oman and should have focused just on *Eco-Challenge*, but my ego was driving my need to "officially" finish with a complete team. Those pressures were made worse by the fact that my personal funds were becoming desperately low. My mother, meanwhile, had developed lung cancer, and I was flying back and forth to England constantly to be at her side. On top of all that, Dianne was due to give birth to our first child sometime in August.

The stresses of life felt enormous. My stamina was at its limit. I didn't feel I could handle anything more.

In the middle of all this, on August 22, my son James was born. The incredible joy I felt that day buoyed me. I realized that I was now completely responsible for someone other than myself, which gave me the resolve to work all the harder toward making *Eco-Challenge* a success. This was followed shortly by the good news that my mother was winning her battle with cancer. Life was improving.

So I was stunned when, three weeks later, on September 16, my mother suddenly died. It was a terrible loss, made all the more horrendous because I had totally believed she was recovering and had many more years to live. She had never even had the opportunity to hold baby James. I can truly say that losing my mother was something that could have made me grind to a complete halt. I was devastated. I gave the eulogy at her funeral to about a hundred former factory coworkers, friends, and relatives. I still don't know how I got the words out. But something came to me that seemed important to share. Despite all my crazy adventures—the Parachute Regiment, moving to the United States, becoming a nanny, selling T-shirts on Venice Beach, and racing in the Raid—she had never once criticized me or tried to hold back my dreams. Instead, she would motivate me and help me think through how to achieve things. As I shared these truths, I wept. I owed who I was to her.

Shortly after returning from her funeral in England, I decided that what my mum would want was for me to continue chasing my dreams. I owed it to her and to baby James. In some kind of weird way, I felt she lived on in him. I decided to honor them both by wearing small, laminated photographs of Mum and James around my neck when I raced in Madagascar.

Despite my heartbreak, I had to jump back into training for the Raid, which was only a month away. I arranged a training evolution for a couple of days near my home with the three Navy SEALs I had enlisted as my new Raid teammates: Pat Harwood, Bruce Schliemann, and Rick Holman. Not only were they in top physical condition, but their belief in the power of teamwork as a means of helping one another achieve personal goals was inspiring. Training with them gave me a momentary break from the sorrow and financial pressures that had enveloped my life like a bad dream.

Wearing full packs, we trekked for miles in the hills around my Topanga Canyon home. The terrain was rugged, a continuum of steep, grass-covered hillsides and oak savannahs. Once we finished, the SEALs grabbed a quick drink of water and prepared to drive the three hours back to their base in San Diego. But looking out across the mountains to the north, we saw an ominous black storm cloud heading our way. Just out of curiosity, we climbed the small hill behind my house to get a better look. That's when we saw that the storm cloud was actually thick, black smoke from a wildfire. Even worse, a ten-foot-high wall of flames was racing over the hillside, just a few miles away from my home.

There was no way I was going to let my house burn down without putting up a fight. Without even discussing it with each other, the SEALs began unpacking Bruce's truck. They were going to help me. "We're all part of a team," Pat told me. "This is what being part of a team means."

We quickly got to work. I packed the car and sent my family off to a friend's house. Then the SEALs and I pulled blankets from a closet. We soaked them in water and put them over our backs like capes. We also soaked thick towels in water and wrapped them around our heads. Though we looked comical, this wet clothing was our only protection against the intense heat of the flames. We then climbed up the hillside, armed with shovels and a hose. By then, the fire was less than fifty feet from my house. There was little we could do but try to wet the ground as much as possible and dig a fire line. Just then, in one of those coincidental acts of providence that made me feel as if my mum was definitely looking out for me, a firefighting helicopter flew overhead. Seeing us battle the flames, the pilot dumped his entire supply of water on top of the fire. Just like that, the flames threatening my home were extinguished.

The fire was still raging in other areas of the canyon, however, and the four of us stayed up all night, continually hosing down the roof and watching the fires raging all around us just in case the wind turned it our way again.

As I've said, tests like these take the measure of a person. That arduous day and night bonded our team. We proved that we were calm, cool, and bold under pressure. We became stronger through the test and learned that we could trust one another when the going got rough. However, when all was said and done, I realized that the house didn't really matter. I could have lost the house and it wouldn't have been the end of the world. What was important was that my family was safe and I had teammates I could count on. My other troubles—*Eco-Challenge*, personal finances, sorrow—felt insignificant by comparison.

Shortly after the fires, my teammates and I went skydiving over the Southern California desert. I hadn't skydived since my army days ten years earlier, but it was a Madagascar Raid discipline that I needed to brush up on. Luckily, Bruce Schliemann, Pat Harwood, and the ever-capable Rick Holman were all SEAL skydiving instructors. Even though I was a bit rusty, it was reassuring to know that, in the event of an emergency in the sky, the three of them would find a way to make things right.

We leapt from the plane at thirteen thousand feet, then linked arms and fell in formation until we reached five thousand feet. If you've ever skydived, you know the intense rush of dropping from the sky at 140 miles per hour. The freedom of flight merges with an unsettling terror that something, somehow, will go wrong. I love the romance of leaping from a plane but am too much of a realist to deny that it scares me like few other undertakings. In the Parachute Regiment, I had seen parachutes fail to open properly, seen the mess of broken legs and sprains that accompanied even a minor malfunction, heard about the craters made by bodies hitting the ground after two-mile free falls.

One by one, we separated from our plummeting formation to release our pilot chutes. Pat and Bruce separated first. I reached for my own pilot chute, and I assumed that Rick had already done the same, making me the last one free-falling. I placed my hand on my right hip and pulled the rubber ball that would release my pilot

Stay calm under pressure.

chute, which would then release my main chute.

Nothing happened. The pilot chute, that small drogue that precedes the main chute to ensure an orderly opening, was stuck. Even as the ground raced toward me, I was strangely calm and reached again to tug the pilot chute free. No joy.

Needless to say, this was a desperate situation. But I was aware of everything around me. Out of the corner of my eye, I noticed Rick still free-falling. When he saw I was in trouble, he delayed pulling his own chute to help me. He was using his body as an aerodynamic platform to fly to my assistance. What a guy!

So we're free-falling, unable to speak because of the wind, and communicating through facial expression and sign language. Rick mimed pulling his rip cord, asking me what was wrong. I pointed to the pilot chute. He could see that it was stuck, and pointed to his own reserve chute, miming that I should forget about the pilot chute and pull the reserve. I was sure that the problem was me, not the pilot chute. So, embarrassed, I kept tugging on the little rubber ball.

Meanwhile, an increasingly exasperated Rick, seeing that we were running out of altitude, motioned that he would fly closer and pull my reserve for me. That's a dangerous maneuver under any conditions, but even more dangerous so close to the ground. If we were to accidentally smack into each other or become entangled as my chute deployed, both of us would be done for. Rick, with a wife and two small children at home, was literally risking his life for me. That woke me up.

I needed to set aside my pride and pull the reserve immediately.

I shook my head at Rick. He understood. He had gotten through to me. He changed his body attitude so that he tracked away. I checked my altimeter. I had fallen ten thousand feet and was now at only three thousand feet. It was now or never—I pulled my reserve. It opened with a hard thud, and blossomed into the most wonderful sight: a lime-green, fully formed chute. What a glorious, welcome sight. I floated safely to the ground, awash in the euphoria of being alive, but also racked by the post-adrenaline-jag questions of "what if?" What if I'd been unable to open the reserve chute? What if Rick and I had become tangled? What if, what if, what if?

As Rick landed close by, I was struck by the realization that I could have panicked up there. But I had reminded myself over and over to stay calm. Nothing fruitful would have come from panic then, and I'm sure I would have left an ugly hole in the ground. I smiled at discovering that I could—and would—stay calm in a tight situation.

Rick, meanwhile, was furious. He immediately confronted me about my skills. Why, he wanted to know, had I been unable to perform such a simple task as pulling the pilot chute? With our trip to Madagascar just weeks away, it was obvious that the SEALs had concerns about my skydiving abilities.

By then I had taken off my chute and laid it on the ground. He reached for it, in order to demonstrate the proper way to pull the pilot chute. He gently pulled the rubber ball. But the pilot chute wouldn't budge. He tried again, this time yanking hard. It still wouldn't budge.

You may forget how you behaved when the going got tough, but others will not.

He actually pulled so hard that he lifted the entire chute off the ground, and still the pilot chute was wedged inside. It turned out that on this particular chute the pocket holding the pilot chute had been sewn so tightly that the pilot chute was stuck fast. There was no way I could have gotten it out.

In a strange way, I was thankful for the trial by fire. You never know whether you'll be able to remain calm and thinking clearly in a quickly approaching death situation. By remaining calm, I proved to my new teammates that when push came to shove I had the right stuff. More important, I could trust myself.

That trust became crucial during the Madagascar race. Late in the competition we undertook a forty-hour nonstop walk across a desert known as the Mikea Forest. The lead teams were only hours ahead, and we were sure the forced march would catapult us to victory. The French had told us of a mythic tribe of little people living in the Mikea Forest, but we had assumed that it was just local legend, like the fairies of the English countryside.

The Pygmies that surrounded us after midnight, however, were quite real. The hard looks on their faces betrayed hostile intent no less effectively than the spears leveled toward the four of us. Saying nothing, wearing tunics of the brightest red fabric, they were a mini version of East Africa's Masai warriors. I might have thought I was hallucinating if I hadn't heard Rick and Pat discussing ways to defend ourselves. "I'm taking the safety off on my pencil flare," Rick said, speaking of the emergency illumination provided by race organizers. Per race rules, we had no weapons of any kind. A flare would have to do in a pinch.

"Okay. Me, too," Pat said. "I'll take the ones on the left." It was second nature for my SEAL teammates to lapse into a military posture. We were outnumbered six to one in this showdown. But even if Pat and Rick and Bruce managed to take out a handful of men, there would still be plenty of angry Pygmies to finish us off. Clearly, a different approach was needed.

Negotiating secret: If all else fails, make them laugh.

I looked at the spear of the man standing before me, then slowly—an inch per second—I began extending my right hand toward the tip. The warrior could see what I was doing, but made no attempt to stop me. He just watched. Perhaps he thought I was a fool.

Soon the other Pygmies began watching my hand's inch-by-inch journey toward the razor-sharp spear. There was no turning back. All eyes were soon on me, even those of my teammates. What in the world, they had to be wondering, was Burnett up to? Was he trying to get himself killed?

Delicately, I pressed my finger against the point of the spear as if testing its sharpness—and man, it was sharp.

I had crossed the point of no return. Either my strategy was about to save the day or I was about to look like a total moron, and get a spear through my gut.

I pulled my finger back quickly, howled in great comic pain, then collapsed to the ground as if shot. I rolled around on the ground and continued to scream in pain.

For a moment my howling was the only sound echoing off that dark desert. Then one Pygmy laughed, and another, and another. Soon, all the Pygmies burst into uproarious laughter. They'd never seen such a foolish man in all their lives. Spears were lowered, and relieved exhales were emitted by my teammates.

Making people laugh, even when things are dire, is not always the obvious course of action. But I'm living proof that it's the best.

Team American Pride finished ninth in Madagascar. As well as managing to make a little history by becoming the first American team to ever finish this race, I had also managed to convince KCAL Channel 9 in Los Angeles to pay to send their on-air sports reporter, Mark Steines, to Madagascar to produce a one-hour special about the exploits of our team. It was my second venture into pulling together a television deal, and this one was a significant improvement over my Oman deal. Earlier, I had convinced the Raid Gauloises organizers to provide me free copies of all the footage their ten camera crews would shoot at the Madagascar Raid. In return, I would get the Raid Gauloises publicized on American TV. The other side of this deal was that I convinced KCAL to accept this footage and have Mark Steines edit it, at KCAL's cost, into a one-hour special. The Raid was happy to have gotten an American show to publicize their unknown French race, and KCAL was happy to end up with a one-hour show that would have cost over a million dollars had they shot it themselves.

But the best part of the entire deal was that KCAL would get to air this show only once, then the show became my property to distribute. I had simultaneously arranged a deal with ESPN to accept the KCAL one-hour show. Essentially, they were acquiring free programming. In return, ESPN would provide me with thirty percent of the commercial minutes available during their broadcast. I then sold these commercial minutes to my Team American Pride sponsors. Looking back, it was a pretty audacious scenario, but it worked, and the ESPN show got fairly good ratings. I was learning how to be bold and creative in putting together a national television deal. These newfound skills would serve me well later.

Since this early adventure in Madagascar, Mark Steines has moved on to national prominence as the anchor on *Entertainment Tonight*, and we have become close friends. He often still laughs with disbelief that KCAL, the Raid, and ESPN agreed to my crazy deal.

I have not been back to "the Red Island" of Madagascar since racing the Raid in 1993, but I can honestly say it changed me forever. The months leading up to it were a painful emotional learning process, the race itself was more physically demanding than anything I had ever done before, and I had jumped through countless hoops to make it all work from a business point of view. All those tests before and during the Raid made me stronger and savvier. My personal journey to the Red Island marked a career turning point. I knew that, no matter what, I had gained the confidence necessary to make myself into a success. What I didn't know was that I had one last vital lesson to learn.

Chapter Five

Eating Humble Pie

Within a month of returning from Madagascar, I made the mistake of letting our ninth-place finish and my national television deal go to my head. I decided to race the Raid again in 1994. This time, in Borneo, my reasons were selfish and ego-driven, and could actually be detrimental to the success of *Eco-Challenge*. But I didn't care. The first time I had done the Raid I had finished with an incomplete team, but in ninth place. This time I wanted to lead the first American team ever to win.

Big mistake. That chapter of my life should have been over. It was time to turn my energies from six months of training and racing each year into making my dream of *Eco-Challenge* come true. I'd endured the hardship of actually racing and observed the logistical nightmares of Raid officials as they struggled to keep track of fifty teams spread over hundreds of miles of wilderness. I admired their hard work but knew I had to improve upon their methods. American racers would expect flawless execution. Also, any TV company that financed me would expect American-quality production. I planned to produce an efficient *Eco-Challenge* and more than double the number of film crews covering the race. I wanted to produce a dynamic television show about racers questing after this Holy Grail. I wanted *Eco* to be more epic, more dramatic, more bombastic: a David Lean film come to life. I'd learned what I needed to learn by racing. I should have moved on. But I was stupid, and decided to take on both racing in Borneo and simultaneously producing my first *Eco-Challenge*.

Recognize when it's time to move on.

I immersed myself in raising money, finding a course location, and convincing teams to pay to race in *Eco-Challenge*. I was irked that people kept comparing it with the Hawaiian Ironman competition, when, in fact, *Eco-Challenge* would be far tougher. In response, I ran a two-page advertisement in *Triathlete* magazine that said, "This Little Race Eats Ironmen For Breakfast." Such confidence made me an easy target for those in the endurance racing world. They questioned my ability to make such a claim, particularly since I hadn't ever competed in Ironman. My response was always that I'd completed two Raids, though I knew that that wasn't sufficient pedigree to quiet the most savage critics. More than ever, I wanted to win the Raid Gauloises to show that I had the right stuff. Since even Ironman competitors grudgingly agreed that Raid was the toughest race on earth at the time, winning would mean never again having my credentials questioned.

The problem was that I was immersed twenty-four hours a day, seven days a week, living, eating, and sleeping my development of *Eco-Challenge*. I wasn't training properly for the Raid. When I arrived on the island of Borneo for my third and final attempt to win the Raid Gauloises, mentally I was still in Southern California preparing for *Eco*. Making matters more daunting, the Raid field was the toughest in history. If Team American Pride was going to win, it would take a supreme effort.

We flew from Los Angeles to Kuching, a small town on Borneo's northern coast. As always, I arranged for sponsors to finance the cost of flying the team, and to provide all the team equipment and food. The tasks of raising the sponsorship money, making the logistical arrangements, trying to train, and trying to develop *Eco-Challenge* had me arriving in Kuching mentally and physically exhausted. I needed a vacation, not an endurance race.

From Kuching, it was a seventeen-hour odyssey to the starting area via turboprop, an insecticide-reeking express boat (a sleek, enclosed passenger boat resembling a DC-10 without wings), a four-wheel-drive Jeep, and a ten-mile walk through the rain forest. The Raid contingent of athletes, journalists, and assistance crews—over 500 people in all— marched in single file.

The deluge began early in our hike. Water gushed from the heavens as if shot from a fire hose, and my every inch was soaked. The ground was mud—yellow like mustard and slick as ice. Walking uphill meant stooping on all fours and using roots and tree trunks as makeshift ladder rungs. Walking downhill was worse, and I spent more of it sliding on my backside than actually trekking.

As luck would have it, we arrived at our destination of Ba Kelalan just as the rain stopped. The village was small—just an airstrip, a school, and scattered huts. The local children serenaded us as we marched in, their angelic voices and scrubbed faces in sharp contrast to the sodden, weary competitors.

My teammates and I stowed our gear on the hardwood floor of a schoolroom. It was not luxurious, but a roof over our heads would be welcome when the inevitable midnight monsoon struck. An Australian team shared the space. Between the two squads, the level of nervous energy was stifling.

I needed to get out, be alone, clear my head. I went for a walk, trying all the while to figure out how I'd gotten myself so emotionally detached from the enormous undertaking I was about to embark upon. The Raid would mean days and nights of immense suffering. There would be endless confrontations with personal fear as we trekked through claustrophobic jungle choked with leeches, wild pigs, cobras, and man-eating reticulated pythons. I don't know how I had fooled myself into thinking I would finish, let alone win, but somehow I had done just that.

But even as I tried to summon passion for my teammates and the race, my mind wandered back to my office and the thousands of phone calls I needed to make if *Eco-Challenge* was to become a reality. I interrupted my walk time and again to tell other teams about this exciting new American event, the *Eco-Challenge*. It would be held in April 1995, just six months after the Borneo Raid. The title sponsor was Hi-Tec Sports, the same company sponsoring Team American Pride.

Right up to the moment the gun sounded, I was soliciting other teams to race *Eco*. I was a lone man on a mission, justifying my actions by seeing the big picture: The Raid was small in the scheme of things, only a small stepping-stone to future success. Clearly, I was in Borneo for Mark Burnett, not Team American Pride. I was not mentally prepared. I had taken on too much. It had been an insane decision to even come here, a fool's errand.

When we finally got under way, foolishness was replaced by optimism. My entire team expected to win. I finally set aside thoughts of *Eco*. My forty-pound pack felt uncomfortable on my back as we trekked quickly from a small clearing into the jungle. Sunlight went from being an equatorial spotlight to being filtered, and almost blotted out, by the green canopy. My Navy SEAL triad of Rick Holman, Pat Harwood, and Bruce Schliemann were navigating. Then—and I don't know the precise moment it occurred, but I remember thinking it was awfully early in the Raid for such a thing to happen—we got lost.

The 1994 Raid Gauloises had barely begun. We were supposed to be looking for a trail that would take us up a mountainside. Instead, we were utterly, completely lost, stumbling off-trail through wall after wall of vegetation. The confusion of being lost in the jungle is mind-boggling. There are no landmarks to orient north, south, east, or west. Maps are useless. Forward movement means hacking trail with a machete—arm-numbing work that brings exhaustion quickly in hot equatorial climates.

We despaired when darkness fell. We hadn't seen another team in almost twenty hours. We endured the terror of marching all night through primitive jungle, never quite sure whether those pink eyes reflecting from our headlamps were going to attack. In all that time, we didn't hear or see another team. Finally, at noon on the second day of the race, we entered a small village nestled in a clearing. Our joy was beyond words.

Then we looked around. Everything looked familiar. The houses, the airstrip, the school. . . . We were back in Ba Kelalan! We had walked in a circle. The Raid Gauloises was twenty-four hours ahead of us.

The smart thing to do in that situation would have been to review what I already knew about the Raid—that twenty-four-hour gaps can be overcome; that my team was strong enough to march nonstop to make up that gap; that things could only get better. Instead, I focused on the negative: My invincible Navy SEALs had gotten us lost; my team sponsor, Hi-Tec Sports, could use our failure as an excuse to pull their financial commitment to *Eco;* and finally, I would become the laughing-stock of the entire outdoor industry.

As producer of *Eco*, this was a nightmare. For the SEALs, the specter of being disgraced in the Special Warfare community loomed. The trouble was, none of us had a clue how to get out of Ba Kelalan. I took control of the untenable situation and held a team meeting. We agreed to pay a local guide to show us where that elusive trail was located. We were breaking Raid rules, but we didn't care. Forward progress was paramount. Meanwhile, we began squabbling as the strain finally hit us. The squabbling drained us much more than the physical effort. The Raid had become a misery, and none of us wanted to be there.

Bruce was forced to drop out two days later because of a twisted knee, he had no choice—the joint had swollen to grapefruit size. Now not only were we still in last place and arguing, we were also officially disqualified. I was depressed. It couldn't have been worse.

Never quit.

Two days after that, in a bamboo forest somewhere between the fifth and sixth checkpoint, frustrated that instead of challenging for first place we were now still in last place, I also decided it was time to go home. It was time to quit.

Quitting is the most cowardly of all acts. The American public will forgive many indiscretions, but not quitting. It's a sign of weakness. In a team situation, quitters fail not only themselves, but also their team-mates. I didn't quit right then on the spot because I didn't want it to be an impulsive act. After my decision, and just to prove a silly point, I trekked with the team for two more days all the way through the harsh, "hellish" jungle section to the beginning of the "fun" river rafting sec-tion of the Kubaan River. Wandering down to the river with a bar of soap, I washed myself and decided it would be here—at the *easy* part—that I would quit. I went back and told my teammates. I said something like "I don't need to be kicked in the balls to know it hurts," as a way of reminding them I had already finished this race twice before and had nothing to prove by finishing my third Raid. They tried to talk me out of it, but my mind was made up. I was quitting. I was joining the ranks of those men and women who prefer the easy way out. I rationalized it a hundred different ways in my mind, but the bottom line was that I quit. Borneo 1994 was not my finest moment.

Now I'm glad it happened.

The path to success twists and turns, and bumps and grooves can make the journey frustrating, but these difficulties also make the desti-nation even more rewarding. Truthfully, I didn't deserve to succeed in Borneo. I'd juggled work, sponsorship raising, and the all-consuming preparation. My fitness was sufficient, but my focus was blurred. I'd flown halfway around the world with too many other things on my mind, then seen my dreams of winning the Raid dashed in a maddening twenty-four-hour jungle walkabout, wandering around in last place, be-fore being disqualified. If I hadn't quit, chances are, I would have begun viewing myself as some sort of Superman. I would have grown to think that my gut feelings no longer mattered. I had known before I started the Borneo Raid that it was a mistake, but my ego had deafened me to my intuition. I should have listened to my inner voice.

Quitting was my wake-up call. I learned valuable lessons that propelled my career to the next level. If you set out

> **Focus: If you set out to accomplish too much at once, you will fail.**

to accomplish too much at once, you will fail. I didn't belong in Borneo. My focus should have been wholly on preparing to produce *Eco-Challenge*. *Eco* was my future and my passion. I was emotionally invested in *Eco*. Finishing, and hopefully winning, the Raid was a distraction because I'd moved into a new season of my life. I *wanted* to win the Raid, but I *needed* to work on *Eco*. Nowadays, when I get the urge to take on too many tasks, I remember Borneo. I force myself to make hard choices about what I *want* to do and what I *need* to do. When I've made my choice, I move forward immediately, putting all my energy and focus into what I need to do.

When I flew home from Borneo, I wasn't sure whether my quitting would negatively affect *Eco-Challenge*. I dwelled on it quite a lot on the flight, trying to think of clever ways to explain my actions to sponsors and the media. That's when my gut told me not to. As British prime minister Benjamin Disraeli said, "Never complain and never explain." I decided to move forward, ever forward. Yes, my pride was hurt, and I knew many in the adventure community would disparage me behind my back for quitting. I would have to endure the wounded pride, the disappointment of not finishing. Hurtful things all, but hardly fatal. If I let them get in the way of *Eco-Challenge*, it was nobody's fault but mine.

Never complain.
Never explain.

I heard somewhere that "when all else fails, the future remains." So before my plane landed in L.A., I'd set Borneo aside. It was over. I immediately got to work on producing *Eco-Challenge*.

I never want to quit anything again: Nowadays, people use words like "driven" and "dogmatic" to characterize me. They're right. But Borneo 1994 gave that side of my personality a substantial underpinning.

The failure in Borneo was a blessing in disguise. Through failure, I gained the additional strength that I needed to make *Eco-Challenge* a reality. Through the devastating act of quitting, I gained a valuable incentive to persevere, if only so I would never again experience that awful sensation. I don't think I would be where I am today if it weren't for those setbacks. Remember: If you're not failing, you're not taking enough chances. Babe Ruth failed seventy percent of the time when he stepped up to the plate. And while he's remembered

> **If you're not failing, you're not taking enough chances.**

for hitting home runs, it should also be known that he was baseball's strikeout king, too. That never stopped him from swinging for the fences.

When failure strikes, take a deep breath, evaluate what went wrong, then change your approach and push forward again. Ever forward. It was with this in mind that I attacked *Eco-Challenge* with renewed passion.

Chapter Six

How the West Was Won

I have found I work best when I act as an individual, thinking on my own and not following the sometimes very wrong nature of the group. There is a clear difference between working alone, however, and neglecting the need for teamwork when it is necessary. In those situations, I learned through adventure racing, not just any team will do. Proper teammates are essential. Chosen wisely, teammates will support every goal, no matter how outrageous or seemingly impossible. However, the poorly chosen team makes even the easy quest arduous, and it is destined to unravel.

Choose your companions before you choose your road.

The Moors of North Africa have a brilliant proverb to describe how to build the optimal team: "Choose your companions before you choose your road."

So how was I to build my great *Eco-Challenge* management team? Where would I find the dynamic individuals willing to work long hours tilting at windmills? How would I motivate them when that inevitable ebb set in?

Eco-Challenge, should it succeed, would be my dream business and, for my employees, a dream job: traveling the world, staging adventure in exotic locales, and living there three months of the year. That management team came together quickly in the form of Brian Terkelsen, Lisa Hennessy, Amanda Harrell, and Tricia Middleton. All were extremely intelligent, they were not afraid of hard work, and they had a passion for adventure. This core group became *Eco-Challenge.*

Originally, the first member of my team was supposed to be Gerard Fusil, founder and producer of the Raid. Because of the staggering size of an expedition race, his expertise would be crucial. The staging of an expedition race is not unlike a military invasion, with personnel and helicopters and kayaks and white-water rafts. There is always a headquarters, complete with a satellite communications center, video editing bay, motor pool, field hospital, and media center. Out in the field during the race, there are search and rescue, coordination of volunteers, transportation of gear . . . the list goes on. Each location presents a different logistical nightmare, based on the host country's unique physical and cultural characteristics. Never having coordinated such an undertaking, I planned on getting my money's worth out of Gerard's field expertise. Gerard's consulting fee was in the six-figure range, but he was the only person who had successfully pulled off several expedition races, so I gladly paid it.

Soon after, I received crushing news: When Gerard signed our agreement, he was already under contract with the Raid's parent company, Pub Event. Twenty-five days before signing on with me, he had signed with them to provide a similar and exclusive service. Their agreement expressly stipulated that he was forbidden to work for any race other than the Raid.

I had been deceived. Short of flying to Paris and filing suit in a French court, there was no way of retrieving my money. With Gerard out of the picture, I was faced with the brutal realization that I was now the sole technical and logistical mastermind behind *Eco-Challenge.* It was like a linebacker being sent into the Super Bowl without a playbook. Problem was, I'm not a linebacker. I'm a quarterback—a leader. My strengths lie in creativity, production, and coordination. But as I said earlier, when it is all on the line, I'll do any and every task necessary to see a goal completed.

I was scared—I didn't even know what I didn't know. Gerard had been like a security blanket that provided courage. Now I was alone.

I took a deep breath, thought through the hundreds of logistical riddles and technical obstacles looming before me, and found the resolve to go forward. It wouldn't be pretty, but this was definitely the sort of sink-or-swim scenario in which I thrive. I could not, however, do it alone.

What I needed was someone smart to share ideas and strategize with. I had the vision, but no formal training. I brought in Brian Terkelsen, an investment banker from New York who had abandoned Wall Street to make a living at adventure out west. We talked over pizza and beer. Not only was he brilliant and driven, he also truly saw the enormous financial possibilities of the adventure market. He had done his homework. Brian informed me of research showing that family travel adventures such as white-water rafting on the Snake River and mountain biking atop the slick red-rock trails outside Moab were becoming enormously popular, even as hotel rooms in traditional travel destinations like Waikiki were going begging. Americans were stepping outside the comfort zone. Brian confirmed my gut feeling. This new trend was a lifestyle shift instead of a short-term travel phenomenon. Better yet, we would be among the first to capitalize on it.

After joining my team, Brian's first act was crunching numbers to check the plan's viability. He then designed a five-year plan for the new Eco-Challenge Lifestyles Corporation. He forecast earnings based on the several different indicators that might prove my hunch about America falling in love with adventure. To my relief, we were right. The dollars were out there. We just had to go get them.

The ordeal began in earnest in early 1994. From the creative vision already in my head I could see that the three greatest obstacles to a successful *Eco-Challenge* were, in no particular order: (1) obtaining a proper location; (2) obtaining the necessary permits; and (3) raising funds.

Brian and I tackled the most logical, and easily solved, dilemma first: location. I chose Utah. The deciding factor was participation by the state's governor, Mike Leavitt. He allowed me the use of his private plane to fly all over the state for my initial survey, seeing with my own eyes the canyons and rivers and deserts so perfect for *Eco-Challenge*. Beyond that, he made it clear that hosting *Eco-Challenge* was a priority. This unexpected wooing carried tremendous heft. Having the governor as an ally was vital. His participation would smooth the permit process. We needed those permit approvals for the use of public lands—a notoriously tedious and expensive undertaking.

I spent a month studying maps and flying low over Utah in the governor's personal plane, deciding where to put the course. In the end, I chose a route honoring Grand Canyon explorer John Wesley Powell's journey of a century before. Starting just south of the snowcapped Uinta Mountains, the route would loosely parallel the languid Green River as it made its way toward the Colorado River. The finish, fittingly, would be a seventy-mile kayak paddle from the roiling Colorado into the placid water of Lake Powell. I envisioned fireworks announcing the winner and a gala postrace party under the stars.

I hired a series of guides (white-water, climbing, etc.) to set the course. Then I personally trekked, climbed, mountain biked, rafted, and canoed parts of each section. The beauty and isolation were stunning, and it was almost impossible to believe that the neon and glitz of Las Vegas were just a few hundred miles over the desert horizon.

America's cities can feel so crowded that it seems the entire nation is a dense mass of humanity. But in the desert of southeastern Utah, hearing no sound but my footfalls or the roar of the wind, marveling at the land appearing just as it did when time began, I knew the peace only solitude and communion with nature can bring. Utah was the right choice.

Course maps in hand, I strode into the State Tourism Department a few days later, expecting to march back out with a satchel of permits. "This course looks great," they enthused. "Fantastic."

"Thanks," I said. "Can I pick up those permits now?"

They looked at me as if I were an idiot. "Permits?"

"Yes. To get access to that land for the race."

"Permits?"

"That's right."

There was an embarrassed silence. "Oh, no. We can't give permits for federal land." So much for having the governor on my side. What followed was a six-month, quarter-million-dollar wrangle with the Federal Bureau of Land Management. Precious sponsorship dollars I'd accrued to cover race expenses went into hiring consultants to perform environmental impact reports. The free permits I'd expected became very expensive. Then environmental groups noted that bighorn sheep and peregrine falcons lived on the course. My April race date conflicted with the mating of the sheep and hatching of falcon nestlings. The environmentalists feared that my athletes would disturb them.

It was bad enough having to battle the Bureau of Land Management, but the irony of environmentalists opposing my race was surreal. My *Eco-Challenge* was designed to *heighten* public awareness of the earth, not destroy it. The land we were traveling through was used year-round by ranchers to graze cattle and was open to four-wheel-drive vehicles. I couldn't understand how a few hundred people passing through in five-person groups on foot over a weeklong period could be any more disruptive than thousands of cattle eating and sleeping and defecating there on a daily basis. Not to mention our planned route: Ninety percent of it was regularly used by off-road vehicles tearing it up every weekend. The *Eco-Challenge* standards for leaving land as we found it were so stringent that it was a mandatory requirement for teams to carry out all trash—including bodily waste—or face disqualification. Not so much as an energy bar wrapper would be left behind.

Clearly, we weren't going to cause an impact, and would promote ecotourism. But *Eco-Challenge* was a lightning rod for attack because we had the backing of the Republican governor and the national prominence gained from selling television rights to MTV. Environmental groups chose to focus on attacking us instead of on a coal plant being built in the same region. Despite the coal plant being a far bigger environmental concern, attacking it wasn't sexy and wouldn't draw big media attention.

Would *Eco-Challenge* lead to an increase in ecotourism in Utah? Definitely. And that was the crux of the discussion. The various wilderness alliances saw land use as a bad thing. In some ways, I saw their point. Ongoing use of the land would be harmful. However, I believed that the benefits outweighed the negatives. With responsible and regular usage by the public comes a sense of propriety and desire to protect. In the long run, that land is less likely to be developed because people have had a chance to appreciate its beauty, and will fight to preserve it.

On the opposite side of the argument, Utah's cattle ranchers also fought against *Eco-Challenge*. They saw "Eco" in the title, read about MTV's involvement, and lumped us with those environmentalists who have decided that cattle are bad for the land and must be banished entirely. However, I totally disagreed with the hard-core environmentalists who forgot that many of the ranchers were from the same families that had done the hard physical work of taming the West a century before. Some of the fringe environmental groups were even sniping at cattle with guns, and threatening to do the same to *Eco-Challenge* athletes!

I had walked into the firestorm that defines land usage in the modern American West. I had unwittingly added new fuel to the fire, with friends on neither side.

The lesson learned was about education. I hadn't studied the powers of the governor's office, nor had I studied which agency owned the lands on which I wanted to race, or read up on the land wars between ranchers and en-

> **Make sure a business can really deliver.**

vironmentalists. In hindsight, would I have still staged my race in Utah? Yes, but I still wish I had known that my most politically connected teammate, the governor, had no power over the lands I needed.

Never again would I enter into a team relationship without learning exactly what my new ally could and could not offer. It was bad enough to have to raise sponsorship, find teams, and secure a TV deal. Now I had an uphill battle for the permits that I had thought were my easiest task.

This permit process dragged on for months and became a bureaucratic nightmare. Again, it all seemed too much, and most friends told me to go back to the easier world of marketing or even back to selling T-shirts on Venice Beach. But I knew my destiny.

Chapter Seven

Don't Sell Out

A year before the looming disaster of my first *Eco-Challenge* I had been standing at the Raid finish line in Borneo, talking with an American journalist about the essence of adventure racing. He spoke of the beauty of nature, the purity of competition, and the stunning way in which teams can dissolve in the face of enormous hardship.

"There's one other thing you forgot," I told him. We were standing in the shade of an enormous banyan tree, on a bluff overlooking a clear, fast-moving river.

"What's that?"

"Money," I told him.

He looked at me incredulously, like so many people who didn't see the enormous potential for combining business and adventure. "You've got to be kidding."

"Look." I pointed to the sponsor's logos affixed to each competitor's uniform, the banners across the finish line, and the massive, multicolored logos affixed to the race organization's very prominent vehicles. Then I pointed at the cameras filming the whole thing for worldwide broadcast. "Do you really think the organizers have flown halfway around the world

> There's a crucial difference between selling and selling out.

and risked their lives in this snake-infested jungle to put on a race of this enormous scale just because they believe in the purity of competition? It's about money, too."

> There's nothing wrong with pursuing a dream to make a profit.

There was nothing wrong with seeing adventure racing from that perspective, just as there's nothing wrong with pursuing a dream to make a profit. The dilemma comes when a dream that has been cherished and pursued for so long is corrupted—or, as I was to learn with *Eco*, entirely sold—for the sake of money. It's crucial to know the difference between selling and selling out.

For the inaugural *Eco-Challenge*, lining up race sponsorships proved to be an altogether different sort of hurdle than our political snafus. Our budget was $1 million, a figure we hoped to achieve through sponsorships, entry fees, and the MTV rights fees. While designing the course and fighting to secure permits, I was also working the phones and flying about the country to wrangle financing. I didn't see the *Eco-Challenge* as just a race but as a lifestyle brand that applied to all men and women, so I didn't limit my search to corporations aligned with the outdoor industry. Other than alcohol and tobacco, I believed that every product had a place with my competition. I pitched *Eco-Challenge* to companies ranging from airlines to auto manufacturers to soft drink bottlers, assuring them that my offbeat event would someday be the standard by which all endurance competitions—and adventure itself—would be measured.

It helped that the athletes already believed in what I was doing. Thanks to that "audacious" ad in *Triathlete*, which boldly pronounced that *Eco-Challenge* ate the Ironman triathlon for breakfast, I had no shortage of eager squads. The fifty-team limit was met a month before race day. However, few corporations saw my vision and came on board with the sort of massive financial commitment I needed. I had to have seven-figure deals, and was getting high five and low six ones. The money to meet budget requirements was accumulating, but slowly. Just as with the permits, there would be no race if I couldn't procure enough backing. I worked eighteen hours a day during the first five months of 1995, half of that time with a phone pressed to my ear. I tried to remain calm, but the pressure was enormous.

It was then that the Easy Way Out tempted me. A large, well-known shoe company called with an offer that would put an end to my woes. For $500,000 they wanted to buy the race sponsorship, substituting their company's name for the word "Eco" in the race title. They were happy to be associated with the adventure aspect of my race but didn't believe that the ecology part would hold long-term value. How wrong they were. In addition, they would own the event, the name, the rights—everything. I would walk away with a half-million dollars free and clear, but still have the headaches of producing the "Shoe Company" Challenge. The alternate side of that was that if I turned down the offer and *Eco* didn't happen for lack of financing and permits, I would be left with nothing.

I refused their money. It was tempting to quit. The problems with permits and financing were growing. My gut told me to persist.

It sounds crass to use the term, but at this time in my life, having balls counted for everything. That company wouldn't have shown interest unless they saw the same enormous potential in *Eco-Challenge* that I did. If they were willing to spend such an enormous amount of money, so would others. Yes, I was out of cash, depending on advances from credit cards to pay the mortgage. But taking the Easy Way Out would undermine the purity of my *Eco* quest and cheapen my dreams. The clock was ticking, and the money was rolling in slowly. I would just have to work harder.

And I did. Amazingly, my proposals found their way into the proper hands, and several lucrative deals ensued, most notably with Hi-Tec Sports and JanSport. Once we reached the $1 million benchmark, I was free to focus my energies on securing permits. The relief was enormous.

Then a week before the race was to begin, as competitors had already begun arriving in Utah to acclimate to local conditions, Brian arrived with bad news. There was, he told me, "a mistake" in our budget numbers. "How big a mistake?" I asked, not sure I wanted to hear the answer.

"A half-million dollars."

I sagged. In reality, when it comes to budget deficits, I've always found that it's practical to double any figure. Upon further analysis, I was unfortunately proven correct. I was looking at a million-dollar shortfall just one week before the start of the most pivotal event in my professional life. Where in the world was I going to find a million dollars?

Huge problems tend to make me calm and focused. I would find the answer. Combing the list of corporations we'd sent sponsorship packets to, we noted that few had the financial wherewithal and were small enough to turn on a dime to pay us a million dollars within the next seven days. I made hundreds of calls, narrowing the list down further, weeding out those corporations that would not act quickly. The list was still too long, and time was running out. I needed to pinpoint one company. It was all or nothing. No time for anything else.

I had a gut feeling about MET-Rx, the dietary supplement company. They were young, aggressive, and eager to crack the competitive energy bar market. They also had loads of capital. I arranged a meeting, and pitched *Eco-Challenge* with an enthusiasm (and desperation) I'd never known before. The MET-Rx people were dazzled, and it seemed like they might actually do this. I worked literally around the clock from small motel rooms near the racecourse in southeastern Utah negotiating a deal. I felt like I was willing to do anything to save my race, except change the name to the MET-Rx Challenge. We all compromised, and they agreed to come on board as race sponsor for $650,000. The race would go off with a deficit, but it would go off. My staff could not believe I had done it. They danced around the production office and hailed me as the Pied Piper.

So here we were, almost financed, less than a week before the race was to start. Onsite, fifty teams, MTV, *Dateline NBC*, *Good Morning America*, forty journalists, and hundreds of volunteers had arrived in Utah, expecting a race. All that was missing at this very last stage were the permits. Everyone would have had to turn around and go home (though not without putting a price on my head) if those damn permits weren't approved.

I felt incredibly calm throughout those last few crazy days. My gut was right again because at last, four days before the start of the first *Eco-Challenge*, the final permits were approved. The race was a go. My vision was about to be realized. Very few people ever realized how close we'd come to failing both financially and for lack of permits until the 11th hour. Keeping a calm demeanor had again paid off.

When I think back on the wonder and calamity of that first race, a series of images crosses my mind: the start at sunrise, with teams galloping across the desert on horseback while ABC's *Good Morning America* broadcast live from our location; the canyoneering section, where the narrow chasms were often filled with rivers fed by snowmelt; courageous competitors, realizing that swimming those frigid waters was the only means of forward progress, boldly tackling the challenge; Horseshoe Canyon, where teams rappelled. I can still see how antlike they appeared against those massive, biblical cliffs. And the finish on Lake Powell, with flares shot into the sky to celebrate the arrival of the victorious French squad, Hewlett-Packard. (The team's corporate sponsor showed considerable vision by subsidizing a team whose impact wandered far beyond HP's core business unit.) Only forty-two percent of all teams finished, proving how tough my race was.

But most of all, I remember Team Operation Smile and a wonderful seventy-two-year-old woman named Helen Klein. This team's goal was to raise money for an international organization whose corps of doctors traveled to Third World countries performing surgery to repair cleft palates in children. This simple procedure, so common in America, is almost unheard of in developing nations.

Team Operation Smile had a roster of true adventurers—a few were from Europe, a few from America. All, with the exception of Helen, were in their thirties and forties. Helen was their senior by decades. She had come to exercise late in life, taking up running as a means of staying fit in her forties. Within a decade she was completing marathons and ultramarathons. Eventually, she and her husband put on a race of their own, the Western States, a one-hundred-mile trail race in Northern California's Sierra Nevada mountains. Helen not only coordinated the competition, she completed the entire course several times.

Despite this endurance racing background, Helen looked old and frail compared to the U.S. Marines and twenty-something triathletes populating that first *Eco*. She got more than a few odd looks. Only Team Operation Smile saw the potential greatness in this tough great-grandmother.

> *How* teammates communicate can mean more than what is verbally said.

The goal of Helen and her teammates was to finish, not necessarily to win. So they raced slowly. They worked together, helping and encouraging each other. During the mountain bike portion, Helen somehow managed to fall off her bike on a flat section of ground. For no reason, she just fell. None of her teammates moaned or rolled their eyes or gave her a hard time in any way. None of them had that strained look on their faces that translates into "We shouldn't have brought this old lady along." Instead, they stitched up the open cut above her eye, helped her back on her bike, said a few encouraging words, and got on their way again. They genuinely cared for her.

Their actions showed that Team Operation Smile was cognizant that *how* teammates communicate means more than the communication itself, and that unspoken communication can be more powerful than words.

I have seen the effects of improper communication, especially the unspoken variety.

We only have so much energy within us. That energy has to get us through each day, whether it be at work or on the *Eco-Challenge* course. But every time we have a negative encounter with another human being, that energy gets drained. Human problems drain energy like nothing else. Just as the bathtub is full of water, so the *Eco-Challenge* athlete begins the race with a full supply of energy. The bathtub is full; there are ten days to race. You can't put any water back in the bathtub because you have only a certain amount of energy to last the race. The moment you start the race, the plug is pulled ever so slightly from the drain. Ideally, only ten percent of that water (energy) drains from an athlete each day. If the athlete paces him- or herself well and is a fair and compassionate human being, always focusing on the team's goals, he or she will reach the finish line ten days later, just as the last bit of water empties down the drain.

Negativity drains energy.

But when communication goes awry, energy is drained from the bathtub at five to six times the rate it should be. The team is yanking the plug from the drain, instead of peeling it back just a crack. When one team member berates another, saying they should have trained harder, they're not fit enough, or they're letting the team down—all of which is completely pointless—it's obvious that that person is going to feel much, much worse for being yelled at. If someone's feeling bad, it's much harder to carry their pack. I'll never forget the team that was screaming at one another, pointing fingers of blame for this mistake or that mistake. Of course, that sort of thing happens all the time at *Eco*. But what made that particular team special was their name: Faultless.

Energy can also be drained through unspoken communication of the negative variety: the dirty look, the deliberate bump, and worst of all, faking compassion. Saying to some poor guy, "Don't worry, I'll carry your pack, you just carry yourself," but doing it without compassion, in a condescending way, makes that person feel terrible. Those insidious forms of poor communication destroy teams. Anger festers inside both parties. All remaining energy is lost, and the team fails.

This philosophy applies in exactly the same way to everyday life. Unresolved conflicts, whether relationship or work based, drain your energy much more than just working to avoid energy-draining people at all costs. You must choose teammates in life and in business wisely.

I think energy loss through poor communication was why a fit team that included some U.S. Marines didn't finish the 1995 *Eco-Challenge*, but Team Operation Smile, with its little old lady, did. True, they finished in last place, but they finished. They achieved their goal. Team Operation Smile showed one of the true secrets of *Eco-Challenge*: It's not just about the fitness and the skill, it's also about the energy retained through positive, honest human communication.

Team Operation Smile conserved its energy by avoiding negative communication. When team members did communicate, it was always in a positive, reinforcing manner. They didn't blame one another when things went wrong. They were humble and flexible. If a problem arose, such as getting lost, Team Operation Smile never bickered. Instead, they'd look at the situation and say, "We're in this together, let's deal with this."

Helen was a smart, tough lady. Once, when she and her teammates had run out of water, they came across a puddle in the desert. Another team was already there, staring at a dead cow lying in the water and wondering whether the water was safe to drink. Helen didn't hesitate; she got down on her knees and began drinking. "It's drink or die," she said. "It's fifty miles to the next water and you'll never make it without drinking now. If you get sick, it'll be after the race and that's okay." But it was probably more to the credit of her teammates that

> On a good team, ordinary people can do extraordinary things.

Team Operation Smile finished. They didn't complain, they supported one another the whole way, and they kept their egos in their backpacks.

I realized, after watching Helen's team paddle across the finish line on Lake Powell, that having her on the team was actually a gift for Team Operation Smile. Women in general—and an older woman like Helen, specifically—are actually better in the *Eco-Challenge* than men. They're willing to give and receive help without attitude. Men are resistant to asking for help. They think it will make them look weak. Often a woman will size up a situation, admit that she can't conquer it alone, and then ask for help. Or she will say, "I can't carry this pack. Do me a favor, carry the pack for me over this hill because you look strong." Can you imagine a guy saying that? A guy would rather die. In most cases, though not all, when a guy's exhausted, he's not thinking about the team's goals; he's only thinking about looking good. He doesn't want to admit being in trouble.

On good teams, men and women don't worry about how they look as individuals. They worry about the team. The person in trouble is not a man or a woman, but a teammate.

The greatest lesson I learned at that first *Eco* was how ordinary people on a good team can achieve extraordinary things. But highly skilled team members who have focus, know how to communicate, and really care for one another as a team are unbeatable. The group I've got working for me now—producers, camera operators, sound engineers, editors, assistants, course designers, mountain guides—is just such a team. We've stood by one another through thick and thin, driven by loyalty and focus on the goal. They are the best.

I'm reminded of something oil billionaire J. Paul Getty said: "Take away the oil fields and the factories, but leave me my fifty best people and I'll have it all back double in five years."

Eco-Challenge was a success, but instead of being an easy springboard to a second race, it saddled me with a few hundred thousand dollars of debt. Exhausted, I flew home to Southern California, hoping for several weeks of much-needed rest.

I didn't get it. ESPN was already calling, wanting me to set up an *Eco-Challenge* at the X Games. Two great things came from that second *Eco-Challenge:* First, my fee paid off the Utah debts once and for all, putting my business into the black, where it's been ever since. Second, we had a chance to immediately produce another *Eco-Challenge*, putting into practice all we had learned in Utah. The X-Games *Eco-Challenge* went extremely well and helped my production team gain and keep the enormous confidence they still exhibit today.

When MTV balked at airing another *Eco-Challenge* without a stipulation that all competitors be between the ages of eighteen and twenty-five, I secured meetings with ABC, Fox, NBC, and CBS to pitch *Eco*. All of them turned me down; however, my relationship with the Big Four networks had begun. I didn't know it then, but I'd be visiting them often over the coming decade.

Though I could have stayed in Los Angeles and developed other projects, adventure called. I needed to be in the bush. There I find solitude and beauty and purity and focus. That's where my heart lies. So I began planning the 1996 *Eco-Challenge*. And even though it would have been easier to keep the race in America (considering I didn't have a TV deal) I decided to take it beyond American borders. I wanted the race to have a more international feel. I was thinking that British Columbia, Canada, would be ideal.

It was an exciting and frightening time of my life. The number of outrageous obstacles my team and I had hurdled to realize the previous *Eco-Challenge* were now forgotten as we focused on the 1996 race. We had to find a TV partner and produce our first international event. A lot of people thought I'd lost my mind by going international, but my gut told me I was on the right track.

Competition is healthy.

Never underestimate what a great team can accomplish.

That was my mind-set after finally

getting *Eco* off the ground. I had achieved success, I had completed the first part of my *Eco-Challenge* goal, and I knew that bigger roadblocks were ahead. Step one had been to produce an *Eco-Challenge*. I'd now produced two. The next step was to make *Eco-Challenge* the premier expedition race on the planet, usurping all other races, including the Raid. The way to do this was through better television. I began an active search for a network that would allow me to produce the sort of epic *Eco-Challenge* television show I had in mind. Through proper production and distribution, the medium of television would make *Eco-Challenge* and *adventure* synonymous.

I'm not frightened of competition. It can only make you better. Strangely, the idea of competition has taken on negative connotations in the past decade or so. The implied aggressiveness scares some people and has made competition politically incorrect.

Life is competition. And the *Eco-Challenge*—as the perfect blend of sport, human dynamics, and adventure—is the epitome of competition. Athletes race against other teams, against nature, against the environment, and against their own limitations. Whether competing in the *Eco-Challenge*, vying for a CEO's position, or racing for that last spot in a crowded mall parking lot, everyone on earth is in the game.

Denying an attraction to competition is a form of fear, like procrastination or rationalization. People often feel that they need to be one hundred percent sure they'll succeed before starting something difficult. What they're really saying is they're afraid to compete and fail. But are there really any sure things in life? Are you ever one hundred percent sure it's the right time to start a business, change jobs, get married? Of course not. My philosophy is that I'll Jump In and commit, even if I'm only *forty* or *fifty percent* sure it will succeed. Mike Sears, who served as producer on the first *Eco-Challenge*, was once quoted as saying, "Burnett is the kind of person who would walk down Fifth Avenue in New York, saying 'Come on everybody, let's follow the parade,' even when there's no parade. But within a couple of blocks, people follow him to the parade, and he'll be leading it. I can't decide whether he's courageous or crazy."

Maybe I'm both. But there's no denying that the pressure of competition sharpens me, pushes me, makes demands of me. Instead of denying the attraction, I embrace it. In competition, as in failure, are sown the seeds of success.

It was lucky for me that I believed in this because now I had *no* TV network, little money, and no *Eco-Challenge* location secured. But I still knew I was on to something big. I was going international.

Chapter Eight

Adventure TV

With no TV deal, I had only seven months until the start of the British Columbia *Eco-Challenge*. Then I had some luck. A friend of mine, Tom Wertheimer, arranged a meeting between me and Greg Moyer, president of the Discovery Channel. The Discovery Channel International had already expanded into more than one hundred countries and needed the programming to give itself a genuine worldwide brand. What Greg saw in *Eco* was an adventure Olympics. We ended up marrying the Discovery Channel and *Eco-Challenge* over a cup of coffee at the National Association of Television Executive Producers Conference in Las Vegas. The deal, signed on a scrap of paper with numerous handwritten changes, gave the Discovery Channel global multimedia rights in exchange for a production fee and a rights fee. With about six months to spare, I'd pulled another rabbit out of the hat.

The challenge for me would be personal and professional. On the professional level, attempting to narrow hundreds of hours of footage into five hours for broadcast would be daunting. That our deadline to deliver the show was just ten weeks after the race ended made it all the more demanding. More than ever before, as we expanded, I would need to focus on my duties as executive producer and choose the right teammates.

Personally, I had never worked within a corporate structure. My company is not like other companies. We don't dress in suits and ties. The atmosphere is collegiate, yet workaholic. Instead of glitzy office space, we work in a nondescript building. With the amount of time I spend on location, and the fact that we rarely have visitors who we need to impress (we let our shows do that), fancy office space would be a waste.

Discovery, on the other hand, was a $7 billion corporation with thousands of employees. Discovery would be able to put *Eco* in 140 million households in 130 countries.

To ensure that the production would go smoothly, I promoted a young coordinator named Lisa Hennessy to producer. She'd worked on both previous *Eco*'s in different capacities and as a producer. She proved to have enormous bandwidth, nerves of steel, and good financial management instincts. To ensure that the majestic British Columbia course would challenge competitors even more than the one in Utah, I enrolled a highly respected senior mountain guide named Scott Flavelle to set the route.

The differences between how I produced a show and how Discovery produced a show soon became obvious. We were used to getting by with a small, casual, smart, shoot-from-the-hip team. If we held a production meeting, it was likely to be over coffee, lasting no more than fifteen minutes.

Discovery favored structured, formal production meetings. They had a public relations crew sending faxes and Internet transmissions worldwide, touting the event. Corporate sponsors had been flown in and were being treated to first-class accommodations. To say that I was uncomfortable in Discovery's presence would be an understatement.

I was so busy trying to fit Discovery's corporate image of what a successful executive producer should look like that I stopped being myself. There was a lack of spontaneity and spark. Instead of eagerly anticipating its start, I just wanted to get the race over with.

It was only after things started going wrong that I became my true self again—which happened less than an hour into the race, then continued for its remainder.

The start took place in a vast meadow along the Lillooet River. Teams were supposed to ride horseback for twenty-three miles, then ford the freezing river and begin trekking over the dense, forest-shrouded mountains toward a glacier field. But a course-marking error caused the leaders to ride off the path after just a few miles, toward an abrupt chasm 150 feet deep. The bridge over the chasm was washed out, so horses and riders would plunge over the edge if the athletes weren't careful. The situation couldn't have been worse.

With the people at Discovery looking on, I had my helicopter pilot fly low in front of the lead teams and literally herd them back the right way. Then I stopped the race clock, gathered all the teams at the offending junction, and restarted in order of their appropriate time differences—this time going in the right direction. Body language and confidence are everything in dealing with these kinds of situations. I showed no uncertainty. I simply made the decision and got things back on track. The competitors went along with the adjustment without grumbling.

It's amazing what you can get people to do through clear, concise decision making. The opposite can be disastrous.

British Columbia turned out to be a turning point for *Eco-Challenge*. The international roster of athletes saw that our course was every bit as tough as—if not tougher than—the Raid or any other race. On the professional side, the February 1997 broadcast on Discovery was a ratings success, for which I received my first Emmy nomination.

Eco-Challenge is a metaphor for life, in which men and women are thrown together and told to get along every minute of every day, despite being cold, tired, wet, hungry, and miserable. The brave souls entering my race endure the mountains and rivers and jungles gladly. Normal people under normal conditions know better than to venture outside in the brutal weather my teams endure. I'm proud to say that *Eco-Challenge* expedition racers accept it as part of the game and never complain about the hardship. In fact, they embrace the hardship. And that—more than nature, being on television, or physical fitness—is why people race *Eco-Challenge*. They know that hardship is the only way they can find out what they're truly made of—whether they'll back off when the going gets tough, or whether they'll find the courage to be bold, and become their own hero in the process. It doesn't matter whether they win or lose, but how they play the game. The purity of that notion is inspiring.

When I delivered the rough cut of the 1996 *Eco-Challenge* show to the Discovery Channel people, they were unhappy. My creative team of Mike Sears, Tom Shelly, and Jay Bienstock had raced against an impossible deadline. They were expected to produce a show in half the time we currently use. And they did. Not only was it the first time in TV history that an adventure race was to appear on television as a five-hour miniseries, but those guys managed to whittle several hundred hours of race footage into an action-packed television adventure in just ten short weeks.

Discovery had asked for a show with no narrator, and we did it. We felt it didn't work, but we agreed. It was our plan to add narration and change the show as soon as Discovery saw that their idea did not work. But, instead of realizing their error, Discovery conveniently forgot that the show was bad *because* their "no narration" plan did not work! To make matters worse, and with only five weeks until the air date, they gave our finished show to another production company, with orders to make changes to hours one, two, and five. We were horrified. The changes were no different from what we'd proposed, yet we weren't being trusted with our own program.

It was around this time that my second child, Cameron, was born. The birth of a child reawakens one's core values, such as perseverance and being true to a personal vision. It's as if newborns are a reminder to be our best, because they will later emulate our behavior, good or bad. I was disheartened by Discovery's attitude, but emboldened by Cam's birth, quietly vowed to continue fighting to make *Eco-Challenge* look the way I wanted it to. Anything else would be a form of selling out.

With the exception of the three segments Discovery ordered recut by the other production company, I was successful. Later, when it came time to submit an *Eco-Challenge* episode for Emmy consideration, I chose to send hour four because it was one of those that was entirely finished by us. When we received word of the nomination, we were ecstatic because we knew it was for our work, not the other production company's.

A creative rift developed between Discovery and me. They envisioned *Eco-Challenge* as a pure documentary show focusing on nature—trees, animals, glaciers—with the athletes and the race as secondary elements. I strongly disagreed. *Eco-Challenge* was not a documentary but a reality drama about men and women in harrowing, torturous personal circumstances. The animals and nature were bit players in the race's larger drama.

Unfortunately, the Discovery people had total creative control of what aired on their network. Though I controlled the actual production, it was their vision of *Eco-Challenge* making its way onto television. I realized there was no way I could win. At Discovery's urging, I signed over control of *Eco-Challenge*'s television production in 1997. It was a three-year deal, giving Discovery exclusive rights until the summer of 1999. I would remain as executive producer, but the actual control was Discovery's. They decided to use another production company to shoot the race.

Discovery, however, soothed my anguish by doubling my salary. I figured it was a pretty good deal to get double the money for half the work. I swallowed my pride and took the money.

Despite working shoulder to shoulder with the Discovery Channel's most experienced executive producer, Angus Yates, who became a close friend, the first production under the new arrangement was hard. Discovery's accounting and production management departments split the budget into two business units: a television production and a race production. I knew that this was insane and far more expensive, but the issue was out of my control. I was in charge of the race budget, and could only chafe at the money wasted by separating race and TV budgets. My dream was being absorbed by a corporate entity, and I was in the awful position of standing to the side and watching. Just two short years after Utah, when I'd had the courage to tell a major company that I wouldn't take its money, I was only too happy to sell out to Discovery. One could argue that I was being paid quite a bit more money, but the money mattered less and less. I believed that the point of *Eco-Challenge* was human drama, not a factual natural history documentary with a few people thrown in for color. Discovery's point of view was wrong, and violated every tenet of my *Eco-Challenge* dream. Nevertheless, they were in charge. It was an awful feeling.

That sensation permeated the 1997 race in Australia, but by the 1998 race in Morocco, things became substantially better. Angus had gained more control and as a result had brought in a new supervising producer, Paul Sparrow. We all got along great, and Paul agreed that it should be a drama about human relationships. That was gratifying because it was my fourth *Eco-Challenge* and I saw it in my head before we even started shooting. My creative muscles were developing. Honestly, it all goes back to what I said about trusting your gut. I had developed a keen intuition for what works and doesn't work on television.

For instance, when I envisioned the start in Morocco, I had a crystal-clear image of competitors atop camels, sprinting across that hard desert sand like a vision from *Lawrence of Arabia*. And that's how I started the race. It worked brilliantly. Through hours of watching rough cuts of shows and collectively deciding what to keep in, what to keep out, and what elements needed to be added, I learned how great television should be structured. Combining that new knowledge with my gut instinct fueled the growth of my creative ability.

Paul Sparrow had trusted my instinct, and we'd worked well together. Our Morocco show was incredible, and I won my first Emmy. My ego was soothed, and I fooled myself into thinking that qualms about Discovery's control over *Eco* didn't bother me. In fact, when Greg Moyer, the man who'd brought *Eco* to Discovery as his pet project, made me an offer in 1998 that would provide for my family for many years to come, I agreed to the deal. Discovery would own *Eco-Challenge* outright—television rights, race production, everything. It was a financial dream come true.

Then just as we were about to sign the deal, Greg Moyer abruptly resigned from Discovery. In the confusion that followed at Discovery's corporate headquarters, the offer to purchase *Eco* was taken off the table.

I was panicked. I had stopped everything because of the anticipated deal, and now, without it, my race might die.

However, just months later, in the spring of 1999, Discovery came to me with an alternate offer. What had recently become pleasant now soured. They no longer wanted to buy the race, but they still wanted to produce it. However, they would cut my fee in *half*, cut the race's budget in *half*, and then have me solicit corporate sponsorship dollars to make up the difference. Their argument was that they'd spent $40 million on *Eco-Challenge* between 1996 and 1998, beaming the television show into those 140 million households in 130 countries. Despite the fact that they'd earned a handsome financial profit on their investment, Discovery acted as if I was in their *debt*. They were gambling that I would feel so beholden to them (and so incapable of finding a better deal elsewhere) that I would lose my nerve and blink, taking whatever scraps they offered.

I admit that I seriously considered it. Half a paycheck is better than none at all. By this time, I had a wife and two sons. I told Discovery I would think over their offer and return with a reply. But I was bummed.

Even worse was that I had discovered a new idea called *Survivor*, about a group of castaways marooned on an island, and I had hoped Discovery would be the ones to buy that as well. When they turned *Survivor* down, I knew our relationship was worse than ever. Discovery sealed our fates in the summer of 1999 when they let their exclusive option on *Eco-Challenge* lapse. I'd gone from one secure show, with high hopes for a second one, to zero in only a few months.

It was time to stop selling out and take control of my dreams. I had to admit that I was no longer an adventurer dabbling in television, but a television producer with a passion for adventure. I needed to focus on being the best television producer I could be. I would take *Eco-Challenge* to another network, and focus totally on the human stories.

> **Stand by your dreams. Don't sell out.**

Oddly enough, I had a *Survivor* pitch meeting with Steve Chao at the USA Network shortly thereafter. He quickly passed on *Survivor,* but before the meeting was over he told me he was interested in the rights to *Eco.* I was stunned and thrilled. Instead of the world rights Discovery had previously owned, I boldly told Steve I was only interested in selling American rights to the show. He agreed, and we signed a deal. I then made another deal with the Borneo state of Sabah for sponsorship worth $2 million U.S. Then I brought in Columbia TriStar to handle overseas distribution because they're known as being the best in the world at that facet. The result? A year of enormous growth. *Eco-Challenge* would be seen by over one billion people in 2001. The ratings on USA more than doubled my Discovery ratings, and the show was critically acclaimed. The best part was that the show was a human drama instead of just extreme adventure and nature—what I'd wanted all along.

Thank God that Greg Moyer resigned and they took that offer off the table. At the time I had been sick to my stomach, but looking back, it was the best thing that could have happened. Through that twist of fate, I learned a hard lesson about being true to my dreams. They are guideposts, showing the way to success. Altering them or selling them out can only lead to regret. Standing by your dreams is an act of perseverance that builds immense character, empowering you as you dream anew. So stand by those dreams, even when the temptation to sell out is strong.

. . .

Before filming the Borneo *Eco-Challenge* due to the USA Network, I owed Discovery one final *Eco-Challenge* television show. I traveled to the Patagonia region of Argentina in November 1999, fully in charge of what would truly be the toughest race in the history of expedition racing. Athletes would race almost four hundred miles through a host of disparate ecosystems: riding horseback across the grassy pampas, bushwhacking through a bamboo forest, paddling alpine lakes and rivers, climbing to the summit of Monte Tronador, a fourteen-thousand-foot Andean glacier on the border of Chile and Argentina. It was undoubtedly the world's premier endurance competition, and athletes expected—I would even say *demanded*—a course as severe as that in Patagonia.

Patagonia was an odd experience. Not only was I working with Discovery, with whom I now had an otherwise nonexistent relationship, but I was also working side by side with the same Argentinian government officials—and in many cases, military leaders—whom I'd fought so hard against in the Falklands War. My Parachute Regiment had taken heavy casualties during the advance on Port Stanley. At one point during my 1999 visit to Argentina, I even walked into a military barracks and saw photos on the walls of the very same units I'd seen combat against. It reminded me, somewhat sadly, of my friend Bob Wade. We had grown up a few miles from each other, and had served together all over the world during our time in the Parachute Regiment, getting shot at numerous times. During the Falklands War, he had been enormously selfless. Once, after marching all day through a bog, I felt as if my wet feet were frostbitten. I was cold, wet, and miserable. Bob gave me his last pair of dry socks. When I first came to America in October 1982, I had expected Bob to be joining me within a matter of months, but he was tragically murdered in London by a moron in a bar disagreement. Knowing that he died so stupidly after being shot at so many times during warfare made me even more personally motivated to live my life to the fullest.

That trip through the Argentine barracks was both poignant and surreal—it was made even more surreal by the fact that they knew nothing about my British military background. They thought I was born and raised in the United States.

As I've said before, every race has its peculiar logistical problems, and every moment is tense—from my yelling "go" through a megaphone at the starting line to the inspirational moment when the last team trudges across the finish line. So there's never really a sense of ease accompanying my midrace moods. This year it was the weather that nagged at my intuition.

All mountains are notorious for their abrupt weather changes, as their shape and breadth have the capacity to alter the pattern of the wind. Patagonia is an extreme case in point. Its location in the infamous "Roaring 40s" wind belt (named for the forty- to fifty-degree latitudinal range) meant that powerful Antarctic winds raked the region.

The weather was good for the low alpine section of the race—dusty and extremely hot, with no wind. Competitors had brought tents and sleeping bags, but had no need for them. The fastest teams dropped theirs in a transition area in order to travel lighter and faster. Then, as the lead teams headed into the jagged Cathedral Spires region of the course, the worst storm in ten years struck. Full whiteout conditions meant that all helicopters were grounded, so I could only sit in the communications tent at headquarters and listen to the radio for confirmation that all teams were accounted for.

As night fell, the storm cleared. I relaxed. Then, awful news. Three teams were still missing: Team Red Bull from Spain, Team Vail from the USA, and Team Argentina. They had been battling for a spot in the top ten when the storm set in, and they were definitely in the heart of the mountain wilderness. The temperatures were lowest there, not higher than ten degrees. That cold, combined with wind and snow, created the perfect recipe for hypothermia—and death. I tried to sleep that night but could not. My *Eco-Challenge* motto is "four out, four back," meaning that the four team members always traveled together. That night, however, the motto took on new meaning as I feared that, for the first time in *Eco-Challenge* history, teams might not come back.

At 4 A.M., I called on the radio for a status check. Neither USA, Spain, nor Argentina had wandered into the safety of a checkpoint. The storm had temporarily stopped, however, and I gave the order for my pilot to warm up the helicopter. Along with course manager Kevin Hodder, we took off at first light to search for the missing teams.

The mountains now looked deadly instead of gorgeous as the pilot eased the helicopter into the sky that clear, crisp dawn. I no longer saw scenery or television visuals; instead, I recognized the force of nature, silent and foreboding, waiting to swat aside my brave competitors. The ground was blanketed with three feet of new snow that glittered in the pale purple morning light. I felt a chill just looking down on it. How could any team survive a night out in conditions like that without tents or sleeping bags?

We flew over the course for three hours, checking every possible location. There was no sign of the missing teams—no footprints, no campfire smoke, no distress signal. They were gone. As I told the pilot to head back to headquarters, I looked away so he couldn't see me. I had a tear on my cheek. In my anguish, I must have asked Kevin the same question fifty times: "Do you really think they could possibly survive all night without sleeping bags?"

"I hope so," he answered each time. "I hope so."

The radio crackled to life. It was a jubilant call from the rappel checkpoint—USA, Argentina, and Spain had just arrived. They had marched through the night together, encouraging one another to keep moving to avoid freezing to death. No one was hurt. And they were eager to continue racing.

I was in awe of what they had accomplished, and very, very relieved. When I arrived in Patagonia at the beginning of *Eco-Challenge*, I very much expected the next *Eco-Challenge* to be produced for the USA Network. I could finally produce a TV show about *Eco-Challenge* that focused on the human stories. Also, with great excitement, I anticipated producing my first *Survivor*. Year 2000, the start of the new millenium, was also going to be my new beginning. I'd been preparing for this moment for many years.

But when those three teams got lost, I truly didn't care about future *Eco-Challenge*s or my first *Survivor*. There were lives at stake. It's important in business and in life to be able to prioritize and to be able to dump well-laid plans as the need arises.

Fortunately, *Eco-Challenge Patagonia* ended well, with everyone safe and a great TV show produced. But those two days of fear reminded me that, when dealing with nature, anything can go wrong. Nature is so powerful that no matter how successful you are, or how big your production is, a powerful snow storm in the mountains, a tropical squall on the ocean or a desert sand storm can remind any of us just how insignificant we really are.

With this in mind, I began the new year. I knew I had enough experience under my belt to deliver to America a whole new type of television—with the best natural backdrop ever seen. But I would not underestimate nature and I would not overestimate my skills.

Chapter Nine

Pitching *Survivor*

I first heard the idea that was to become *Survivor* in 1995, while at Fox television in Los Angeles pitching *Eco-Challenge*. Lauren Corrao, the exec hearing the *Eco* pitch, told me about this game show concept in which a bunch of people starve on a desert island. They compete for luxuries such as food and pillows. Meanwhile, a host living a sultan's existence on a luxury yacht offshore eliminates them from the contest, one by one.

The brain behind this game show concept was Charlie Parsons, a prolific British producer. Lauren loved the idea but believed it would take someone with previous experience in producing large-scale adventure-reality TV in a remote setting to pull it off. In her mind, *Eco-Challenge* qualified me. In the days and months after that meeting, I constantly thought about the island game show, though I saw it more as a drama. When I traveled for business I would look about the plane at my fellow passengers and imagine us crash-landing on an island. Where would I fit into our new society? Who would lead and who would follow? Who would find the ordeal overwhelming?

I made it my goal to meet Charlie and show him *Eco-Challenge*. We hit it off, and I ended up buying the North American rights to his island show in 1998. I had a gut feeling that I could make this great concept even greater. My *Survivor* would be bigger, more dramatic, and more epic than any nonfiction television ever seen.

But first I had to convince a network to pay the production costs, which would run into millions of dollars. I would get only one chance to pitch it to a network or cable channel, and I didn't want to blow it. As practice, I pitched the idea to friends and acquaintances at dinner parties. I didn't tell them they were guinea pigs—but at some point during dinner, someone would invariably ask what I was working on next. I would smile, take a deep breath, raise my voice just a notch for greater emphasis, then explain *Survivor* as brilliantly and boldly and seductively as I possibly could.

> **Practice your pitch on your unsuspecting friends.**

At first the pitch came out long-winded and overcomplicated. My dinner companions would lean back in their chairs, heads nodding vacantly as if listening, even as their eyes glazed over and their thoughts wandered. They would hear me out, but then the conversation would diplomatically shift to another topic.

As I perfected the pitch, however, making it faster and more fluid and always exciting, I noticed my dinner companions leaning in to hear each syllable. Their eyes sparkled. They peppered me with questions, all of which I learned to answer with the same polish I used to deliver the pitch itself. By the time I walked into the Discovery Channel's headquarters in 1999 to pitch the show for the first time for real, I was capable of selling it to anyone, anywhere.

Or so I thought. Mike Quattrone at Discovery turned me down flat. He said it wasn't right for their brand. I was stunned. Discovery had been my partner on *Eco-Challenge* since 1996. We had a solid working relationship, and the network was the natural place for a show about adventure, nature, and drama. Mentally, I had counted on them buying the show. I was devastated.

But, as is my modus operandi (moving forward, always forward) I pitched *Survivor* everywhere it seemed appropriate—and was rejected at every turn. At the USA Network, Steve Chao turned it down in less than thirty seconds, then announced out of left field that he wanted to buy

Eco-Challenge. At Fox, David Hill said I should first produce and televise it in Australia to see whether it worked. He warned that if I messed up my first network show in the United States, it would be my last.

By the way, Steve and David are now friends of mine. Both are brilliant TV minds who are highly unusual in their willingness to laugh publicly at their *Survivor* passes—something less-confident execs would never admit.

The passes continued: NBC, then ABC, and finally CBS. Yes, CBS passed! Tom Noonan, president at UPN, loved the concept, but the fledging network couldn't offer enough money for me to put together a quality production. Although I was tempted, I knew exactly how I wanted *Survivor* to look and feel, and for that I needed a sufficient budget. Knowing it was for the best, I mustered up my courage and turned UPN down.

Then, unbelievably, I got another chance to pitch CBS. This time it was Ghen Maynard in CBS's Drama Division. Ghen immediately liked what he heard and took the idea to CBS president Leslie Moonves, who was intrigued but wanted to hear me pitch it in person. I should have been nervous going in to see one of the legendary tough guys of network TV, but I had never been calmer. Confidently, my skills polished at all those dinner parties and previous pitches, I walked into Leslie's enormous office and delivered the pitch of my life. I began by handing him a mock copy of *Newsweek* with *Survivor* on the cover. I wanted him to know how big I believed this idea was. During this pitch I also added that I was certain I could help CBS pack the advertising into sponsorship packages similar to those for large sporting events. He bought the show, approving a large enough budget under the condition that I help line up advertisers before filming began. He wanted to see whether the advertising community would embrace this novel program, and whether I could deliver on my sponsorship concept.

The moment Leslie said yes was one of the most exciting and horrifying of my life. I was finally in the big leagues. I'd sold a television show to one of America's three biggest networks. Anyone in America with a television could watch my show. Cable wasn't a prerequisite. The potential audience was massive, which was enormously frightening.

Survivor would mean a nationwide contestant search followed by thirty-nine days of filming in the South China Sea. The logistics were incredible. Was I good enough to pull it off? Would America embrace my quirky little show or would they laugh at my surreal Tribal Councils, native "art direction," and overly serious confessionals? Beyond my dramatic intentions, what if someone died? And what about the promise of helping to sell commercial minutes before production began? Had I been crazy to make such a promise?

> **Be bold and exude confidence, no matter how nervous you may be.**

I took a deep breath, quieted the doubts, and remembered that I needed to believe in myself. The show would work. I had always surrounded myself with good people. I had made quality adventure-reality television for five years. Plus, I had always played a huge role in securing advertisers for *Eco-Challenge* on the Discovery Channel. I knew my stuff. As long as everyone did their jobs and I did mine, *Survivor* would turn out fantastic.

I got down to work, sending location scouts around the world to find the ideal *Survivor* island. Then I attacked the financial issue. I worked with CBS Advertising Sales to design sponsorships instead of merely commercial time, offering advertisers on-air product placement if they put their money behind *Survivor*. The sponsorship product-placement concept was relatively new for a network television series, though I had been doing it for years as a necessity for *Eco-Challenge*. I learned it through studying the financial sponsorship model for the Olympics. I was positive the sponsorship model would work with *Survivor*, too—and it did. Advertisers embraced the new show. Every sponsorship was sold before we began filming. *Survivor* was already a financial success! All we had to do was get the same number of viewers that CBS would ordinarily get from summer reruns. I was sure we could do that.

Of course, I still wanted to get huge ratings. I pride myself on crafting absorbing television. Earning the money is fine, but at the end of the day, my biggest rush comes from overhearing people honestly rave about something I've produced.

The filming of *Survivor* presented one challenge after another. Nothing I'd filmed for *Eco*—not the sandstorms of Morocco, not the cyclones off the Great Barrier Reef, not the blizzards of Patagonia—compared with the travails of Pulau Tiga. From the tempestuous equatorial weather to the sea snakes to the daily spectacle of competitor Richard Hatch's nudity, there was never a dull moment. And the excitement didn't end when we flew back to civilization. The five short weeks between the end of location filming and Memorial Day weekend were a whirlwind of editing, publicity, high-level secrecy, and meeting after meeting after meeting with CBS to make sure the show had the perfect tone for the network's audience demographic. The first show was now "locked"—finished, in TV talk—but I was feeling edgy. Even I, who always decided not to stress out about that which I couldn't control, simply could not put up with the idea of America disliking my show.

In hindsight, those fears were unfounded. *Survivor*'s astronomical success now seems like a given. But before the show aired—before America met Pulau Tiga and the sixteen original castaways, and before Jeff Probst made "the tribe has spoken" part of the national vernacular—there were no guarantees that anyone would tune in for thirteen consecutive weeks. Television history offers plenty of examples of new shows bursting onto the screen full of hope, then slinking off to anonymity a few weeks later.

Just two days before the *Survivor* premier, my worry level was at an all-time high. My family and I were in Malibu, celebrating at the home of Burt, my former boss and mentor. His beach house sprawls across four oceanfront lots. As we chatted while drinking chardonnay on the deck, it struck me that the setting couldn't have been more idyllic: Before me on the sand my two young sons played near the Pacific. The sky was a cloudless blue. And the combination of salty, soft breeze and dry white wine lent a distinctly Californian touch that was a far cry from my childhood in London's grimy East End. I felt more than a little awed that I'd gone from being Burt's servant to being his holiday guest.

As if reading my thoughts, Burt pointed to the sprawling beach-front home next door. It was a single-lot teardown, but the view and location meant that it was selling for $3.7 million. "That house is for sale," Burt said. "Whoopi Goldberg was over looking at it the other day."

Jokingly, I said, "I should make an offer and buy that house. That would be the epitome of the American dream. From rags to riches. Everything would come full circle."

"No. You got it all wrong. You should buy *this* house and *I'd* buy that house," Burt corrected, laughing. "You'd be living on the big property, while I move into the small place next door—*that* would be the American dream coming full circle."

Legendary screenwriter William Goldman has written of what he calls "movie moments"—real-life coincidences so stunning and pivotal that they normally occur only on the silver screen. That Memorial Day, sipping chardonnay with Burt, I experienced a movie moment. It literally flashed across the sky, for as we sat there an airplane towing an advertising banner flew along the beach, just a hundred feet above the ocean. I ignored it at first—such airplanes are common in Southern California, especially on holiday weekends. But when I finally read the banner I was shocked: It promoted my *Survivor* premiere airing in three days' time. Burt and I gazed at it in disbelief. I felt more than a little proud that my old boss was witness to this aerial demonstration of how far I'd come.

If that had happened in a movie, the audience would immediately recognize the banner as foreshadowing great things to come. That's how I chose to approach it in real life. The airplane was the reassurance I needed. *Survivor* was destined to become a hit.

The challenges and adventures of *Eco-Challenge* had taught me to rely on my gut, but it was *Survivor* that made me put that skill to use each and every day. It was one tough decision after another. And you know, I can honestly say that few were wrong. For instance, when it came time to select a host, I watched more than a hundred audition tapes. But the minute I viewed Jeff Probst's, I knew he was the perfect fit for *Survivor*. He wasn't famous, nor was he an expert adventurer, but my gut told me he was the one.

I also had a gut feeling all along that *Survivor* would catch on with the American public. Who could resist watching sixteen strangers building a new world, then destroying it week by week, vote by vote? The subject matter was universally interesting.

I put that philosophy to the test two months before production began, while I was still in Patagonia for *Eco-Challenge*. The race was done, and it was our last night before heading home. By then, a press release requesting *Survivor* applicants had made the front page of *USA Today*, yielding six thousand homemade audition videotapes. My casting director, Lynne Spillman, had narrowed that initial bunch down to eight hundred, then further whittled the field to fifty "gold star" finalists. Lynne placed their videos on a single VHS tape for me to review, then FedExed it to Patagonia. Rather than watching the tape alone in the vacuum of my hotel room, I invited the crew to come have beers in the alpine chalet by the finish line. Many of them were booked to work on *Survivor* eight weeks later, and I thought they might like to discover what kind of men and women they would soon be seeing on a daily basis.

Secretly, however, I wanted to gauge their true reactions to the show. My strategy was similar to what it had been when I practiced the *Survivor* pitch at dinner parties. From the minute I popped that videotape in the chalet's VCR, everyone was captivated by those crazy tapes. The crew watched, enthralled, as the would-be castaways creatively demonstrated why they should be on the island. Sean Kenniff, who made the final cut, shot his video in the shower, surrounded by rubber snakes and spiders. Sonja Christopher played the ukulele and sang. The *Eco-Challenge* crew was totally captivated by the *Survivor* casting tapes. It was a great sign.

I flew home from Patagonia and began to focus exclusively on *Survivor*. The question I was asked most often in the weeks and months leading up to production was "How will it begin?" People were buying into the dramatic pretext of the show, but I think they sensed that a great deal of its legitimacy hinged on how we actually got the castaways onto the island. The television audience needed to see these people being marooned.

My gut told me that forcing the castaways to jump ship a mile offshore and swim to the beach would make a stunning visual, and elicit a strong emotional response in viewers that would make them want to watch more. Who wouldn't be titillated at the idea of literally leaping into the unknown?

When I'd gone to Borneo in June of 1999 to scout locations, the helicopter had flown over a small fishing village. It was primitive and obviously indigenous, set in a small bay fronting the South China Sea. The houses were on stilts, with longboats and native fishing boats tied off on the stilts. It looked like something straight out of *Apocalypse Now*, and had the visual and cultural appearance that would immerse viewers in the exotic location immediately. I never told anyone at the time, but that village was where I was determined to shoot the opening moments of *Survivor*.

When you know you are right, always stick to your guns; you *must* trust yourself.

I had a visual inspiration, looking down on the village. Not only would the castaways leap from a boat into the water, they would also board the boat at this fishing village. This would say to the American public that not only were the castaways about to be marooned on a forbidding jungle isle, but they would get there by leaving from a totally foreign, tiny, Third World fishing village.

However, when I returned to Borneo just prior to production, eight months later, the location scout didn't know what village I was talking about. He took me to a different village, one he felt was perfect for the opening. I took a look at the village he had in mind. It wouldn't work. When I described the village I'd seen before, he looked at me like I was crazy. He said that no such place existed. We flew up and down the coast for hours one day, searching only for that village—and found no sign of it. I went back to my hotel room thinking he was right: I'd imagined the place.

I dug out the photographs I'd taken during that initial visit. There was a huge stack, and I examined each photo, searching for some sign of that elusive, perfect village. I despaired, thinking that I would never find it, and *Survivor* would lose a vital bit of its essence and flavor.

Then I found a stack of photos I'd misplaced inside a zippered compartment on the side pocket of my luggage. There it was: the one and only picture I'd taken of that village. When I showed it to a few local guys the next day, they told me exactly where my lost village could be found. My location scout and I flew there, and saw that it was as I remembered. Perfect. I had made the decision to shoot in that village, and stuck by it, even when told I was mistaken. Some might call that stubborn (it is), but belief in gut decisions means sticking to your guns, even when others say you're wrong.

The next step in making that opening scene perfect was finding the proper boat. We found the *Mata Hari* moored in the harbor in Kota Kinabalu, outside a luxury hotel. She was a native sailing ship, built by hand, without the use of nails. Her hull was yellow, with an orange image of the rising sun on her stern.

The owner was happy to participate in *Survivor*'s filming, but she also let us know that the *Mata Hari* was more suited to coastal cruising than open-ocean travel. She had made the fifty-mile passage to Pulau Tiga once—and just barely. What's more, the journey took seven hours. This presented a pair of problems: first, safety. Would there be enough space on the camera boats to pull the castaways inside if the *Mata Hari* sank? Second, cost. Filming every minute of a seven-hour trip would

cost me a fortune. My dilemma was
simple: Either I accepted the risks and
financial obligations of filming on the
Mata Hari, or my opening segment
would have to be changed. But to what?
I couldn't very well have sixteen people
leaping from the afterdeck of a fiber-

> Nothing great
> is accomplished
> without risk.

glass trihull. If I were going to do that, I might as well be filming an island version of MTV's *Beach House.*

I risked it. On the morning of March 13, 2000, *Survivor* production
officially began. The call time was 4 A.M. The crew and I took speed-
boats out of Kota Kinabalu harbor to the fishing village of Sabang. It
was pitch-black as we left the marina outside the Magellan. The boats
had no running lights. Roaring into the predawn darkness was like entering one of those scary fun-house rides—I couldn't see what lay before me, but I knew the next thirty-nine days and nights of *Survivor*
production would be a thrill.

The castaways were also taken by speedboat in the gray dawn from
their hotel to Sabang. They looked scared as they walked through the
village in the early morning light. They donned orange life jackets, and
climbed into two colorful launches owned by the villagers. Then they
motored out to the *Mata Hari,* bobbing at anchor in the harbor. They
sat like victims, knees drawn close, helpless. At this point in the competition, they were not allowed to speak to one another. I was struck by
how normal they looked against the indigenous Sabang backdrop and
how unprepared they appeared for what was about to happen to them.
"Weird to think," a crew member said as I stepped into a boat to board
the *Mata Hari,* "that soon all of America will be talking about them."

The cruise to Pulau Tiga went flawlessly. It was a seven-hour, "one-
take" day, and we had a total of twenty-three cameras shooting almost
continuously throughout the voyage, then flawlessly segued into shooting island reality once the castaways paddled ashore. That two-mile
journey took several hours in the equatorial sun. I felt extremely bad for

the castaways, but happy that they had learned right away that *Survivor* was no picnic. I couldn't have asked for a better day. I knew as soon as I saw the rough-cut footage of Jeff Probst ordering the sixteen surprised castaways to take what they needed and leap from the *Mata Hari* that the show had a perfect beginning.

That decision got the production off on a good note, which was vital. We were trying to accomplish something that had never been done before on American television. Reality was being suspended in favor of "dramality" (drama and reality). Not only would the audience have to buy into that premise when the show aired, but the crew had to buy into it as we filmed. A majority of them had worked with me on *Eco-Challenge*, so they knew my approach to filming adventure-reality television. But *Survivor* was a test for all of us. A crew with the wrong attitude could unwittingly film the show as parody or farce or as pure documentary instead of a real-life struggle to endure thirty-nine days with all the inherent drama of living with fifteen judgmental peers. That made the Jump In decision-making process that much more vital.

Chapter Ten

Lessons in Reality

Going into the first *Survivor*, I knew that for the competitors, living on Pulau Tiga would be a scary experience. The island was only a mile wide and three miles long, and had been created just one hundred years before, when a volcano shoved that speck of land from beneath the sea. The jungle was formed from birds dropping seeds carried from Borneo; the animals had been stowaways on passing ships, then had been left on the island during refueling segments. My location scouts had been specific in listing island hardships: Pythons, malaria, mosquitoes, monitor lizards, rats, sand fleas, sharks, equatorial heat, and sea snakes were just a few. When it thundered across the sea and deluged Pulau Tiga with lightning and rain before continuing its march, the weather was horrendous. Finally, the living conditions left something to be desired. We wouldn't live much better than the castaways, sleeping in hastily built hooches with lukewarm running water and no air-conditioning. Our daily diet would generally be fish heads and rice.

All in all, it was an environment conducive to fearful, emotion-driven decision making. *Survivor*, however, was my leap into the big leagues. I didn't want to blow it. Before making any decision, I reminded myself to set aside any foreboding or irrational anxiety. Only then could my gut tell me the way to go.

Once we were all on our little island in the middle of nowhere, life was considerably better than I had imagined. Castaways were on one side and crew on the other, separated by a mile of swampy, thick jungle. The island took hold of the castaways, the crew, and everyone else involved with the production. The hardships of everyday living became an accepted fact.

For all the contrivance of filming a television show there, life on Pulau Tiga was a true adventure. And just as there is danger in adventure, there are also jungle splendor, exotic sunsets, and the wonder of watching monkeys and eagles and monitor lizards thrive in their natural habitat. Life on the island became an odd juxtaposition of deprivation and enchantment; we all began to enjoy Pulau Tiga very much. I cannot begin to describe the simple wonders of life on a deserted tropical island.

Nine days into filming, my gut told me that the castaways, the crew, and even the island were converging into a dynamic television show. On that day, as a tropical storm of enormous proportions drenched the island, I made a series of decisions that reinforced exactly the type of quality and commitment necessary to do the show the way I had previously visualized it.

Turn your anxiety into excitement.

The first council had been a nervous affair, as neither castaways nor crew yet realized that a visit to the Tribal Council could literally change a person's life. The person getting voted off wouldn't just be sent home but would also miss out on the tremendous wealth and fame afforded the *Survivor* champion.

I can only imagine that the first visit to the Tribal Council was incredibly surreal to the castaways. There they were, living in a makeshift shelter on the protected side of the island, subsisting on rice. Other than a few camera crews, they saw no other people. Their bodies were slowly adapting to the rhythms of sunrise and sunset, and planning sleep patterns accordingly. It was primitive—and very real.

They walk through the jungle in the dark for an hour, which is truly horrifying. Snakes are everywhere. They enter a clearing and—*voilà!*— a set decorated with faux ruins, a fire pit, and a gong. A jib camera hovers over the set, and six camera crews are staked out around the stage. Jeff Probst stands before the fire pit. The lights overhead are bright and hot.

Surreal.

Sonja, the nice older lady from Northern California, was voted off at that first Tribal Council. She walked off politely, not sure where to go or what to do. Had she experienced an adventure during her three days on Pulau Tiga? Perhaps. However, her fellow Tagi tribe members were genuinely sad to see her go, which brought the show closer to the vision I had for the Tribal Council—a tense, dramatic proceeding where an individual faces what they truly stand for by having their actions and words recounted and questioned before their peers. The game had a real edge to it. The Tribal Council was foreboding.

Three days later, at the second The Tribal Council, B. B. Andersen, the Kansas City contractor, was sent home after a raucous, irreverent council. I knew the American public would pick up on their sarcasm. Would it affect the show? I didn't know, but I did not want to take that chance.

In discussing the matter with Jeff before the third Tribal Council, I decided to accentuate the drama as much as possible. I wanted Jeff to ask deeper, tougher questions of the castaways, not letting them dodge anything. I wanted to coordinate the logistics of the council so that everything went off in crisp, punctual fashion. Keeping to a strict schedule would accentuate our control.

What I didn't plan for was the weather.

A by-product of island living is an unobscured horizon, so we were able to watch every moment of a line of thunderclouds as they marched toward Pulau Tiga. We could see the clouds stretching from the sky down to the water, marching our way, black and billowing like the jaws of death; the lightning crackles, horizontal sizzles zigging diagonally to the ocean surface.

By seven o'clock that night, as the Tagi tribe was led from the jungle onto the set, the storm was on top of us. The ripping gale dumped rain in buckets. The sun had gone down an hour before, and we'd turned off all island generators—save the Tribal Council's—to enhance the darkness. The crew wore rain ponchos, hiking boots, long pants, and shirts as they made final adjustments to their positions. Ninja Lynch, our jib operator, had one eye on the set and one eye on the sky, afraid lightning would strike his tall black metallic jib.

From then onward, when I think of thunder I remember the indescribable loud booms that night on Pulau Tiga. Like a light switch being flipped on and off quickly, lightning would turn the night into day, a split second would pass, then a deafening roar would descend on the earth and shake the ground. The thunder was so close, so powerful, it felt like it emanated from inside my head. Standing in the rain on Pulau Tiga that howling night, I knew again where fear, everyone's childhood fear of thunder, came from.

"Do we stop?" asked a crew member standing at my side. He was trying to be subtle, but the rain and wind forced him to yell directly in my ear. He was afraid one of the two-hundred-foot-tall banyan trees would topple onto the set or that a bolt of lightning could strike us all.

"No." I was firm. Having filmed through the blizzards of Patagonia, the sandstorms of Morocco, and countless thunderstorms, I thought that the gale now besieging us would not harm our production. I would never expose my people to undue risk. The storm would be nothing more than a tremendous nuisance. Still, to be absolutely certain, I asked my location manager, a Borneo native, Eric Thein. He told me the lightning was flaring horizontally across the sky, which meant it was a harmless phenomenon known as sheet lightning. We were in no danger of it reaching the ground and striking any of us. As for the wind, no banyans were close enough to fall on the set. The trees nearby were much smaller. Finally, the rain didn't bother me. I ignored it. A little water never hurt anyone.

We all got soaked that night, particularly Jeff Probst, who didn't

> **Embrace life's storms. The biggest storms can produce the most dynamic results.**

have the luxury of wearing a raincoat during filming (though the castaways did). We were plunged into total darkness twice when the storm knocked out the Tribal Council power. But we worked as a team and came through. Afterward, the crew threw a spontaneous, cathartic party that night. Even as I used the single island phone line to call CBS in Los Angeles and apprise them of the situation, the camera operators and sound technicians and dozens of other people who made *Survivor* possible cavorted. We were our own tribe.

From that night onward, I had complete faith in myself and my vision for the show.

There's a saying that people use on all my productions: "It's all decided—until the last minute, when Mark changes his mind."

I tweak and tune up until the moment filming begins, making sure everything is just right. I'm very aware that when filming begins there are one hundred crew members following a plan that I have set in motion. I've got them going down path X, and they're happy to go that way. But then I'll get a

> **Always be brave enough to change your mind when you know you should.**

nagging thought . . . something isn't quite right. I know how I want something to look when it finally appears on television, and I know I won't be happy with myself or the final product if it doesn't look just the way I envision it. So very often I'll tell those hundred people walking down path X that I've sent them the wrong way. My fault entirely, I tell them, but they're going down the wrong path. To accomplish our objective, they must head down path Y instead. I'm not afraid to look stupid and admit that I was originally wrong. The bottom line is that only results count. How you arrive at them does not.

I'm reminded of a scene from my army days. I was on the parade ground, watching a regiment drill in formation. Of the one hundred men marching, ninety-nine were in step, but one poor guy was off. "Look at him," I remember saying to a friend, "they're all in step except for that one guy."

My friend studied the formation. "You're wrong. Look closely. They're all out of step. He's the only one marching right-left, right-left to the sound of the drum as he should. He knows what he's doing."

Sometimes in life, everyone will act like you're out of step. It's okay to believe it for a while, but you must learn when you're the one in step, driven by the beat of the drummer in your head, and everyone else is off. There were a score of moments when I felt others viewed me as out of step during the filming of *Survivor*. Before filming began, for instance, I had a vision of filming interviews in reality. A castaway would be interviewed about his or her opinion of another castaway, even as that other castaway wandered by or even worked on their shelter in the background. A couple of my producers told me it wasn't done like that. They said that interviews should be done away from the group, in a controlled setting. But I saw *Survivor* as a completely new type of TV show that deserved new rules. I stuck to my guns and told them at least half the interviews should be filmed in reality. Once we tried it, we were all amazed to learn that the technique was incredibly effective. We even invented a name (actually an abbreviation): O.T.F., which stands for "on the fly" interviews. These could be done at any time, even with other cast members in the background. O.T.F. interviews really work.

Or take the Tribal Council lighting. Now, before I tell this story, know that I have absolutely no knowledge of lights or lighting. I don't know the lights' names or what they do or how they work. All I knew on Pulau Tiga was that I wanted the Tribal Council set to appear as if it were lit entirely by the fire and the moon. The castaways should not ever see a light.

The lighting crew went to work, laboring for days on the installation of a beautiful array of natural-looking lights. But during rehearsals for the first Tribal Council (crew members acted as stand-ins for castaways) I knew things weren't quite right. I told them that I needed all the lights changed. They were flabbergasted. The set was lit perfectly. They had all done their job.

And they were right. It was perfect—too perfect. I knew that the lighting crew had done the job to the best of their abilities, but I needed them to do it differently. I needed them to forget everything they knew about traditional methods of lighting a set and find some ingenious way to light the Tribal Council in a distinctly *Survivor* fashion. No visible lights. Let the castaways feel as if they are in a real ruin, lit only by firelight, rather than on a set lit by studio lights. It had to be authentic.

The lighting department told me it couldn't be done. Lights were located in certain places for a reason. Hiding them or getting rid of them entirely and still having enough light to shoot quality television was out of the question. It was a mark of their talent and professionalism that their true interest lay in getting the job done instead of fighting me. They put their heads together and found a way to light the set *Survivor*-style.

I also had a crazy idea to use the lighting on the Tribal Council to represent my belief that the Tribal Council was a metaphor for the weekly death and rebirth of the tribe. This came to me from reading Joseph Campbell's philosophy, part of which states that stories involving death and rebirth are timeless and give hope. At the Tribal Council, the tribe is essentially killing one of its own. Jeff Probst utters the words "the tribe has spoken" and then metaphorically kills the person who has been voted off by snuffing the person's torch. At this point we change the music to be more like a funeral march, as the "dead" tribe member walks off through the jungle and into a blue light before disappearing from the show. Jeff allows the ensuing silence to speak volumes, as the seriousness of the moment grows in sadness. The audience is always emotionally moved. But each week must have a happy, "hopeful" ending. That's why, when the cameras come back to the Tribal Council and the remaining "living" tribe members are still basking in the warm glow of orange firelight, Jeff offers them the week's moral story and sends them back to their tribe camps, telling them he will see them tomorrow. His reference to the next day, coupled with the upbeat music as they walk off, is their rebirth. It offers hope, and leaves the audience feeling positive toward the next week's show.

When I first suggested this, I know my lighting guys thought I had lost my mind, but they delivered for me anyway and, as subtle as these touches were, they worked.

It was the last week of filming. I was five days from the wrap party and looking forward to the flight home and the hectic process of postproduction, when a group of advertisers came to the island to see firsthand what we were up to. I felt a little Kurtz-ian showing them around, as the crew was all tanned and barefoot, totally in tune with island living. I was fascinated that this little subculture I'd created had morphed into something so powerful and pervasive. We ate, slept, and breathed *Survivor*.

The visitors, however, were jet-lagged from their trip and obviously wary of the island. They knew of the snakes, poisonous spiders, giant lizards, and malaria. I smiled as I remembered our own early days on Pulau Tiga before we all went native. I gave them a tour of the crew compound, served them a barbecue lunch on the beach, then took them for a boat ride around the island. Later, the advertisers got to watch a challenge being filmed at the mud volcano. That night, it was back to the crew compound for dinner and a glimpse at the rough cut of the first show, which would air in less than two months.

Despite all my gut decisions and hard work, I was tremendously insecure as those dozen men and women got a first peek at *Survivor*. Every single decision I'd made since the time we arrived on Pulau Tiga was about to be tested by that group. They would return home and vote with their advertising dollars.

The advertisers laughed in all the right places, showed awe and fear—all good things. But I knew we'd accomplished the results we'd been aiming for when one of them shook my hand. "I was expecting *Real World*," he said, in reference to the MTV television show, "but this is a feature film."

Another agreed. "I've got chills," she said.

After they left, I called the crew together to tell them that we were on totally the right track. *Survivor* would break new ground. But even I didn't know just how big our little show would become.

When you are the leader, you must make decisions. You must lead, and you need to convince your troops to follow you. What you must avoid is the "emperor's new clothes" syndrome. I don't want people telling me exactly what they think I want to hear. I've taken pains to surround myself with a small group of men and women who will talk to me honestly, all the time. If they don't agree with me, I want them to tell me. I may overide it, but at least I will have heard and considered other options. You cannot lead by consensus *or* by ignoring your troops. The best solution is to hire people who are smarter than you are, people who will stay focused and who will speak up in pursuit of a better product. But in the end, someone has to lead.

> **Listen to every viewpoint and then be decisive.**

Decision making is a tough task, but how you live life and how you achieve your goals depend upon it. So be right or be wrong, but don't be afraid to make a decision.

Chapter Eleven

How in the World Do I Top *Survivor?*

Before *Survivor* became the biggest summer television show in history, I was prepared for a certain degree of publicity. But I don't think any amount of planning could have prepared me for the sudden onslaught of national attention. People walked up to me on the street, in airports, in coffee shops, telling me how much they loved the show. It was beyond comprehension. My life had changed. If *Eco-Challenge* had brought me a little bit of attention, I had no idea what *Survivor* would bring. We were on the cover of every magazine. Talked about on David Letterman's show. I was even a guest on *Larry King Live*.

I was juggling my life between the ever important edit bays and preparing to produce yet another *Eco-Challenge*.

By the time I left the country again to fly back to Borneo to produce my first *Eco-Challenge* for the USA Network, every day was a surreal whirl of interviews, high-level meetings, and CIA-like secrecy to promote the show and keep America from learning the name of *Survivor*'s winner. At first I was afraid I would slip up during an interview and say "Richard Hatch" out loud, basically detonating the surprise finish. My paranoia about that happening was incredible. But in time I became so closemouthed that saying his name became an impossibility. I never spoke his name aloud, not even with people in my office who knew he'd won. I don't think I could have formed the words if I'd tried.

It was actually a relief to be back in Borneo. The host hotel for *Eco* was familiar ground—the Magellan Sutera in Kota Kinabalu, the same establishment we'd used for *Survivor* scouting and as a base for *Survivor* office operations during production. All in all, I'd spent about five months of my life in and out of the Magellan. Also, I was familiar with Borneo from my Raid debacle in 1994. The irony of my greatest failure and my greatest triumph taking place on the same remote island was not lost on me. Borneo was my geographic talisman, reminding me how far my dreams had taken me.

When my driver pulled up to the front entrance of the Magellan, a crowd of ten employees waited to welcome me—everyone from the manager to the chief bellhop. "Welcome back, Mr. Burnett," the manager said as a hostess stepped forth and placed a garland of orchids around my neck. "No need to check in. We've already taken care of that. Let us show you to your room." Then I was led to room 6260—the very room I'd left at 4 A.M. one black morning months before to begin shooting *Survivor*. I took it as a positive sign.

A segment of the race would take place through the Danum Valley, a primeval jungle populated by pygmy elephants and only recently explored for the first time. You have to see this spot to imagine its lush beauty and danger, choked as it is with cobras and leopards and leeches so insidious that one actually crawled into a competitor's penis. The rivers raged brown and swollen, often rising several feet within hours. The jungle was so impenetrable that when one competitor crashed his bike and punctured a lung, my helicopter pilot had to use the tail rotor to cut branches to make an impromptu clearing so we could land to make the rescue. To say I was in a place diametrically opposite the luxury and glitz of Hollywood would be a huge understatement.

However, that's where I was on August 23, 2001, when the final Tribal Council was aired on American television. Three weeks had passed since I'd arrived. Countless journalists on-site had asked me how it felt to be missing out on the big night when a record forty million viewers were expected to tune in for the *Survivor* finale. The questioning was constant, and led me to ponder why I was in Borneo instead of in Hollywood. What I realized was that though success was incredible, my dream had been to make a great, epic show and I'd done that. Now I was where I belonged: in the jungle on another adventure race, in an incredible place. Later that day, eight thousand miles across the Pacific Ocean, the secret I'd carried since April 20 was revealed to the American public: Richard Hatch had won *Survivor*.

Mark Steines of *Entertainment Tonight*, who'd covered the Raids in Madagascar and Borneo and had since become a close friend, was with me again at *Eco-Challenge*. We had talked in-depth many times about *Survivor*, but the subject of who won had always been off-limits—until then. "I guess you can talk about it now," he said.

Steines and I walked to the top of a small hill. Below were a few camera crews lounging, many of whom had worked on *Survivor* and already knew the outcome. They were the ones who laughed the loudest and most knowingly when I took a deep breath and shouted the winner's name to the world: "Riiiiiiichaaaaaaard Haaaaaaaaaatch!"

Then I climbed down from the hill and got back to the task of continuing to produce the Borneo *Eco-Challenge*. If

Revel in success, then find a new challenge.

you look at the Borneo show, it was one of the most adventurous and successful *Eco-Challenge* productions I've been involved in. Yet, it had come more easily to me. Lisa Hennessy, my co–executive producer, is so talented that she handled logistical details perfectly, freeing me up to be wholly creative. I had new confidence. The USA Network helped me feel that way by maintaining a hands-off attitude. The race was dangerous, inspiring, mysterious, and epic—everything *Eco-Challenge* should be—and we pulled it off without a flaw.

Toward the end of the race, when the final ocean leg was in its night stages, I could do nothing but wait at the Dragon Inn, a floating resort, which doubled as the finish line. I felt so confident, so relaxed, that I even allowed myself to enjoy some midrace party time with the crew. I look back on those few nights as pivotal to my growth as a person. Better decisions are made by relaxed people.

After the final team arrived at the Dragon Inn, the race concluded. We all flew back to Kota Kinabalu and ended up back at the Magellan. As I checked in, I felt like a new person. Our closing party a day later involved more than a thousand people and took over the entire open-air restaurant.

A headhunter priestess, who had skulls hanging from her clothes, opened the proceedings. The lights were turned off as she came in, chanting and followed by warriors from her tribe who carried spears and blow darts. Just fifty years earlier, Borneo had been a land of headhunters, and this formidable woman had been one of them. The government had brought her in to ward off the evil spirits that they believed had followed us from the jungle—and would follow us home if she didn't chase them back to the jungle. She was led to the stage in a trance, making eye contact with no one. During the next twenty-five minutes I didn't believe she was actually in the room. Her body was with us, but she was on the Other Side.

I've spent enough time in remote places with primitive people to know that the spirits they believe in are not to be doubted. I always respect local spiritual beliefs. Remote people have not lost touch with this other world in the way we city dwellers have, distracted by our electronics, steel, and glass. I guarantee that everyone in the room that night will remember it as long as they live. Even the Malaysian locals looked scared stiff of this woman and her belt of human skulls. I get chills just writing about her.

The Borneo closing party was an all-nighter for most people, but I went back to my suite early. Later, as I lay in my bed in room 6260, I knew that my third Borneo experience had been the best—a time I'd never forget.

I arrived home late on September 3, just in time for Labor Day. The journey was long, and I was still asleep when the doorbell rang the next morning at 8:30. I shuffled out of bed in sweats and a T-shirt, then walked bleary-eyed downstairs. As I walked through the kitchen, I had to step around my two dogs dozing on the tile floor. Clearly, after months of craziness, the household was long overdue for a rest.

I opened the door to find two well-dressed executives holding an envelope. They were serious and respectful, and reminded me of Secret Service agents. "Mr. Burnett," the taller of them said, "we're from CBS."

"Oh . . . good morning. Do you want a cup of tea?" My British sense of decorum made me feel sorry for them—what could be so important that Leslie Moonves would drag them out of bed this early on Labor Day?

The tall one handed me the envelope. "This is from Leslie Moonves. We need you to read it in front of us."

"All right." I shrugged. Inside the envelope was an extremely warm congratulatory note from the president of CBS. I would later frame it and hang it in my home office.

"Ah, that's great. Wonderful," I said. "Thank you very much." I said good-bye and waited for them to walk away so I could close the door without being rude. I was extremely touched that Leslie considered me important enough to send the note, even while I also felt bad for the two executives. More than anything, however, I wanted them to go away so I could get back to bed.

But they weren't going anywhere.

"No, you don't understand, sir," the tall fellow said. They presented me with a large basket filled with fruits and cheeses and wines. A toy car was nestled inside the basket.

"Wow. That's great." These guys probably wanted to go back home and get on with their holiday. "Thank you very much."

And still they wouldn't leave.

I began closing the door, not noticing the puzzled looks on their faces.

"Sir . . . I don't think you understand. The reason we're here . . . it's behind us." He gestured to a new champagne-colored Mercedes 500 SL parked in the driveway behind them. Still tired and confused, I thought, "Why are they pointing at their car?"

"Mr. Burnett," the tall man said finally. "Please let us show you around your new car. Compliments of CBS."

> Expect greatness, and fantastic surprises will find their way into your life.

Only then did I understand. The tradition of giving a car as a gift was one of the ultimate symbols of Hollywood success. I had arrived. I can still recall the jubilation at receiving an unexpected token of validation.

So often the unexpected has an ominous ring. But sometimes the unexpected is a package delivered to your doorstep, thanking you for a job well done. Be an optimist and a dreamer. Expect greatness from yourself, and the best kind of unexpected surprises will find their way into your life.

Accomplishing goals is often a long, drawn-out process. Sometimes it takes just weeks or months, but the process can also last years. *Survivor* took four years to transition from Christmas party conversation to television production. A goal may seem elusive over such an elongated time frame. It's easy to lose heart, abandon the goal as unattainable, then shift your life's focus to something else.

> Little victories: When setting long-term goals, benchmark your progress.

To avoid such a situation, I practice the philosophy of "little victories." You might like to think of them as "baby steps." These are minigoals, easily attained, steps on the ladder leading upward to the ultimate goal. Whenever you are setting a long-term goal, it's vital to have these benchmarks along the way as measures of progress and a means of keeping hope alive. By setting realistic, attainable goals you'll avoid frustration;

achieve small, empowering victories on your way to a larger one; and gain momentum as each success is realized. Some people call that being on a roll. Well, the roll is merely the result of each small success making you feel more confident.

When *Survivor* became a summer phenomenon, I was pleased to have accomplished my goal and ecstatic at the success. But it's important to note that the two weren't the same. Success was an incidental by-product of fulfilling my goal, which had been to produce the best possible television series I was capable of.

My goal for *Survivor 2* was to learn from the first show, then produce a tougher, more cinematic, and more engaging contest. Hard task, that. As with all sequels, *Survivor 2* would be compared endlessly with *Survivor 1*. That was the gold standard.

I had no control over the ratings or critical acclaim of *Survivor 2*. The public would make those decisions. Instead, I set three preproduction goals: (1) Find a proper location; (2) design and build a better Tribal Council set; and (3) prepare an incredible opening segment.

First things first. Step one was finding the location. The location is the seventeenth character on *Survivor*. It needs to be mysterious, epic, and inspiring. Pulau Tiga had truly been the centerpiece of *Survivor 1*. "There's something about an island," one of my producers had said when I told him I was thinking of a landlocked location for *Survivor 2*. "I think maybe you oughta go to the Bahamas or something."

That was certainly an option. But I needed a place whose wildlife and topography were even more daunting than those of Pulau Tiga. As much as I wanted to spend six weeks sunning in the Bahamas, *Survivor* meant building a civilization from the ground up, not Club Med. The viewer should never have the impression that a water-ski boat is going to appear over the horizon, towing a tourist.

For *Survivor 1*, I had chosen a place I was familiar with from the Raid in 1994. That familiarity had paid off. For *Survivor 2*, I would follow that same strategy and go to another familiar place. The place I had in mind was in the Australian Outback, on a beautiful part of the 1997

Eco-Challenge course. It had everything. The vast Outback, full of red earth dotted with eucalyptus trees, also had kangaroos, snakes, wild dingoes, and aboriginals. A truly magical place, it also had very real danger. One of my great fears during *Eco-Challenge: Australia* had been saltwater crocodiles. These prehistoric renegades are the scourge of the Australian rain forest, growing up to twenty feet long and attacking people without provocation. Their name, by the way, is misleading. They live in the ocean, but also thrive in freshwater, and are transient beasts given to traveling miles and miles inland. To my way of thinking, saltwater crocodiles—"salties," in Aussie speak—are basically great white sharks that can swim up rivers and wander around on land. A terrifying thought. I'd hate to come face-to-face with one of those beasts.

Portions of the 1997 *Eco* course had been held along the Herbert River, almost one hundred miles inland from the ocean. I scouted much of the course by helicopter, and was sure the area was free of saltwater crocodiles. As had been my practice since *Eco-Challenge* had begun, I'd asked every local I met about what given dangers lurked at every location. In the case of Australia, my constant questioning had been about whether or not salties had been found this far upriver. All the local and even national park officers had laughed at me: "Of course not." One local outfitter even ran kayaking trips through the Herbert River gorge.

At one point during the scouting, the pilot, course designer Scott Flavelle, and I landed on a small beach abutting the sparse eucalyptus forest. The day was brutally hot. After looking all over the beach for the telltale signs of crocs, we stripped and went for a swim in a giant pool at the base of a massive cliff over which a mighty waterfall tumbled. The water was black and ice-cold, but it felt good on the hot afternoon. I decided the idyllic pool would make a perfect addition to the course. As we choppered away after an hour of swimming, I was inspired by the majestic beauty of this remote place.

A few weeks later, as it became obvious that the Herbert River would be part of the racecourse, I decided I needed documentation for insurance purposes, proving there was no saltwater crocodile danger. I hired a wildlife biologist to fly over the course with me. Scott Flavelle flew with us. When we flew low over the place where I'd gone for a swim, I strained my eyes looking for crocodiles, but saw nothing. Afterward, at lunch, I said to the biologist, "I guess you can sign off on the fact that there are no salties here."

Between bites of his sandwich he said, "I think we should have another look, just to be safe."

I'm thinking to myself that this guy loves helicopter flights, part of some male testosterone thing. Hey, I love them, too. Helicopters are great. But they also cost a lot of money. You don't just go bumping about the Outback in helicopters as if it were some theme park thrill ride. However, I needed him to sign off on the insurance form, so I couldn't very well refuse that biologist his helicopter ride. Off we went.

Just when we were flying low over the place where I'd gone swimming four weeks earlier, he asked me over the headphones, "What do you see?"

I looked at the water and shore closely. "Nothing."

"Look again."

I studied the beaches below. All I saw were two old tree trunks that had probably been washed there when the river was high. Just then, the biologist asked the pilot to descend to the beach, and the helicopter dropped abruptly. As we got closer and closer, the logs suddenly came to life with immense speed and power. In a second they covered the ten feet between the sand and the water.

The biologist grinned. "Now you know what you're looking for, mate."

Scott Flavelle and I looked at each other, unable to speak. A chill ran down my spine.

"You've got to be kidding . . ." My words trailed off as I realized I'd swum naked in those waters. What saved me from getting eaten? Were the salties not hungry that day? Were they not paying attention? I had no idea.

I still used the Herbert River as part of the *Eco* course, but only the sections above the waterfall. I knew the salties could never scale that cliff, so that pool was as far inland as they got.

Well, for *Survivor 2*, I decided to use the Herbert again—above the falls, of course. The top of the pink granite cliff was a thundering majestic waterfall and the site of my new Tribal Council. This and the surrounding eucalyptus forests, with the kangaroos, emus, and wild pigs, would raise the *Survivor* bar. By hiring Karen Jones, my old location manager from *Eco-Challenge*, to make the necessary phone calls to Australian officials, the Herbert River became the site of *Survivor 2*.

That was my first little victory.

The second goal was designing a Tribal Council location that met my new ideas of how it should look. For the first *Survivor*, I'd visualized overgrown jungle temple ruins. It was intentionally claustrophobic, matching the sensation of being trapped on an island. For *Survivor 2*, I wanted an aboriginal-meets-Stonehenge appearance. It would be open and imposing, matching the limitless, unrelenting nature of the Australian Outback. There would be no roof, not only to match that Outback sensation, but also allowing us to shoot down on the set from a helicopter. I huddled with Kelly Van Patter, the brilliant production designer who is responsible for the look and feel of the show, telling her my Stonehenge ideas and stipulating that the broad, pink granite plateau atop Herbert Falls be the location. Kelly's trademark is an unerring ability to make the impossible a reality. I had no doubt she would design and build the ideal Tribal Council set.

If only it were that easy.

Australian officials made it clear that we could use Herbert Falls. However, the rock must not be harmed in any way. No bolt holes, no drilling, no anchoring of the set into the granite whatsoever.

I saw the wisdom in their mandate. For us to deface the rock would have been a tragedy.

I told Kelly to find a way to build atop Herbert Falls without harming the rock. She flew in a feature film construction crew from Sydney to study the massive site. They said it couldn't be done. Yes, it was possible to build a wooden platform atop which the Tribal Council would perch, and the rock would remain unharmed. But the site was hundreds of feet below a canyon wall. The lone trail from the canyon rim to my would-be Stonehenge was of the same granite atop the falls, and was prone to getting slick like ice from the slightest rain. One misstep and a worker (and soon, a castaway) would slip into the river and tumble over the falls.

So I had my location, but getting men and materials down there was impossible. The solution was an engineering marvel. A freight elevator was built alongside the rock to lower heavy objects (building materials and equipment preproduction; cameras during production). A staircase was also constructed, allowing production personnel and workers to go to and from the site without fear of falling into the river. The Tribal Council location was quickly constructed after that. Kelly solved the final problem—where to place the control booth so it couldn't be seen during helicopter shots—by building a giant booth out of fake rock that exactly matched the pink granite.

Two down, one to go. The final little victory that had to be accomplished before we could begin production was bringing the castaways onto the show. I couldn't sail the *Mata Hari* up the Herbert and kick them overboard to do battle with the salties, even if that would make for a fantastic entrance. No, it had to be something unique and visual. What I decided to do was have them skydive into the Outback. The premise would be a plane crashing into that arid wasteland. The survivors would drop to earth beneath their canopies (emblazoned with the *Survivor* logo, of course), and the reality would begin. I planned to have the castaways secretly trained and certified in skydiving before being flown to Australia.

However, we were due to begin production in October 2000. Though that meant springtime in Australia, it was autumn in the United States—too cold, blustery, and damp for skydiving training. Leslie Moonves also pointed out that *Survivor* was the story of normal people stranded in abnormal surroundings. Would normal people already know how to skydive?

He had a point. Skydiving was scrapped in favor of having an airplane deliver the castaways onto a small, remote airstrip in the Out-back.

I received another invaluable piece of advice when I arrived in Sydney, en route to our location in Queensland. It came during my first-ever meeting with Peter Chernin, president of Fox, and second-in-command to Rupert Murdoch at the vast News Corp. empire. We met to discuss some initial interest Fox had expressed in either acquiring Mark Burnett Productions or signing a deal that would give them first look at all our future projects. We had just made history with *Survivor*, and many such suitors came calling. I was more than a little in awe that Peter Chernin wanted to meet me personally, but I knew in my heart the value of my future company, and gave Peter a dollar amount based on that estimate. What I was asking was at the time too expensive to Fox (if only they had known!), so the Fox discussions went nowhere. However, before we parted he passed along a few simple words that enabled me to build my company to its current size. Peter's advice was simple: In order to grow, I needed to delegate. I needed to use my skills and inquisitive spirit—not on micromanaging every production detail, but on invent-ing new ideas for shows, getting the productions up and running, and then allowing my eminently capable staff to sweat the details. This would give me space to think of new ideas and oversee the storytelling in postproduction. "That's how to build a big company," Peter told me.

I have since incorporated that lesson into my daily approach to doing business, but I conveniently ignored it on the first day of filming for *Survivor 2*, instead preferring to be hands-on during a very danger-ous moment in the production.

It was October 23, 2000, just a couple days after my meeting with Peter, but thousands of miles away. I sat with the sixteen castaways at a small airfield on the fringes of civilization, waiting to board an Aus-tralian Air Force Caribou, the one airplane capable of landing and tak-ing off from the unbelievably short distance allocated as a runway. The planes had been most recently used to fly refugees out of East Timor. *Survivor 2* was the first time the pilots were delivering men and women to a dangerous location, instead of rescuing them from one.

The flight would be in two parts. I would travel with the castaways for the first leg of the journey, using this time to brief them on how the game would begin and splitting the group into two tribes. After an hour's flight we would land at a remote field—literally, just a field—and I would leave the plane, giving my seat to Jeff Probst. Filming would begin at that moment.

The fog was so bad that morning that we couldn't take off. I fidgeted, uneasy about the delay and mentally planning how we might reschedule the afternoon's shooting. The castaways were no better. At this point still not allowed to speak, and glancing uneasily at one another and the camera crews, they were obviously frightened about the adventure to come. Only the two pilots were calm and cool, talking about flying as they sipped coffee and looked at the sky now and again. Their banter made the morning easier, for I could tell they were confident professionals.

We finally boarded and were lifted into the Australian sky. The Outback sprawled three thousand feet below us, and the two-engine propeller plane was buffeted by winds. The castaways and I sat facing one another across the cargo section of the small fuselage, perched in fold-down seats made of parachute webbing. My years as a paratrooper meant I'd spent countless hours inside planes such as this, but I must say that the flight was as rough as any I can remember. I wasn't surprised when several castaways threw up.

When we finally arrived at the rendezvous, the pilots circled the landing strip to plan the approach. Below us was thick, heavy cloud cover with only one small hole revealing the Outback. The only solution was for the pilots to abruptly spiral to earth rather than angle casually toward the ground. My previous paratroop experience gave me a clear mental picture of how the spiraling would take place, with the plane descending three thousand feet almost vertically, then flaring for a jarring kiss with earth. My five-point safety harness was loose at the time, so I tugged on the straps to cinch my body securely into the seat. Noting this, several castaways did the same.

What followed was a landing unlike anything I visualized, and wilder than any I've known. The pilots began by opening the cargo doors at the rear of the fuselage. Wind rushed into the cavernous orifice, and I could feel the plane's aerodynamics alter as the open doors became air brakes creating drag at the back of the aircraft. Then the nose pitched forward until it felt like we were plunging straight down into the ground. Using the open cargo doors as a pivot point, the pilots then began corkscrewing the plane in tight circles to the ground. The engines revved higher until it felt like they were screaming, and the wind rushing over the wings made that sound universally associated with planes about to crash. The castaways were doing their best not to show emotion—after all, their game had effectively begun—but screams and the smell of vomit filled the air.

I'd like to say I witnessed the entire spectacle with detached bemusement—the method producer sagely enduring terror—but that was not the case. In all, we descended three thousand feet in thirty seconds. The plane set down on solid ground with a few bumps and bounces. Probst, who had watched the entire incident from the ground, probably didn't know whether to laugh at what we'd endured or be frightened that it might happen to him in a few short moments. Either way, he put on his game face as he greeted the castaways stoically. Then he boarded the Caribou, along with the camera and sound crew consisting of Ninja Lynch and Fred Wetherbee, and took off. The process of taking those castaways into the game, through the disorientation of a flight across a strange land in a strange plane, effectively shut them off from the outside world. I'd earned the three little victories necessary to get production under way. *Survivor 2* was off and running.

I've often said that my shows are metaphors for life. *Eco-Challenge* shows the drama inherent in group dynamics, then adds a pain-and-adventure quotient that makes the competitors peer into their souls. How they relate to others during the stress of the race becomes a lesson on how to optimally interact with family and coworkers.

Paratrooper days—me *(left)* with two members of my patrol on an operation, 1980.
My good friend Bob Wade is on the right.

(Mark Burnett)

Nanny days—keeping the kids and myself fit, 1983.

(Mark Burnett)

Mum and Dad, 1985.
(Mark Burnett)

The infamous triple black.
(Casey Capshaw)

James Burnett, "the first white kid ever in the village." *Eco-Challenge* Fiji, 2002.
(Mark Burnett)

Cameron and James with toys for the Maasai kids. Kenya, 2001.
(Mark Burnett)

James's eighth-birthday celebration. Kenya, 2001.
(*Mark Burnett*)

"The Snake Catchers," James and Cameron, sole protectors of
the base camp, cast, and crew. *Survivor* Thailand, 2003.
(*Mark Burnett*)

Cameron's mahimahi. *Survivor* Pearl Islands, Panama, 2003.
(Rachael Harrell)

Jeff Probst and me. *Survivor* Amazon, 2002.
(Chris Wilkas)

Trump and me preparing the *first* ever boardroom. *The Apprentice*, Summer 2003.
(*Kevin Gilbert*)

Trump and me at the 2004 NBC TCA summer press tour for *The Apprentice*.
(*Aussenard-WireImage*)

Sugar Ray Leonard and me out for some fight-night front-row action. *The Contender*, Fall 2004.
(Kevin Gilbert)

Conrad and me having a "sponsor talk." *The Contender*, Fall 2004.
(Kevin Gilbert)

My partners and me at the
2004 NBC TCA summer
press tour for *The Contender*.
Left to right: Jeffrey Katzenberg,
Sylvester Stallone, Sugar Ray
Leonard, and me.
(Aussenard-WireImage)

Martha and me—my triumphant
success with the T-shirt challenge.
Skylands, Maine, 2004.
(Martha Stewart)

With *Survivor,* that metaphor for life is a function of time and deprivation. The castaways cannot escape their fellow players and still accomplish their goal of winning the game. The hours and hours together force these men and women to interact. Their arguments and anguish are not a function of stress and danger, à la *Eco-Challenge,* but mirror the hours families and friends and coworkers spend together. A habit or mannerism that might be only mildly irritating at first grows into a source of loathing and contention. Arguments explode. Petty rage blooms.

While *Eco-Challenge* and *Survivor* showcase drastically different methods of connecting (or not) with other human beings and carrying on a successful and happy life, they share one vital component: Things go wrong. Smart competitors expect the unexpected. They absorb the shock of a new obstacle or calamity, find a solution, then reach for their goals. Winners are always flexible.

Lesser competitors become stymied and angry when things get tough. The problems of day-to-day life aren't more common for these people, but they seem to happen more frequently and with greater impact. They seldom realize their goals.

The cast of *Survivor 2* was adept at expecting the unexpected. They weren't innocent virgins playing the game for the first time, in the manner of the cast of *Survivor 1* (with the notable exception of Richard Hatch). The cast of *Survivor 2* had all watched the first series over and over. They came to play. When conflict arose, they were much more able to handle it because they knew it was coming. They didn't know when or how, but they were certain it was coming. When people ask me the differences between *Survivor 1* and *Survivor 2,* that's what I tell them—*Survivor 2*'s castaways knew how to play the game. They expected the unexpected.

On the crew side of the production, I observed a brilliant example of an individual adapting under pressure to realize a goal. Russ Landau, the composer responsible for *Survivor*'s singular musical sound, was on location for a few days to observe firsthand the Outback musical experience. His plan was to return to Los Angeles and compose. While in the Outback, Russ met with David Hudson, the world's premier didgeridoo player. A didgeridoo is an aboriginal wind instrument. It would replace the conch of *Survivor 1* as the indigenous sound of *Survivor*. Whereas I see the world in a visual way, Russ sees the world musically. It was helping him to hear David's didgeridoo as he absorbed the sounds and sensations of the Outback. All those experiences would find their way into the music he composed back home, so that when the music was finally played for *Survivor*'s viewers, they would be musically transported to the Outback.

Adapt to your surroundings.

At the same time Russ was visiting, a small army of international press was on-site. For security reasons, all visitors were limited in what they could see and where they could go. They could not, for instance, attend the Tribal Council. Nor could they visit the camps. Journalists had been allowed to do both those things during *Survivor 1*, but the first show's immense popularity now meant greater speculation about which castaways left this show, in which order, and the name of the final winner. Secrecy was paramount. Our goal was no leaks to the media about any aspect of the show. The media were understandably disappointed at the limitations on information about *Survivor 2*, so I found myself searching for a way to make their experience memorable. I showed them a rough cut of the first episode and walked out with them to observe the survivors' camps from about fifty meters away. But that was all pretty tame and unmemorable. I wanted to find a way to make them feel appreciated. My solution was asking Russ to play a little of the new *Survivor 2* theme music for the press. I expected a rough demo—the musical equivalent of doodling on a notepad. I thought the media might like to hear some of that well in advance of the general public.

Russ went one better. He took the next afternoon, working with his laptop and some other electronic synthesizer equipment, to redo his

"Ancient Voices" theme à la Australia. The next morning the press was hearing a *Survivor* symphony in the middle of the Outback.

I admired the way Russ didn't make excuses when presented with an unexpected obstacle. In fact, if I didn't know better, I'd say he'd planned on cutting that CD in the Outback all along. He expected the unexpected. Survivors always do.

In making *Survivor 2*, I was surrounded by a championship team: my crew, most of whom had worked with me for years. They're tough. Many shot *Eco-Challenge* in Borneo, then flew directly to *Survivor 2*, still picking the leeches out of their navels. I also made the acquaintance of several new crew members from Australia—total professionals, with impressive résumé listings such as the latest *Star Wars* and *Mission: Impossible* films. The scenery was incredible and motivating, a sprawling canvas of land and weather and animals that made me appreciate how lucky I am to do what I do for a living. I'll never forget the sound of kookaburras in the morning or the kangaroo families hopping by the crew compound.

There were challenges, too: three crew members bitten by snakes, and forest fires that threatened to shut down the entire production. Viewers were able to see a portion of those fires during the airing of *Survivor 2*, but it didn't translate well to the screen. But I have never seen fire roar out of control like that. The flames reached the tops of the eucalyptus trees, and there was absolutely no way of stopping the fire's march toward the Herbert River. At one point, I was just about to give the order to evacuate when the rain finally set in to douse the fire.

But what was most incredible about the experience was the outcome: *Survivor 2* was a great success. We beat the popular sitcom *Friends*, a ratings feat almost no one expected. We also demonstrated that we were quite deserving of Leslie Moonves's decision to air the first episode immediately following the Super Bowl. We held our lead-in audience quite nicely. (In fact, over the entire thirty-plus-year history of the Super Bowl, few shows have maintained the viewing audience as well as *Survivor*.)

Most of all, *Survivor 2*'s success proved beyond the shadow of a doubt that the results of the first *Survivor* were not a fluke. My brand of reality television was here to stay.

Chapter Twelve

Epic TV

I'm an adventurer. It's my nature to seek out new challenges and experiences. Even while I was in the Outback shooting *Survivor 2*, I was already looking forward to *Survivor 3*. Some of the moments I enjoyed most while in Australia were downloading Internet photos from the *Survivor 3* location scouts in Africa. There was a romance and intrigue to Africa, an adventurous calling.

When it comes right down to it, I needed a new challenge. Success begets success, and it also begets a desire to continually seek new adventures.

I went into the *Survivor 3* filming with lofty expectations of myself and the production. My aim was twofold: to make my show look just like a movie, and to reinvent television in the process. I thought about certain films with an African adventure quality: *King Solomon's Mines*, the *Indiana Jones* movies, *The African Queen*. All of them stress hardship and action. But the one movie that stood out most in my mind was *Out of Africa*, with Robert Redford and Meryl Streep. There is a romance to Africa that I find appealing, and it came through wonderfully in that movie.

Adventure is romantic, and the thrill of adventure is also motivating. As I've said, one way I define adventure is by pushing limits, sometimes subconsciously. For instance, it was my goal to make the next

Survivor with the same lush cinematography as *Out of Africa*. More than ever, I wanted my television show to look like a movie.

I was less nervous about *Survivor: Africa* during prep than I had been during the prep for *Survivor 2*. I knew then

> **Make each successive success unique.**

that more than anything else, casting was the key factor for the second season. Everyone was already asking me how I could possibly find another Richard Hatch, another Susan Hawk, another Rudy Boesch. I realized that the trick was in not looking for new Richards, Susans, or Rudys. It was in finding sixteen diverse and different new characters that would represent a cross section of the United States.

Africa would be no different. So as I prepped, I knew again that even with an epic location such as Kenya—with its lions, giraffes, elephants, and zebras—the ultimate success of the show would be decided by the casting.

The *Survivor* casting process has become an elaborate science. Even so, casting director Lynne Spillman claims she can't so much as go out to a restaurant anymore without approaching colorful fellow diners to suggest that they apply. Back at the office, Lynne and her staff wade through the estimated fifty thousand audition tapes and applications. They watch each and every moment of each and every tape, and read every application, searching for that glimmer of unique character and personality that makes for a great *Survivor*.

The original fifty thousand applicants are narrowed to eight hundred. The applications are reread closely. Phone interviews are then conducted, marking the first time that the eventual $1 million winner has an inkling that we believe they have what it takes to be the ultimate survivor. Lynne and her staff often fly to major cities to interview applicants in person.

Eight hundred are narrowed to fifty. Those men and women are flown to Los Angeles for a no-holds-barred round of interviews with me, Lynne and her staff, CBS personnel, and members of my production crew. These are conducted inside CBS's headquarters, and with total secrecy. This part of the process can be brutal. No question, no matter how personal, is considered off-limits.

Next, an extensive psychological profile is administered. A thorough background check is conducted. The fifty become sixteen, with two alternates. These names are submitted to CBS for a last round of interviews before we go ahead and begin the formal process of inviting an applicant to play *Survivor* (with the significant signing of nondisclosure agreements that applies).

For *Africa* I found another great bunch of diverse North Americans, including the West Virginia goat farmer Tom Buchanan; a tattooed and pierced surfer from Santa Cruz, California, named Lex van den Berghe; and an extremely handsome Jewish pro soccer player from Boston named Ethan Zohn, who looked just like a modern-day King David.

Similar to our production in Australia, the African location was a tent camp in the middle of an arid region. But unlike Australia, where water was supplied from the Herbert River via the local cattle station, Africa had no such water source. Each day we had to ship in hundreds of gallons of fresh potable water from Nairobi, six hours to the south. And the shipments could come only during daylight hours because of bandits patrolling the roads.

We had chosen to shoot *Survivor: Africa* at the Shaba Reserve in the north of Kenya. This was previously the location and inspiration for the long-running 1970s TV series *Born Free*, about a lioness named Elsa. It was well known as the reserve with the highest concentration of lions in Kenya. In fact, during scouting, when we found the Tribal Council location, there was an enormous pride of lions lazing under the acacia tree that would become the backdrop to the set we later constructed. As fierce as they look, it was quickly pointed out to me that the lions wouldn't really be a danger. The really dangerous problems would come in human form.

Our elaborate base camp was located an hour's drive from the nearest power source. We designed and built a base camp for more than five hundred people to live and work in during the more than three months we would be on location. We had generators, sophisticated water well systems, a water filtration plant, shower and toilet blocks, offices, catering facilities, a bar, and a pool. Row upon row of tents lined the savanna. In short, we had built a small town in the middle of nowhere.

The first night we turned on the lights in our little town, I remember feeling as if I was standing in a stadium. *Whooom!* The lights came on with such power and brilliance that the stars were lost in the brightness. The light carried for miles over the flat plains of Africa. It was a beautiful sight. We had done it; we were prepared to receive the crew that was soon to arrive over the upcoming weeks to shoot S3. The few of us who were there shared a toast to our success.

The next morning, however, brought a surprise of biblical proportions. Tribesmen began trickling into the base camp, coming on foot from miles away. This continued all day long. As it turned out, the tribes in the surrounding area had seen our electric display and sent wise men bearing gifts to our base camp. They actually thought we were the coming of the Lord. Other than their fires and the stars over their heads, they had never seen light at night and presumed we were coming to save the world.

Despite this awesome display of spirituality, that part of Kenya was just south of what we were told was "no-man's-land." This most unholy site was so close to the Somali border and its guerrilla warlords that I asked the American embassy in Nairobi for advice on how to deal with them. You may remember that some years earlier that same embassy was blown up by one of the earliest attacks on Americans by Al Qaeda. Therefore, the embassy that we visited was a new, fortified enclave on the outskirts of the city. When I met with the ambassador and his team, I soon learned that they possessed uncanny details about all the tribal chiefdoms, the level of threat they posed, and how truly dangerous that part of the country could be. It became obvious to me that the ambassador's team included at least a couple of CIA operatives, men who seemed to know intimately the identity and whereabouts of every bad guy in the region. Their advice for me was simple: Have all of our road shipments coming from Nairobi occur in daylight hours, and hire Richard Leakey's Kenya Wildlife Service as our protection.

This struck me as strange advice. Why should I hire a bunch of national park rangers to protect us against the hordes of the north? In fact, I later learned, the KWS were highly trained commandos of the savanna. Their job was to spend weeks at a time out in the African bush with their AK-47 automatic rifles, hunting elephant poachers. I immediately hired ninety KWS armed guards to protect the production.

The KWS then told me that it was unlikely that any terrorists or guerrillas would attack us because of political ideology or for the financial gain of stealing our millions of dollars' worth of camera and editing equipment. Rather, any dangerous encounter would most likely come from Somali silently poaching Shaba's huge herds of tusked elephants.

Sure enough, midway through production, while filming a challenge down by the Shaba River, shots rang out from the forested hillside across the river. The KWS returned fire and were about to go into full attack mode to track down the offending poachers, who obviously had the shock of their life when they saw a couple hundred people right where they expected elephants to be. We obviously couldn't allow the KWS, while on the CBS payroll, to catch the poachers and execute them, which is the penalty in Kenya for elephant poaching—as well it should be. Even though it would be legitimate enforcement, it would also be a bitter pill for CBS and the press to swallow that CBS employees had shot and killed a bunch of poachers. I'm sure the KWS thought we were out of our minds for letting the poachers get away, possibly to return in greater numbers, but it was obvious to us that we had made the right choice. We were all jumpy for days after that, fearing the Somalis might come back. This nervousness was only heightened when, one night soon after, a gazelle jumped the electric wire marking the perimeter of our camp, pursued closely by a full-grown lioness! The two of them tore through the center of camp, oblivious to the 250 tents and the dozen half-naked and terrified editors returning from the showers.

Just another day at *Survivor*.

In preparing the show opening we had convinced some local Masai vil-lagers to help. We asked them to stand in the background as the army truck transporting the survivors drove through in the morning light. Two days before filming was to begin, we showed up, only to find that one of the main warriors we had been dealing with was missing.

When I inquired as to his whereabouts, the other warriors noncha-lantly told us that the night before, a lion had jumped over the *boma* (a protective fence made of thorny acacia branches) in order steal a goat. When the warrior tried to fight off the lion with a spear—as only a Masai warrior would—the lion ripped off half his shoulder. This brought home to us the very real danger of Africa and caused me to in-crease the height of the *bomas* in which our two *Survivor* tribes would be living. I also required that the survivors keep a fire lit in their *boma* twenty-four hours a day, and that someone always be awake, wielding a pot and pan to clang loudly and, we hoped, scare off the lions.

The *Survivor* tribes were named Samburu and Boran, which were subtribes of the Northern Masai. One night during filming, Ethan Zohn, the eventual winner, was on guard duty by the fire when he heard heavy breathing. He peered through the thorny *boma*, only to find himself face-to-face with a lioness. As predicted by the KWS, the lion was just curious about Ethan and the others. Because no animals such as chickens or goats were inside the camp, the lion had no reason to jump the barrier. For that heart-stopping confrontation alone, Ethan truly earned his million-dollar first prize.

Through that encounter and others during filming, I learned that in terms of animal threats in Africa, a lone water buffalo is much more dangerous than a pride of lions. One day while filming, Big Tom Buchanan, the garrulous castaway from Saltville, West Virginia, inadvertently came face-to-face with a water buffalo. Being Big Tom, and showing no fear whatsoever, he probably had the water buffalo more confused than at any other time in the animal's life. It was the water buffalo, not Big Tom, that backed down and walked in the other direction.

I brought my kids with me to Africa because we were filming during July and August, in the middle of their summer vacation. One day, when we visited the local Samburu Masai tribe, James and Cameron noticed that the kids didn't have any toys. So James, then age seven, convinced Cameron, then age four, to give away all of their toys to the local children.

So off they went, back to our camp, and filled Cameron's Buzz Lightyear backpack with toys. Before long, every single one of their toys was stuffed inside the pack. Cameron was obviously just going along with his older brother's scheme. He did not look happy. But I felt certain that as soon as he saw the happiness he'd brought to these local kids he'd warm up. We returned to the Masai village the next day. As toy after toy was individually given to the children, James, with great delight in his voice, explained how this motorcycle worked or how the robot fired its missile. All the while Cameron was having second thoughts about the grand toy giveaway. He watched with growing despair as, one by one, his toys went to other children, never to return. We concluded and got back in the open-top Land Rover, which had a standing platform, so, from the chest up, you could be looking out. As we drove away through herds of zebra and passing giraffes, I started a discussion with the boys about how good it felt to give to the needy local children. James, of course, agreed because it had been his idea in the first place. Cameron, for the first time, had the biggest grin on his face, which made me happy because he had not seemed at all happy as he gave away those toys. So I said to him, "Doesn't it feel good, Cam, to see how happy you made those little boys?" To which Cameron replied with one short sentence that said it all. "I've still got my back-pack, Dad."

And sure enough, sitting firmly on his back was his empty Buzz Lightyear pack.

A few days later it was James's eighth birthday and he had a firsthand example of the value of giving without expecting anything in return. The Masai had been so appreciative of James's toy giveaway that, upon finding out about his birthday, they decided to give him an experience he'd never forget. That night, as we were preparing to celebrate in our traditional birthday cake way, the Masai, numbering about fifty, emerged from the dark savanna. The first we heard of them was their guttural chants; then we saw them in full crimson regalia. It was an incredible sight to behold. What happened next was an image I will never forget. The warriors dressed young James the same as themselves. He even got his own spear. Then they danced with him for hours on end— just James and the Masai, while the entire crew of four hundred sat and watched in amazement and wonder. It was *National Geographic* come to life. At the end, we treated the warriors to cake. As they were eating, I noticed that the women of the tribe were around the corner. They are never allowed to see the men eat, because the men are considered god-like and the women are supposed to believe the men never need to eat. I had politely asked the warriors if it was okay for us to also give the women some cake, to which they agreed. For the first time ever, the Masai women tasted sugar. Their smiles almost rivaled the one that had been affixed to my face while watching the Masai dance with James.

Africa, however, was not all fun and games. During the early days of filming, a CBS news producer who had worked on *60 Minutes* visited us to do a news story on *Survivor*. Over a few beers one night she told me that she had recently covered the story of the AIDS epidemic in Africa. Then she told me an astounding statistic: Of the thirty-three million people with HIV worldwide, a whopping twenty-two million of them live in sub-Saharan Africa, also known as "Black Africa." Moreover, she told me of another enormous tragedy—that a pregnant mother has a fifty percent chance of not passing the HIV virus on to her fetus if she takes a single $8 pill called Novoprine. The problem is that most women either cannot afford the drug or have no access to it at all.

Throughout that night I lay awake thinking, "Here we are, a multi-million-dollar TV production, when for $8, half the children born could be HIV free." I resolved to start a foundation under the banner of *Survivor* to raise money for and awareness of this problem. Upon hearing of my plan, Jeff Probst suggested I put my efforts toward an existing foundation for which he had recently become a spokesperson. It was the Elizabeth Glaser Pediatric AIDS Foundation, named after the wife of *Starsky & Hutch* star Paul Michael Glaser. She ultimately died of AIDS after contracting HIV through a blood transfusion given to her after the birth of her first child, Ariel, in August 1981. Elizabeth unknowingly passed the virus to her daughter through breast milk, and then three years later passed it on to her son, Jake, in utero. Starting in Africa, *Survivor* (and subsequently, *The Apprentice*) began shipping all of the props used in the show back to the Elizabeth Glaser Foundation, to be auctioned off on eBay, which then passed on one hundred percent of the proceeds to EGPAF. To date, well over a million dollars has been given to EGPAF from props that would have been either left behind on location or kept in storage.

The final version of *Survivor: Africa* looked and felt like a film, just as I had hoped. The shoot forced me to constantly set aside my fears and make decisions on a Jump In level. Things were always about to fall apart. The problems seemed to occur almost daily—the location logistics that

Facing your fears robs them of their power.

could have devastated the production if they hadn't come together properly; the Somali poachers shooting at us; the lioness racing around our camp and the potential for lions to invade the survivors' camp. But I knew I had to lead, and I did. I will never forget my home in Africa.

My show—and my life—seemed to be settling into a nice rhythm. I was pleased that, as reality shows became more prevalent on television, mine were the standard by which all others were compared. No longer were we working with the bare-bones budget of *Survivor 1* and *2*, asking the crews to sometimes work around the clock filming reality. Our budget had grown, and with it my desire to ensure that the production resemble a feature film rather than a television show. The process of site reconnaissance ("the recky"), casting, filming, and post-production was flowing nicely from show to show, so that we could likewise flow seamlessly from one *Survivor* to another. With our new connection with the Elizabeth Glaser Pediatric AIDS Foundation, we had even begun to give back in a small way some of the enormous number of blessings we had received. Little did I know that even as *Africa* was proceeding so smoothly and I was enjoying an adventure straight out of Stanley and Livingstone with my boys at my side, the façade of calm and ease would soon be ripped away. My Jump In theories were about to be put to the ultimate test.

Chapter Thirteen

The *Survivor* You Never Heard Of

S ometimes," Walt Disney once said, "it's fun doing the impossible." Note the word "sometimes." Often, doing the impossible takes every last bit of pluck and ingenuity you possess—and then asks for more.

Survivor 4: Arabia—as we were calling it until fate intervened— was the ultimate exercise in the impossible. There was nothing fun about it, but I will always cherish that time as one of the greatest and most focused of my life. Every skill I had learned through my years in the realms of adventure and television came into play. I learned dozens more. And now, looking back, I think it might even have been fun.

What? That doesn't ring a bell? You hard-core *Survivor* viewers don't remember the inimitable *Survivor: Arabia*, where the castaways made a life for themselves amid the unrelenting sand and heat, and the challenge themes were straight out of *Arabian Nights?* You don't remember the challenges on camel back? The Bedouin tents? The falcons?

There's a reason why: We never filmed it.

Arabia was to be the show's fourth edition, shot entirely on location in Jordan, that small nation bordering Saudi Arabia, Israel, Syria, and Iraq. It is the crossroads of the Middle East. I got to know Jordan's King Abdullah II through John Feist, one of my longtime producers, who had recently shot a documentary for the Discovery Channel in that ancient desert land. My hope was to shoot *Survivor* in Jordan in the fall, and perhaps return to film *Eco-Challenge* there in the spring. For *Survivor*, I hoped we could shoot in a region known as Wadi Rum, where David Lean had filmed *Lawrence of Arabia*. The show's opening scene—"the open"—would even take inspiration from *Lawrence*, with all the cast-aways taking a train ride through the desert. They would depart from a spectacular Victorian-era station in Amman, Jordan, and watch out their windows as they passed through the vast Arabian Desert, passing lush, palm-fringed oases and nomadic villages. The moment would be blissful and calm. Suddenly, the emergency brake would sound. Brakes screeching, the train would grind to a halt in the middle of nowhere. Windows would be lowered, and heads would pop out to peer ahead. Blocking the track would be Bedouins standing in the shimmering heat before a small cargo of supplies and leading a herd of sixteen camels— one for each survivor. Then the cameras would pull back to reveal that the castaways were stranded in the middle of a vast, majestic desert.

The Bedouins would direct the survivors to mount the camels for the ride to their camp, which would be in a lush oasis. We had even begun developing a "camel cam" to shoot the scene from atop one of these powerful humped animals as it loped over the sand.

I did the scout in early August 2001, during the filming of *Survivor: Africa*. From Nairobi, I flew to the United Arab Emirates, then on to Amman. My *Eco* and *Survivor* production scout teams, seasoned professionals all, traveled with me. They had worked with me on productions around the globe, enduring months of deprivation, time away from families, danger, and hardship. Little did we know it, but the adventure we were about to endure over the next three months would make previous *Eco*s and *Survivor*s seem like a picnic in the park. It would be the ultimate Jump In moment of my career, forcing me to trust my gut and find solutions to a most amazing series of obstacles.

After our plane landed, the king's guards escorted me and my entire staff out onto the tarmac. The heat was so intense that it felt as if my head was melting. We were led to a waiting fleet of Range Rovers.

In a moment of visually pleasing precision, the king's team of chauffeurs opened all of our car doors at the exact same instant. Then we were driven through the streets at an incredibly outrageous speed. Needless to say, the local people, seeing the king's vehicles ripping down the road toward the palace, stopped and stared. The intersections were blocked in advance by royal police rushing ahead of us, and we sped unimpeded through the streets. I felt like "King for a Day."

Amman is a low-rise modern city in the midst of a biblical land. With its mixture of traditional Middle Eastern cafés and modern restaurants and bars, Jordan's capital felt like an organic ancient Arabia interspersed with bits of Paris and New York. That worldly sensation was enhanced when we subsequently attended a pair of fabulous parties at the homes of wealthy Jordanians. While sipping wine next to their backyard pools, we could see across the Jordan Valley to the lights of ancient Jerusalem. It was hard to believe that one narrow gap separated all of us from the modern-day nightmare of the Israeli-Palestinian crisis. That Amman's ancient name was "Philadelphia" (brotherly love) made the irony all the greater.

Our escort throughout our stay was Samer Mouasher, a close childhood friend of the royal family and a highly successful, American-educated Christian Arab. It was Samer who introduced us all to Jordan's customs and culture. (It's traditional to grab food off a plate with one's hand, for instance, but only with the right hand. To use the left hand is the ultimate offense because that is the hand used for wiping when using the toilet.) And it was Samer who led us away from Amman in a small fleet of SUVs, taking us into the desert as Dire Straits's *Brothers in Arms* CD played again and again on the car stereo. There is a deeply spiritual aura about Jordan, something timeless and pure. I felt it seeping into my very being as we traveled through the low scrub and sand outside the city.

We traveled to where the Dead Sea Scrolls were discovered, and to the tomb of Aaron, brother of Moses, which lies within a white mosque atop a towering peak. Then, finally, it was on to Wadi Rum.

Like most Arabs, Samer was an extremely attentive and warm host. When I had mentioned to him in passing that my vision for *Survivor: Arabia* was that the survivors would live as Bedouin nomads—sleeping in tents so enormous they were capable of stabling Arabian horses inside, traveling by camel, hunting with falcons—he showed deep enthusiasm. But when we arrived at Wadi Rum, it was obvious that Samer had done more than just listen. There, waiting for us, was a large Bedouin encampment at the base of a low mountain range. I've loved the desert since my wonderful times in the Sultanate of Oman while competing in my first Raid Gauloises, and even from the first *Eco-Challenge* in southeast Utah around Canyonlands. Both of those are spectacular, but nothing prepared me for the pinks and yellows and oranges and reds of Wadi Rum. It was a truly spiritual place.

The Bedouin encampment was a huge, U-shaped tent complex with a cooking pit in the middle. Our dinner was a goat that had been cooked by burying it deep in the burning sands, where it was slow-roasted by the sand and sun—but with no flames at all. The meat was succulent and tender. Afterward, we sat with our hosts and smoked fruit-spiced tobacco from the communal hukka, under a pitch-black sky full of dazzling stars. The night was breathtakingly silent. As Samer's private joke to me, we slept under the watchful gaze of Bedouin falcons. I was living as a Bedouin. I felt the desert's power.

We spent the entire week scouting locations at Wadi Rum, sleeping in the pure desert air, reveling in the splendor of Arabia. One night Samer had another surprise in store for us. We mounted camels and rode through the cool night air to the ancient city of Petra for a private midnight tour, by candlelight. Petra became famous to the western world through the movie *Indiana Jones and the Last Crusade,* in which Sean Connery and Harrison Ford rode their horses up to the Treasury House. What an astonishing place! Now in ruins, Petra was once an important trading link between Arabia and the Mediterranean Sea. The nearby cliffs are a deep red and orange color, as are the houses of the city itself. Throughout history, Arabs, Romans, and Franks occupied this beautiful site, with its many buildings carved into the rock. We wandered through Petra in awe, then rode back to our tents, exhausted but also exhilarated.

With every passing day I was more and more certain this would make a great place to shoot *Survivor*, providing us with stunning backdrops of sand and stone, brilliant sunsets, and the sort of deprivation for which *Survivor* is famous. My thoughts were confirmed when the king allowed us to tour the entire country in his personal Super Puma helicopter. It was fast and loud, capable of carrying twenty people. Our pilot was fond of climbing to an extremely high altitude, then plunging straight to the ground before leveling off in a narrow canyon, which he would weave through at top speed. It felt like the "Death Star" scene from the first *Star Wars* movie, at once terrifying and exciting. I recommend it highly.

When we landed outside Aqaba, the legendary city on the Red Sea, to refuel, the temperature was 125 degrees in the shade. For all its beauty and history, Jordan would be a brutal place to play *Survivor*.

I flew back to Africa, then immediately dispatched a fifty-man crew to Wadi Rum to begin preparations. The Tribal Council set had to be designed and built, crew lodging and editing suites needed to be constructed, and the Games Department needed to begin planning, basing many of the contests on local customs, traditions, and legends. I approved the transfer of $2 million in preproduction costs. We were due to begin shooting November 12, which allowed thirteen weeks of preparation.

Then came 9/11, the day the world changed.

I was personally responsible for the safety of my fifty employees, and still had to decide whether we should get them out of there or proceed with preparation for filming. On September 12, as I was lifting weights at the Malibu Gym, I got a call on my cell phone from King Abdullah. "If ever the Middle East needed reassurance, we need it now,

Mark. Film your show in Jordan. Show the world that terrorists cannot alter peaceful plans."

I was humbled. In the great scheme of things, we were just a little TV show—entertainment. But at a time when the world was aghast at this horrific act of terror, a simple television show was considered an important sign of solidarity in the face of the anti-Arab pandemonium sweeping the United States and Europe.

I was deeply flattered by the king's personal request, but it had become clear that the attack on the twin towers was a carefully planned, highly funded terrorist act, not the random machinations of a few disgruntled men. Les Moonves, president of CBS, and I both realized it would be impossible to ask my crew of four hundred to leave their families and spend two months holed up on the Jordanian-Saudi border mere weeks after 9/11. Nothing would ever make us feel safe, and we'd never get the necessary insurance coverage. It would be impossible to film *Survivor: Arabia*. That part of the world was simply too dangerous, especially for a group as conspicuous as an American television show. Even the name *Survivor* sounded somewhat inappropriate. With that decision in place, I made a personal plea to King Abdullah to secure safe passage for my crew back to the U.S. Thanks to him, they experienced no problems at all. Getting my shipping containers packed and out of the region was obviously a whole other problem. Nothing was leaving the Arabian Sea without major delays—king or no king.

Almost every problem has a solution.

Even as all this was going on, there were financial realities that needed confronting. *Survivor* had become the financial crown jewel of CBS. For the show to be ready to air by spring, we absolutely had to begin filming no later than November 12—an impossibility. I knew that *Survivor 4* was not going to happen, and I called Moonves to discuss the situation, thinking he would agree with my assessment. He didn't. "Over one hundred million dollars in advertising has already been committed for *Survivor Four*," he said brusquely. "I know you'll find a solution." Click. He was gone.

Thus began the ultimate producing challenge: Find a new location, get permits, design and build sets and a crew compound, get thirty-five cargo containers of production equipment by ship from Jordan, then pull off a forty-day shoot. The task was impossible—and certainly not the sort of thing they teach at USC film school, not even as some sort of manic case study. But as the Navy SEALs like to say, failure was not an option.

Act fast,

but act smart.

The first question I asked myself was, *What is the safest place in the world?* Or to put it in less-subjective language: *What place was farthest from the world's troubles?*

The South Pacific: It is remote and beautiful, with many islands. (I was beginning to develop a theory that islands and *Survivor* should be synonymous.) But I had already done *Survivor* in Australia, and New Zealand was too cold. As I began considering other islands in the region, I was approached by one of my producers. Kate Hall is the daughter of famous cinematographer Conrad Hall, who shot such great movies as *Butch Cassidy and the Sundance Kid* with Paul Newman and Robert Redford, and *Road to Perdition* with Tom Hanks. He also owned an island in French Polynesia and had personal connections with the territory's president. Because things had to happen fast for the show to begin filming on time, that sort of connection would be vital to opening doors in a hurry.

On September 15, the first day that planes were once again allowed to fly out of the United States, fifteen of my department heads flew business class to French Polynesia. When we landed in Papeete, Tahiti, that Sunday morning, I immediately flew by helicopter with Kate Hall and Craig Armstrong to the private island retreat of Gaston Flosse, president of French Polynesia. He was spending the weekend there with his family and wanted a small group of us to come for Sunday lunch.

Flosse was was a pale, boorish, larger-than-life Frenchman who wore colorful Polynesian shirts, white pants, and sandals. The island was low-lying and shaped like the letter "C." Inside the "C" was a perfect lagoon, leading straight out into the open ocean and the classic reefs beyond. Thousands of palm trees fringed a perfect coral reef, like something you would see in an American Express commercial. There was a private airstrip and a compound of homes fit for a king, which is exactly what this president is. In fact, the president of French Polynesia also holds the office of senator in the French Senate. We spent the afternoon drinking rum cocktails out of fishbowl-sized glasses and poring over sea charts of all the islands of French Polynesia, some as many as fifteen hundred miles distant. Though the situation was idyllic and the rum drinks quite strong, I was careful to nurse my same punch bowl all day long and not lose sight of why I was really there—to find a location for *Survivor 4*. I had only eight weeks to go, and President Flosse, ostensibly the king of French Polynesia, held the golden key. As we looked at his extensive maps and charts, I described *Survivor* as needing as wild a location as possible, with warriors, tribal customs, and remote beaches. "There is only one choice for you, my new friend," he replied in broken English, pressing a stubby finger to a spot almost fifteen hundred miles southwest of his island. "The Marquesas."

The Marquesas are a group of ten volcanic islands governed by France as part of French Polynesia (which also includes Tahiti and Bora Bora). The warm, humid islands were once the home of fierce cannibals. Best of all, they lay in almost exactly the center of the Pacific Ocean, as far from civilization as any place on earth. I wasn't convinced yet that it was the perfect location, but beggars can't be choosers. We made plans to fly there for a reconnaissance the following morning.

Meanwhile, the idyllic afternoon weather abruptly changed. A storm began dumping buckets of rain. The water fell in a torrent so thick you could barely see a hundred yards. It became obvious that we would be spending the night on President Flosse's island refuge. I decided to call the scout team, who were working patiently in Papeete, telling them to await my return to hear our next move.

The president, however, had other plans. He announced that, regardless of the fierce storms and violent seas, we would all board his private boat for a short journey to Bora Bora. I was terrified, but calmed somewhat by visions of traveling aboard a royal yacht. In my mind, a royal yacht was enormous and obviously seaworthy, like the *Britannia*. But, in fact, Flosse led us to a forty-foot marlin fishing boat. Designed for fishing, not comfort, it was the sort of unstable watercraft that would rock you to the point of seasickness on a calm sea.

Now, in my life I have been on all manner of aquatic vessels, in a dog's breakfast of foul conditions. But that journey to Bora Bora had to be the scariest, most hair-raising boat ride of my life. The only thing that gave me a glimmer of hope that we might come out of the ordeal alive was the fact that the president of a country would never get on a boat that was sure to sink.

The thunder and wind of the storm drowned out the sound of the boat's engines as we motored out of the perfect little harbor. The instant we entered the open ocean, the bow began heaving as we splashed through waves twice as high as the boat. Everyone was told to remain upstairs, but I was invited down below to the family cabin by the highly unusual president in the brightly colored Polynesian shirt. He promptly fell asleep on a small bed. He lay there, snoring so loudly I couldn't hear the storm outside. White as a sheet, I lay on my own small bunk, praying the entire way that we'd survive.

After the three-hour journey, we arrived in Bora Bora's sheltered lagoon, which was flat as a millpond. The president woke up. "Ah, voilà!" he said, a smile creasing his face, as if nothing had happened.

My prayers answered, I stepped out onto the dock, looking across at Craig Armstrong, who was no sailor and looked as if he'd endured a particularly vile sort of seasickness. We were both grateful to be on land. Our eyes locked. He didn't need to speak, because his expression said it all: "Only for you, boss. Only for you."

We returned to the hotel, where the scout team awaited news of my meetings. Kate had called ahead and addressed them. "Tomorrow, we scout the Marquesas. Be ready in the lobby at oh-seven-hundred." I smiled when she told me that, knowing that the scout team's first move when they got that call was to immediately go online to find out where in the hell the Marquesas are!

Soon we were all aboard a presidentially commandeered 737, taking us far away from President Flosse, en route to the Marquesas. But something told me that I hadn't seen the last of him.

The flight was three and a half hours long, which reinforced a mind-blowing reality: We were still in French Polynesia, but it was as far from Tahiti to the Marquesas as it was from Los Angeles to Chicago. That's a lot of ocean! I was invited to come into the cockpit and sit with the pilots in the jump seat—a first for me. The view was incredible. As the Pacific Ocean passed thousands of feet beneath us, the Marquesan island of Nuku Hiva suddenly came into view. Its jagged lime-green mountains rose almost vertically out of a deep blue ocean. Waves crashed against the rocky volcanic shores. This was nothing like the president's private island with its sedate lagoon. This was serious ocean. There was something mysterious and foreboding about the Marquesas that I liked right away. This was the perfect location for a *Survivor* shoot.

As we came in to land, the wind gusted hard against the plane, pitching us sideways. The airstrip was perched above cliffs, which made the bumpy landing seem even scarier. We disembarked and were transported by Land Rovers over a muddy mountain pass to a village that had jumped right out of James Michener's *Tales of the South Pacific*. We were met by friendly island women in brightly colored clothes, and warriors with tattooed faces. This was not tourist-friendly Tahiti, but rather a land with its own identity and a colorful history of wars, cannibalism, and missionaries—the evidence of which was shown by a prominent white cross perched high up on one of the mountains, the

Marquesan equivalent of Sugarloaf Mountain in Rio. The thought of how the natives built that big white cross up on that steep mountain, and *why*, filled my mind. I had the rest of the afternoon to ponder that enigma as we toured the island by Land Rover, boat, and even the island's only medical evacuation helicopter.

In 1846, Herman Melville wrote *Typee*, a novel about his time among a cannibal tribe of the same name on the Marquesan island of Nuku Hiva. Later that night of September 17, 2001, after our exhaustive day of touring, in the city of Taiohae on that same island, I called my fifteen-person team together to discuss whether we were capable of producing the show in time. Every single person at the table told me we couldn't do it. Medically, there was not only the problem of malaria, which, though horrific, was curable. There was also the chance of contracting the incurable disease of elephantiasis. (We had seen some women on the island with ankles as big as their thighs.) Logistically, assuming we got our containers released in time from Aqaba, shipping our equipment from Jordan in time would be impossible. The beaches weren't big enough for challenges, and we had no place to house the crew. The islands lacked the infrastructure to handle the needs of such a large number of people, with sanitation being the biggest problem of all—the small septic system in this town of locals could never support the four hundred crew members it would require to pull this off. Under normal conditions we would all live in a tent city, but when I suggested that, producer Dick Beckett pointed out that the groundwater was such that we wouldn't be able to adequately build sewage facilities as we had done in Africa and Australia. So any hope of a tent city would require manufacturing completely new bathroom facilities, shower blocks, and a complete waste treatment system.

> To do the impossible you need the best team.

Last of all, and perhaps our biggest roadblock, was that land use in the Marquesas was complicated. It was controlled by different families and by different tribes who didn't recognize the government of French Polynesia as sovereign over their land. In fact, the more we learned about the Marquesas, the more we realized that President Flosse had little control over this part of his kingdom. The Marquesans viewed themselves as a completely different country!

So as I went around the table that night, I heard all those arguments over the course of forty-five minutes, every one of them saying that filming *Survivor* in the Marquesas would be impossible.

When they finished airing their concerns I stayed silent for a moment before weighing in. My choice was to either heed their concerns and cancel the production or boldly Jump In with both feet, come what may.

I clearly heard in my mind the conversation with Leslie Moonves ten days earlier, when he had calmly told me there would be a *Survivor 4* because he had already sold the advertising. Moonves had also told me in a later call that of all the producers of the CBS shows, he was glad that I was the one who had this problem because he knew I would solve it. He had often bragged to others in Hollywood that he had had far fewer problems from Mark Burnett Productions in Borneo, the Outback, and Africa than he had had with all his other productions down the street in Burbank put together. I'd always puffed out my chest with pride at just how good my team really was. I wasn't about to let his confidence in me prove to be misplaced. Therefore, I calmly explained to the group that we had a job to do.

"Everybody says we are the world's greatest adventure production company, and the current circumstances would cause the fainthearted to put in the production insurance claim and scrap *S4*. However, we are the best. We are going to do *S4*, and we are doing it in the Marquesas. I don't care if we house the contestants in the town hall, every challenge is tiddlywinks in the town square, and the Tribal Council is in the schoolyard. We have just under eight weeks," I concluded, "but this production will happen. Is anyone not on board?"

They were shocked, but not a single person spoke up. "Okay. I take it that we're all in," I said. I huddled with my financial team to figure out the cost.

The next morning, I placed a phone call to Les Moonves and told him, "We will do it, but it will cost an extra five million to pull it off."

"Just do it," he said brusquely, hanging up the phone.

The first great problem had been solved that night around the dinner table. After my announcement that the production would definitely go forward, we had brainstormed till the early hours. The issue of where to house the crew was settled in ingenious fashion: We would hire a cruise ship. Every department head warned me that these solutions had costs, and that in TV and film production, speed can be expensive, but this measure seemed perfectly cost-effective.

After 9/11, nobody wanted to travel, and cruises were being canceled. It gave us the perfect advantage to find a cruise ship that had lost its winter bookings. We found just such a vessel in Seattle. It could sail to the Marquesas and house our crew, including all meals, cabins, showers, and even recreation. It would be the first time *Survivor* crews had slept in beds—albeit while enduring seasickness.

Meanwhile, we began making reconnaissance trips over the various Marquesas islands, scouting locations. One day, as the helicopter swooped low across the jagged landscape, we flew into a dead-end valley. At the mouth of the valley was a waterfall tumbling several thousand feet off a sheer cliff. The pilot knew the significance of the valley, and even as I gazed in awe at the splendor, he leveled the helicopter off at the base of the waterfall. Then he climbed straight up, all the while keeping the cockpit facing the cliff. I noticed evenly placed indentations in the lava rock, but thought little of it at the time. We climbed higher and higher, until the base of the falls was a dizzying distance straight down. And still I noticed those indentations to the side of the falls. My curiosity aroused, I began following their path as we climbed higher and higher. They ended near the top, in a cave whose broad mouth was filled with the unmistakable—but discomforting—sight of human skulls and bones. The pilot explained that they were the skeletons of the island kings. Generation after generation of king had been carried up to the caves by warriors and laid to rest. Their ladder had been the indentations in the rock.

What an amazing sight! One slip and those warriors would have fallen to their own deaths, yet they managed to carry dead bodies up to the cave, then climb back down. What an incredible example of believing in oneself and jumping in to follow the path toward greatness. The warriors who volunteered to carry those chiefs up those cliffs must have possessed great faith in their abilities—clearly able to distinguish the slender but important line between "Jump In" (a conscious decision) and "fall off" (an act of fate)—even though a more rational person would never attempt such a thing.

The Marquesas had all the elements for a great *Survivor—if* we could *really* pull it off. Truly, I didn't know whether we could or not, but I put on a brave face for the crew. If the leader seems unsure or nervous it trickles down to the ranks in a huge chain reaction. The best chance for us to make it was to go forward with confidence. More than anything, what we needed was a really smooth production. Unfortunately, that wasn't meant to be.

Chapter Fourteen

Under Pressure

M ost of us, if we knew the difficulties we would encounter during a long journey, might never step out the door. That was me on the morning of September 19, 2001. I was nervous and more than a little overwhelmed by the difficulties I was sure to encounter over the next two months. I was in Nuku Hiva, gazing down from my hilltop bungalow to the picturesque cove below. The tropical sun was already beating down, illuminating the green amphitheater of jagged jungle peaks ringing the cove. It was a picture-perfect scene straight out of *Tales of the South Pacific*. Small, local fishing boats bearing smiling Marquesan men, their faces covered in tattoos, chugged back and forth across the bay, barely missing the manta rays that were continually surfacing and flapping their enormous fins on the surface. The Marquesas were virgin and wild, and—most important of all—it was going to be the home of myself and my crew until Christmas.

I tried to picture the same scene a month into the future, when there would be a large white cruise ship sitting there at anchor and the local fishing boats would be outnumbered by ship's tenders shuttling our crew back

Jumping in is all about having a conscious faith in your own abilities.

and forth to work on the shoreline. The coast would be ringed by makeshift workshops for our Art and Marine departments and the portable cabins hurriedly constructed to house our back-office staff and Challenge Department. Sprinkled among the tattooed men and vividly dressed local women would be the complex four-hundred-person machine that *Survivor* had become. How would my crew deal with the constant motion of living on a boat? How would we fit into this ancient, structured warrior society? After all, the ancestors of those same smiling Marquesan warriors had tried to eat Herman Melville only two miles from where I sat. And how would our supply lines work out here as they were stretched to the breaking point fifteen hundred miles from Papeete?

> **When you have too much on your plate, be decisive.**

My head was spinning. I still did not have the official sign-off from President Flosse on our shooting permit, which required a number of conditions to be met. CBS hadn't formally signed off on our increased budget, either. I'd learned enough to know that rushed telephone conversations don't cut it. The allocation of that extra $5 million had to be in writing. And on a personal level, I was unsettled from the recent end of my marriage. All that hard work and time away from home had taken its toll. If I had really analyzed my situation at that moment it wouldn't have been so much "jump in" as "jump off"—as in leaping from my bungalow balcony and onto the rocks below. I'd become like some crazy circus performer running between a series of tall sticks, each with a different plate spinning on top of it.

While racking my brains about how to *actually* pull off *Survivor 4*, I also had to quickly reinvent what *Survivor: Marquesas* would feel, look, and sound like to our television audience. That Bedouin theme music that Russ Landau, our composer, had just worked on? Now it was irrelevant, all his hard work and creative genius for naught. I would need to fly him to the Marquesas to immediately record and adapt the sounds of the South Pacific into our music library. Then there was the issue of inventing Marquesan-themed tribe names, challenges, and, of course, the all-important buff colors. And what and where would the Tribal Council be? As if all this wasn't enough, casting director Lynne Spillman was back in the United States, racing from city to city, frantically trying to piece together the new *Survivor* cast. She was calling me every day to find out whether this show was actually going to happen and, if so, where? Every potential cast member obviously wanted to know where they'd be going, but there was no way we could tell them yet. I called Lynne, telling her to trust me and to assure everyone that it would happen, but that she couldn't officially confirm the dates or location for a week or two yet. She was used to knowing the location about eight months before the shoot, and we were now just fifty-five days away. I'm sure she thought I had lost my mind.

My preproduction crew and I were almost entirely shut off from the world. We existed in a frantic cocoon, working like crazy to somehow make the reality show a reality. We would have to work around the clock, and have a lot of luck, too, if we hoped to beat the November 12 deadline for the start of filming. I would later look back on this as the most gut-wrenching three months of my life.

As if the tribulations of *Survivor: Marquesas* weren't causing me to lose enough sleep, I had another, equally demanding, production deadline approaching as fast as a freight train. The ninth edition of *Eco-Challenge* was scheduled from October 17 to November 2, in the snow-covered Southern Alps of New Zealand. That start date was just thirty days away! Without a doubt, it would be the most grueling *Eco* race-course to date, and by far the most complicated high-altitude TV or film production ever. To add to my problems, a local municipal government in the city of Gisborne had cleverly—and somewhat unethically, in my opinion—trademarked the name "Eco-Challenge" in the country of New Zealand. If I didn't either buy back my own trademark or at least make them some kind of a deal, then *Eco-Challenge: New Zealand* would have to be renamed without using the word "Eco-Challenge"— the event's brand name! Fortunately, from a race and TV production standpoint, the ninth edition of *Eco*, unlike *Survivor: Marquesas*, had been in the planning stages for more than a year.

The preparation showed. Scott Flavelle, our trusted *Eco-Challenge* technical director, had developed a risk assessment and management plan that had included hiring a fifty-person team of crack mountain guides, led by Everest veteran Guy Cotter. The guides would rig more than ten miles of safety ropes from peak to peak in case the legendary southern winds blew in a freak storm and reduced visibility to mere yards. My other insurance policy for keeping *Eco-Challenge* on track had been to hire a bunch of local production crew members who had just come off working on Peter Jackson's *Lord of the Rings,* and were up-to-date on the best techniques for shooting in the wildly fluctuating weather conditions of New Zealand's mountains.

Their knowledge would prove vital. The route would see the athletes mountain bike, trek, climb, kayak and raft a route through the Southern Alps. A clear visual reference during the race would be Mount Cook, the highest peak in New Zealand. It was named for the inimitable British explorer Captain James Cook, who survived the slaughter of his men by Maori cannibals on a visit to New Zealand, but was later killed and eaten by Hawaiian islanders on Valentine's Day in 1779. This, I thought, gave the New Zealand *Eco-Challenge* and *Survivor: Marquesas* an eerie, cannibalistic parallel. I hoped that, as our Captain Cook, I would survive both locations unscathed.

The weeks since 9/11 had flown by, and before I knew it I was standing at the starting line of *Eco-Challenge: New Zealand.* I had been spinning plates the whole time, reinventing *Survivor: Marquesas* and overseeing *Eco-Challenge.* During that time I had convinced Gisborne to give me back the rights to the name "Eco-Challenge." In return, I would provide the town, free of charge, a fully sponsored team that would race under the name Team Gisborne.

As I stood at the starting line, I reflected on the evolving nature of *Eco*. Once seen by many as just "sports TV," it had transcended that genre through the human stories we televised of those brave souls who attempted this extreme (and often life-changing) expedition

> **In a crunch, it's better to keep momentum through compromise than to argue to a standstill.**

competition year after year. We no longer just accepted applications to enter each year, as a normal race might; instead, we cast *Eco* in the same manner we do *Survivor*. Teams of elite athletes are selected for their pedigree, but we search for interesting stories and characters, too. In New Zealand, that included Sarah Boardman, a self-confessed couch potato from Chicago, who insisted on leading her Team Moosejaw even though she had far less experience or compassion than any of the other three members. Sarah was on a continual rampage, which drove her teammates nuts but made for compelling TV. We had also cast Team Go, led by an ex–Army Ranger named David Christian, and including Alex Basile, who was way out of his league and whose teammates eventually had to drag him around the course with a rope. This team had failed miserably in Borneo the previous year and had hoped to finish in the top ten in New Zealand. Including Alex had been their biggest mistake.

In addition to the television aspect, what was also interesting was how much the sport of expedition competition in general had changed since I'd first raced the Raid Gauloises in 1992 and subsequently produced the last eight *Eco-Challenge*s. The teams had become exponentially faster and more fit, with many of them making a living racing professionally. Teams no longer used gear designed for mountaineering or backpacking, but raced in lightweight packs and shoes specially made for expedition racing. Instead of trudging through lengthy trekking sections, many teams adopted the practice of tightening their pack straps and running, sometimes for several hours on end. And of the many innovations I had installed at *Eco,* the absence of "dark zones," meaning teams never had to stop racing on account of darkness, had made the biggest impact. Just as in any big expedition, be it scaling Mount Everest or trying to discover the source of the Nile, explorers choose their own sleep patterns. I wanted *Eco-Challenge* to add this extra responsibility and risk.

Those risks were highlighted in spectacular fashion in New Zealand. On any given *Eco,* the elite teams would finish four to five days ahead of the weekend warriors. The two prominent elite teams in New Zealand included the defending champions, an American squad called Eco-Internet, and a team of hardy New Zealanders led by a hulking, incredibly fit Maori named Nathan Fa'avae. The Kiwis, known as Team PureNZ.com, were going to make sure that no Americans would beat them on their home turf.

At the start, Fa'avae announced that he had calculated that his team would finish first in a record four days, an unheard-of feat, just so long as they did not get lost, stop for any reason, or sleep.

It was a stunning announcement. Attempting the course without getting a wink of sleep was a huge gamble. The Americans felt that it couldn't be done. Eco-Internet team captain Ian Adamson stated to the press at the starting line that "knowing when to sleep" was essential. Pushing on without getting at least two hours' shut-eye in every twenty-four hours would result in a big decision-making mistake. He would simply race at his own pace, and when the Kiwis of New Zealand crashed and burned through lack of sleep, he would stroll on by. We knew we had all the makings of a great TV show. It was simply a matter of contrasting those at the front of the pack pushing their personal limits with Sarah Boardman and Team Go at the rear pushing theirs.

September 11 was still a dark cloud hanging over the world as the minutes ticked down to the start of *Eco-Challenge: New Zealand.* Our race start was just six weeks afterward, and many athletes had boarded the flights to New Zealand somewhat cautiously, thoughts of terrorism very much on their minds. So when I asked for a moment of silence before starting the race, it was unlike any other prerace ceremony. It was refreshing to witness the international collection of athletes forgetting their competitive nerves and actually pondering what had gone on in New York—wondering what might happen next to the world.

Then they were off. The race began with a ride and run on the shores of Lake Taupo. Hundreds of competitors atop New Zealand horses thundered across the open plains toward the base of the Southern Alps, where they would dismount and begin their trek up into the serious high-altitude snow and ice.

Over the following days I pretty much lived in a helicopter, setting down at remote checkpoints to greet and encourage teams, or simply to fly in search of missing squads. Early one morning in the middle of the competition, my helicopter landed on a remote peak in the Southern Alps. As I stepped off to stretch my legs I was handed a satellite phone. On the other end was a furious Les Moonves. He had seen the preliminary budget reports for *Survivor: Marquesas*. Never mind that we would begin filming on time, thereby saving the network $100 million in revenue. What bothered him was the money I was spending to make it happen—money I had warned him about. "How the hell could this *Survivor* cost five million dollars more than any of the others?" he demanded.

Trying to hide my exasperation, I explained to Les that things had changed since *Survivor 1*. No longer did I have a tiny crew working round the clock for slave wages and sleeping in primitive huts. The size of my crews had grown as large as—or larger than—those on many feature films. The sum of $5 million was actually small in comparison to what it could have been.

At the time, I was shocked and a little put out. I mean, I felt like I had saved Moonves a great deal of tribulation—at considerable professional risk to myself.

But that day, as I stood on that bitterly cold peak, Leslie Moonves taught me an invaluable lesson. His phone call was my wake-up call to the true nature of big business. When Les had hired me to produce *Survivor 4* he expected results, come what may. Les didn't expect to do it himself or to have long, drawn-out discussions of how I would achieve those results. He just wanted it done. Even the extreme case of 9/11 causing *Survivor: Arabia* to fall apart, necessitating me to come up with an alternate location and begin producing *Survivor 4* just five and a half weeks later was not seen as an exception. He didn't really care how I did it, just that I did. And, of course, I did do it, just as he knew I would.

Hire the right person to get the job done.

This was a pivotal moment. Leslie could confidently tell me to solve the problem and hang up because he knew he had hired the right person. I had already instinctively understood that lesson, but he reinforced it in a direct manner. The reason my production company had grown so large was that I had hired highly competent people to work for me and to promote from within; many of my producers began in entry-level positions. Lisa Hennessy, the producer who has worked for me longer than anyone, had begun by working on *Eco-Challenge* nights and weekends for free.

A subcurrent of the message was an understated warning: Leslie didn't really expect me to reduce my budget. We both knew that there was no way to instantly reinvent a production meant for the sands of Arabia into a seafaring shoot on a Marquesan island—all the while having to replace the thirty-five containers of equipment stuck in Aqaba on the Red Sea, bring in a cruise ship to house my crew, buy entirely new tools for the Art Department, and maintain a supply line for food and other necessities to an island fifteen hundred miles southwest of Tahiti, where things cost double just because they are so far from a major continent. Les knew very well that it would cost this much more. He just wanted to make sure that his star producer of nonfiction television wasn't resting on his laurels and plundering the corporate vault, thinking the extra budget money came easy. In his gruff way, Les had just told me, "Stay on your game, Burnett; watch out for my money."

Shaken up by the call, I got back on board my helicopter, only to find out that a team had been lost in a storm. Rescue efforts were under way. Suddenly Les's $5 million wasn't such a major issue. Human lives were at stake. I've always prided myself on *Eco*'s enormous safety measures. For such a dangerous competition, the level of injury is low, and no one has died. Thankfully, our safety standards again prevented the loss of human life in that gale. Our team of guides and rescue personnel arrived on the scene within moments. Yet another disaster in the sequence of events that began with 9/11 was averted.

The race in New Zealand went on to be one of the most dramatic TV shows I have ever produced. Nathan Fa'avae, the hulking Maori, made good on his promise to push his team, night after sleepless night, through the indomitable Southern Alps. His team of Kiwis was winning the race, just as he had predicted, on the final day of competition. All that stood between them and the finish line was one short mountain hike, then a kayak paddle across a broad lake. Just then, as predicted by Ian Adamson, Nathan hit the wall head-on. His body shut down over the course of a single hour. He was filmed being led around the mountains like a frightened child by his teammate Kathy Lynch. Nathan Fa'avae is one of the toughest and nicest men I have ever met, but when the sleep monster comes for you, there's no choice but to succumb—and succumb he did. In the wee hours of that night, while caring for a freezing, disoriented Nathan, his team was passed by Ian's better-rested American squad.

Team Go finished an entire week later—dead last. They were so far behind that as a joke we had Jessica, the fiancée of their leader, Dave Christian, be the lone person waiting at the finish line while the entire TV production team hid in the trees. Team Go paddled their kayaks ashore with embarrassed faces as Jessica informed them that the TV crew had packed up and gone home, and that if not for her love of

Dave, she'd have left, too. As the team stood there in shocked silence, we all jumped out of the trees. The look on Dave's face was priceless and provided the final scene for the TV series. The members of Team Go were a great bunch of people who totally enjoyed the joke. They knew that, in my opinion, anyone who even finished *Eco-Challenge* was a true winner.

There are a lot of lessons to be learned from *Eco-Challenge* and two of the biggest ones were evident by simply looking at both the first place and the last place teams in New Zealand. The fact that Nathan's team lost because they pushed too hard shows that you are always better off making sure you get enough rest. Rest is invaluable to performance and making decisions when it really counts. When you are a leader, people depend on you. You don't have the right to exhaust yourself to the point of being unable to make rational decisions. Nathan did that to his team. It was a classic case of the tortoise and the hare, as the more cautious and methodical American team walked right past Nathan to victory.

At the other end of the spectrum, Team Go was able to put their embarrassment of being in last place aside and keep their integrity intact by finishing what they set out to do. Many faster teams failed to finish because they let a few setbacks derail their drive and upset their entire equilibrium. It is always better to simply push on and finish, no matter what. By doing that, you will continually beat stronger and more talented people who can operate only when things go well. *Eco-Challenge* is full of similar metaphors for life.

Eco-Challenge: New Zealand ended with a closing ceremony in a Queenstown ski lodge. It was November 2, a rainy night, and although I tried to enjoy the party, my mind was full of the fact that in just ten short days *Survivor: Marquesas* would start filming. This production had seemed snakebit from the beginning, and I wouldn't have been surprised if the disasters had continued throughout. My guard was up, and I was ready for anything. Even a tidal wave wouldn't have caught me by surprise.

One source of optimism was Lynne Spillman's excellent casting choices. The contrasting natures of the contestants' personalities were sure to yield yet another well-played game of *Survivor*, making my job just that much easier.

When I appraise the casting process, I'm constantly startled by the awareness that the road to winning a million dollars on *Survivor* starts with a simple audition tape. There's some sort of urban legend about *Survivor* that leads many applicants to believe that dressing in costumes and performing an elaborate shtick is the way to get a callback. It's not. Costumes conceal the face and distort the voice, making it impossible to get a hint of an individual's true personality. One of the best examples of a person sending in a simple, character-driven tape is Rob Mariano—Boston Rob. In his audition tape, he simply walked around his apartment talking about himself and showing off those possessions that defined him. Everything about him, from the accent to his manner, indicated a true individual. Lynne invited him to attend an interview in Boston, having high hopes that he would make the show.

He bombed. Nervous and reticent, Boston Rob came across as a completely different guy from who he appeared to be in his tape. Thankfully, Lynne had seen enough in that audition tape to put Rob on a train to New York and have him reinterviewed during a casting stop there. The second time around, he loosened up. Eventually, he was selected for *Survivor: Marquesas*. The rest is history.

Not only Boston Rob (a crew favorite who showed a surprising amount of cunning), but personalities like the compassionate Kathy O'Brien and Vecepia Towery, the first African-American winner, put the Marquesas on the map. I later saw a *National Geographic* knowledge test asking U.S. college kids to pinpoint the following locations: Iraq, Afghanistan, and the Marquesas. Less than twenty-five percent knew where to find Iraq or Afghanistan. More than half, however, could point out the Marquesas. We were playing our part in geography education!

Against all odds, *Survivor: Marquesas* started filming on time, with a dramatic marooning in big ocean swells off the coast of Nuku Hiva. The survivors were made to jump overboard with emergency life rafts and begin their odyssey by paddling a whopping two miles to shore. Thus, the *Survivor* that almost never was got under way in spectacular and death-defying fashion. The conniving, alliance building, and week-by-week "voting off the island" had begun.

As expected, however, I hadn't heard the last of President Gaston Flosse. People had warned me that filming in a French territory would be difficult. Time and time again during the course of production, the government of French Polynesia had proven that warning true; their original friendliness turned meddling and obnoxious. This culminated during the last week of production, when the government, which had been outraged about the brilliance of renting a cruise ship to house the crew, abruptly invented a hotel tax to levy against the ship—a tax that would have cost me close to $1 million! And even though our TV show would provide an estimated $100 million in free tourism advertising for the unknown Marquesas Islands and, by proxy, all of French Polynesia, President Flosse was adamant about gouging the Americans. Our biggest fear was that they would impound our camera gear and editing equipment, which was rented from facilities in L.A., thus causing big headaches with insurance and being trusted to lease such equipment again.

My biggest fear was that the lifeblood of *Survivor*—the all-important secrets of who won and who was voted off—would be compromised if President Flosse's government succeeded in impounding our tapes. Those tapes would clearly reveal every secret of our show. This would give the government enormous leverage in collecting their "hotel tax"—leverage I was determined they would not enjoy.

Once lost, our valuable footage could never be re-created. Normally, we wait until the end of production to transport the tapes home, doing much of our editing on-site. For the Marquesas show, we began shipping the tapes home on a daily basis during the last ten days of production. This meant hundreds and hundreds of tapes, of each and every moment of castaway life. Just to be on the safe side, we started with a shipment of blank tapes to see whether they would make it through French Polynesia customs. They did. From then on, we adopted the habit of backing up all tapes, then keeping one set hidden on the islands and shipping the other set home. On the last day of filming, we shipped our final batch of tapes through Papeete. As soon as we received word that the plane had landed safely in America, tapes securely on board, Dick Beckett and Paul Messer retrieved all of the duplicate tapes from hiding, threw them into a huge fire pit, and burned them.

That problem solved, we turned our attention to the cruise ship. My original plan was for the ship to sail directly back to the United States with our equipment on board. It was expedient and inexpensive. Once we learned of the government's intention to seize our gear, that plan became impossible, for the ship legally needed to dock in Papeete before sailing on to America. That meant the government could intercept the ship.

We chose to airfreight our camera equipment the day after filming. Knowing that the government had inside spies on the lookout for crates on the cruise ship that indicated that they contained camera, audio, and editing gear, we manufactured dummy crates, then attached those labels to them. The crates, however, were empty. The real camera equipment was placed in different crates, labeled "clothing." The airfreight bills were similarly mislabeled.

What gave me pause, however, was that all our camera equipment would be on the same flight as I would, and I was terrified that the government planned to arrest me before I could leave the country. We had begun an ugly daily dialogue about the "hotel tax," and it looked as if I would be personally held liable. I didn't help matters by getting into a screaming match with the vice president of the country, telling him how unethical I thought he was. Rumors abounded within the local crew about how mean Flosse could get, and how they fully expected me to be arrested and detained at the pleasure of His Excellency, the President, pending payment of this invented tax. The rumors circulated in my head as I went to the airport to fly home. My biggest worry was that my sons, James and Cameron, would see Daddy being put in handcuffs at the departure gate. So I had them board the plane ahead of me, with their mother, and instructed her that if I didn't board, she should tell them I had been called back to work and would be home in a week or two. It would all work out, and this would keep them calm for now. As I walked through the airport, my heart was beating so fast I could hear it inside my head. I imagined that every suspicious character who walked past was a member of the secret police. I approached the departure gate cautiously.

Lo and behold, as I passed through, nothing happened. No bells went off; no police leaped from hiding to slap cuffs on me. Nothing. The only danger was in my imagination. I joined James and Cameron and their mom and flew back to America. As the plane lifted off the runway, I realized that the French government was content to let me leave, but obviously planned to seize the cruise ship and our phantom camera goods when it docked in Tahiti. A few days later, sure enough, the cruise ship docked and the French Polynesian government seized it. Of course, they found no cameras, no tapes, and no editing equipment. All that was safely back in the United States. I'd like to have seen their faces as they opened the empty boxes.

The first episode of *Survivor: Marquesas* aired on February 28, 2002. Despite the enormous difficulties in producing it, the show was one of the best-produced *Survivor* series ever. Viewers were totally unaware of all the hurdles we had leaped to put the show on the air. Best of all, ratings were much higher than they had been for its predecessor, *Survivor: Africa*. Out of the fire had risen a phoenix.

Of all the extraordinary events that had gone into making *Marquesas* a success, one of my favorite moments came just before the show's finale on May 13, 2002. I had called Donald Trump to discuss renting the Trump Wollman Skating Rink in Central Park as the location for our live show. It was a great honor just to speak with him on the phone. Back when I was selling T-shirts on Venice Beach and getting my start in America, I had read and been inspired by his book *The Art of the Deal.* That book had motivated me to Jump In, take risks, and pursue a career as an entrepreneur. From *The Art of the Deal,* I was familiar with the incredible story behind Trump getting the Trump Wollman Skating Rink built—and had been so inspired by that story that it made me all the more eager to produce the *Survivor: Marquesas* finale there. I also knew that, to him, the rink had a significance that went far beyond ice-skating.

The story is fascinating. When the city of New York originally announced plans to renovate the shuttered ice-skating rink in Central Park in 1980, Trump had been eager to see it completed so that his children could go skating. He could see the rink from his Fifth Avenue apartment in Trump Tower, and he watched with dismay as the city failed time after time to get the rink repaired. For some reason, the pipes they installed kept bursting. After two years of enduring the city's failures, Trump finally got so fed up that he told them he could build them their new rink in twelve weeks. The city initially refused. But after great clamor in the press, the city of New York, thinking it impossible, reluctantly agreed to let Trump attempt the renovation. The first thing Trump did was hire arguably the world's greatest experts on ice-skating rinks, CIMCO, the Canadian corporation that had designed and built the Montreal Canadiens' arena. The CIMCO specialist who flew to New York took one look at the dilapidated rink, its cement surface cracked and pocked from leaks, and told Trump the pipes kept bursting because the rink was using the wrong sort of cooling system—freon instead of brine. Problem pinpointed, Trump successfully completed the arena renovation—which included not only the rink but a restaurant and skater's changing house, too—under budget and in *less than* twelve weeks. Because of the city's initial reluctance to let him do the work, there had been significant media scrutiny. Not only had Trump come through, he had done so under pressure and with enormous kudos from the New York press.

On May 13, ten minutes before the show began, when I got up before the crowd of five thousand people to thank them for coming and to wish them an enjoyable evening, Donald Trump was sitting front and center. I made sure to thank him personally when I addressed the crowd, and to call the arena by its proper name, the Trump Wollman Rink.

> Respect
> and recognition
> are vital aspects
> of networking.

Trump shook my hand and thanked me when I came offstage. It was the first time we had met in person. I told him that I knew the story of the Wollman Rink. He told me to stop by his office sometime so he could get to know me better.

That was the first time the *Survivor* finale had moved out of a cozy studio into the open air. Though we had an arrangement with Donald Trump, there was no arrangement with the Almighty on the weather. The day before the show was to air, a torrential downpour flooded the rink. The rink was actually made to hold water. Draining it was not an easy task. Young men equipped with hastily purchased squeegees duct-taped to long poles were enlisted to try to get the water off the rink. They were mostly—but not completely—successful. Some of the production crew, whose positions during the show called for them to be under a set of audience bleachers, were operating gear while ankle-deep in water.

Regardless of the difficulties of being outside, the *Marquesas* finale was incredible. The backdrop of New York City and the live audience of five thousand people made it epic. We even got Rosie O'Donnell to host the show, which began with *Survivor: Australia* favorite Colby Donaldson delivering Rosie to the stage on the Harley-Davidson she had given him on her show a year earlier. The success of this live finale showed me once again just what can happen when you take a chance and Jump In.

Years before when I had read Trump's *Art of the Deal*, I was inspired, and gambled that I had what it took to try big business. Now I was dealing with him face-to-face and had been invited to a one-on-one meeting in his office high above Manhattan in the world-famous Trump Tower. The moment was both invigorating and surreal. I wondered what might come of it. Little did I know that Trump and I would get to know each other very, very well.

Chapter Fifteen

SURFvivor

Even as I spent a hectic workweek in New York prepping the *Marquesas* finale, producers Tom Shelly and Craig Armstrong and I were compiling a list of various countries that would make a great follow-up site. That is the true nature of *Survivor*—finally finish one and stagger home exhausted, all the while thinking of a new spot on the map from which to begin the process all over again. I am fortunate to have a team of dedicated, intelligent producers who know what makes a great *Survivor* location, and we work together to make the transition from one show to the next, from one location to another, seamless. I normally trust them to give me a list of suggested locations, and I make the final decision based on a combination of my gut reactions and their recommendations about several issues—logistical feasibility, political and physical climate, and real and imagined dangers.

Learn to re-charge your batteries or you will burn out.

For *Survivor 5* I found myself drawn to Southeast Asia, perhaps because we'd been everywhere else in the world but there since *Survivor 1*. I was hoping the next edition of *Survivor* would be more fun—the Marquesas had placed a great strain on myself and my entire crew. So I deliberately chose locations that offered us all a chance to relax as well as work hard. Burnout was a real possibility. We took a long look at Malaysia again, as well as Vietnam, Cambodia, and Indonesia, among others. But one country truly stood out: Thailand. With its Buddhist temples, traditional costumes, and gilded pomp and circumstance, it was both epic and mysterious—sensibilities so vital to a successful *Survivor*.

I had heard horror stories about shooting in Thailand, most of them having to do with governmental obstacles encountered during the making of Leonardo DiCaprio's film *The Beach*. After *Marquesas*, you can be sure that the last thing I wanted was another three months of hassling with a foreign government. But Tom Shelly allayed my fears, telling me that he had a secret weapon—namely, his father-in-law, who worked as a university professor in Texas and had had a student to whom he had become close two decades earlier. That student eventually returned to Thailand and had risen to the lofty position of the nation's prime minister. Before I knew it, we were in Bangkok, touring the city's temples with a government-supplied tour guide. Only then did I realize how independent Thailand was. Other than Japanese occupation during World War II and a Burmese presence in the sixteenth century, Thailand had never been occupied by foreign power. This allowed Thailand's culture to develop without much of the western or Chinese influence evident in countries like Vietnam or Malaysia. The result is an intoxicating mixture of Buddhism and go-go commerce.

Bangkok, situated on the banks of the Chao Phryah River, is a kind of Venice of the east. It is overpopulated and slum-ridden, and it battles an air pollution problem, but the most amazing thing is that even the poorest locals have ornate, glittery decorations on their homes. Traditional shops line most streets, hawking everything from food to sex. The towering Buddhist temples, known as *wats*, number more than three hundred throughout the city and are totally awe-inspiring. One temple, in particular, which sprawled atop an acre of land, is decorated entirely with a ceramic mosaic. Our tour guide, an affable Thai man, explained that the king of Siam (Thailand's former name) had been

awaiting a shipment of pottery during the time of the temple's construction. When it arrived, the king was dismayed to learn that the pottery had been totally destroyed in transit. Rather than waste the
fragments, the king commanded his artisans to adorn the temple with
the broken pottery. It then became a tradition to add broken pieces of
pottery or china to the temple—a practice that continues to this day.

From that *wat* and the others we toured, our production designer,
Kelly Van Patter, drew inspiration for the Tribal Council, which would
be our version of a Thai temple minus any Buddhist elements (so as not
to offend the Thai people). *Survivor: Thailand* clearly had a different
feel from every previous *Survivor,* which had all been earthy in their art
direction. We knew from that moment on that this version of *Survivor*
would be a departure.

While scouting Bangkok, we attended a local kite-flying festival
outside the Grand Palace, once home to Siam's kings. Thousands of
people were flying ornamental kites. We soon realized that these large,
intricately decorated kites, some with wingspans twelve feet wide,
dancing lightly on the Bangkok breeze, were, in fact, not as innocuous
as they seemed. This became clear when what sounded like a World
War II air raid siren suddenly went off. As we stood dumbfounded,
hundreds of people fell to the floor and covered their heads. A kite flyer
had lost control of his contraption, which was now wildly dive-
bombing the lawn at what seemed like eighty miles an hour. It was only
when we had a near miss that we, too, hit the ground. Clearly, the Thais
had played this game before, and for the next few days every time we
heard any kind of siren we would instinctively duck.

During the scout, we were all jet-lagged and running on fumes,
thanks to the long flight across the Pacific and the cumulative fatigue
from eighteen nonstop months of production. I decided to give everyone Sunday off so we could vegetate in our hotel rooms and catch up on
our rest. A big meeting with Thai government officials was scheduled
for Monday morning, and we needed to be at our best.

It is noteworthy that grinning and laughing are important cultural courtesies in Thailand. Any kind of a grimace is seen as a form of criticism. No one likes to be criticized, but Southeast Asian culture in particular does not tolerate criticism well. Come Monday morning, feeling rested and ready, Tom Shelly and I ran into each other in the elevator on the way down to the lobby. We exchanged pleasantries and soon realized that we had both spent our Sundays lying in bed watching movies and eating from room service. Both of us, it turned out, had watched *Austin Powers: The Spy Who Shagged Me*, with its various incredibly stupid but funny scenes. Somehow in that short elevator ride we got on the subject of the character Fat Bastard, played by Mike Myers. During a key moment, Fat Bastard says to Austin Powers, "First things first, where's the crapper, I need to take a shit." As I said, stupid, but very funny. Taken out of context, it may not seem that way, but trust me, it's a hilarious scene. Especially when you're giddy from jet lag.

Tom and I were still laughing hysterically as we exited the elevator into the lobby, much to the confusion and amusement of the rest of the scout team. Our giggling continued uncontrollably in the minivan on the way to the government building, and even into the lobby as we awaited our big meeting. It seemed that every time Tom and I looked at each other, we would simultaneously crack up. This even carried on into the actual meeting itself. Tom's father-in-law and Craig Armstrong kept telling us to hold it together, that we were going to blow the deal if we didn't.

Though we tried desperately, neither of us could stop. Tom and I giggled through the entire ninety-minute presentation, and somehow it became so infectious that the government officials were laughing harder at every humorous part of our pitch. Thankfully, at the end of the meeting the government officials agreed (with big smiles and giggles of their own) to support *Survivor 5* in Thailand. One of the tourism officials escorted us to the elevator. "I think it really helped that the prime minister saw how happy you were every time we spoke of *Survivor: Thailand*," he said to Tom and me. We stared at each other, our grins bigger than ever. The deal was closed. Thank you, Fat Bastard.

In the final days of casting, the chosen survivors are placed under a serious gag order to not speak, look at one another, or flash hand signals to communicate with one another in any sort of way. When it comes time to fly to the location, they all board the same flight but are seated in random locations throughout the cabin, next to total strangers, with orders not to utter a single word. Those violating this order will be immediately booted from the show, and an alternate flown in to take their place. Upon landing, the new survivors are transported by car to a hotel and then ultimately to a location that we call the Ponderosa, where they are housed until the beginning of the game.

All the while, they are taking their meals and meetings with the producers without looking at one another, speaking to one another, or divulging any information that would offer any explanation of their character or personality. They are not to be overheard speaking by any producer or contest handler until they hit the beach. It is like a loner convention—the contestants look at the floor at all times in an effort to avoid eye contact. This is why they frantically try to communicate to one another who they are as characters and as people the instant the filming actually begins.

Over the years, the contestants have said that this early part of the competition feels like being in solitary confinement while surrounded by a group of people. Pregame, they tend to come up with nicknames and character description guesses for one another. They cannot verbally communicate with anyone for a week, even while having a weird and wonderful experience for the first time. No doubt this is why they are totally exhilarated and talk a mile a minute when they are finally allowed to speak. Believe me, this gives us producers great reality-TV moments. From the show's inception, we realized that this pregame silence was vital to making the initial moments of filming vibrant and organic.

In the days leading up to *Survivor: Thailand,* we held the sixteen contestants in small, private beach chalets nestled on the sands of the South China Sea. They would gladly have traded their beachfront accommodations for the simple opportunity to speak to one another, so difficult did they find their solitary confinement. We had again chosen a great cast, featuring the Gen X skateboard kid Robb Z (Robb Zbacnik); fifty-year-old mother of four Jan Gentry; six-foot-five African American IBM computer tech/ex–pro footballer Big Ted Rogers; and the woman who later almost ended his marriage, our very own diva, Ghandia Johnson.

Our first traumatic scenario with Ghandia was while she was confined to her beach chalet to prevent all contact with other contestants and hotel guests. She heard an impatient knocking on the sliding glass door leading to the beach and knew it could only be one of the *Survivor* contestant handlers because *Survivor* security had cordoned off the entire area and all the other contestants were also confined to their chalets. Wrapping her rather voluptuous body in a Thai sarong, Ghandia approached the glass door. At that moment she realized two things: First, she was incredibly glad the glass door was closed, and second, the dangers of Thailand about which I had warned the castaways were not an exaggeration. There, tapping on the clear glass door, was the hooded face of a twelve-foot king cobra, striking at its own reflection in the glass. Her screams brought the local Thai security force, who merely chased the snake away. I then called together the other fifteen contestants and told them the cobra story. I could see their eyes widen as they sat silently before me. They now knew that Thailand would be no walk in the park.

Sure enough, the entire production was plagued by all manner of snake: king cobras, pit vipers, and even the massive amethyst python, which can grow to thirty feet long. However, when my sons, James and Cameron (who were spending another summer break on location), heard about the profusion of snakes, they were far from scared. In fact, they convinced me to let them join a team of locals we had hired to catch and relocate any snakes they found too close to either our production base camp or the survivor's tribal camps. Late every day, James and Cameron would return to camp looking like a couple of Huckleberry Finns, clutching a burlap sack full of newly captured snakes. Before the snakes could be relocated, however, James and Cam wanted to make sure their dad saw what they had been up to. One particular day they brought in a bag they told me held a six-month-old amethyst python. I had a vision of a small, thin baby snake. Much to my shock, the ranger dumped an eight-foot monster from the burlap bag. I jumped back in horror as James and Cameron gleefully laughed at their prize, which then wound itself into a tight coil and refused to move.

The ranger, a model of professional understatement, pointed out that this snake would soon grow to be big. No shit! As I stupidly took a long stick and tried to get the motionless python to leave the area, it struck at me with lightning speed, barely missing me, even though I was almost six feet away. James and Cameron thought this was hilarious. I'm quite sure my heart almost stopped there and then. Never again would I underestimate the power of a python or assume that it is slow.

I needed a better understanding of exactly how my boys were spending their days, so I accompanied them on their next snake-hunting mission. The following morning we set off into the jungle just after breakfast, staying close to three barefoot park rangers. After an hour we had seen no sign of snakes anywhere near our camp. We moved on to a river about five hundred meters behind the survivors' beach. Then one of the rangers froze and spoke excitedly in Thai to James and Cameron. Although they spoke no Thai, the boys seemed to know exactly what he was saying. When I looked curious, they pointed upward into a tree. Sure enough, coiled twenty feet above our heads and hanging in the branches above a knee-deep jungle river, was a huge python.

I, of course, suggested that we leave it where it seemed happiest and move on. In answer to this, Cameron explained, "No, Dad, that's the whole point. We can't leave it. What if it crawls into the survivors' camp?" So like any concerned father, I moved the kids thirty yards downstream while the ranger poked and prodded at the snake with a twenty-foot bamboo pole. When the python finally got fed up, it un-coiled itself. But rather than slithering farther into the tree, it plopped right into the river, sending up a massive splash. James, Cameron, and I were standing knee-deep in the water, at what I thought was a safe distance. But the python swam underwater directly toward us. I picked up Cameron, grabbed James close to me, and froze.

"Dad, what are you doing?" the boys screamed as they squirmed to get away from my clutches and join the rangers, who were plucking the enormous python from the water and proudly waiting to show it to their youngest team members. James and Cameron gleefully let the snake coil the smallest part of its tail around their arms.

I returned to camp, none of my worries appeased. In fact, I became even more acutely aware of the dangers of Southeast Asia in a most immediate fashion soon after.

One day, I took a few hours off to go scuba diving close to an outer island. The water was beautiful and cool, and it felt nice to be out of the heat. Unbeknownst to me, the South China Sea was not as benign as I imagined. After I arrived back on land and was eating lunch at base camp, I was handed a local newspaper. It contained a story about a ten-foot tiger shark that had been caught off the same island where I'd been diving. When the shark was cleaned, the remains of a person were found in its stomach! This picture was prominently displayed on the front page. Pete West, the Aussie who headed our Marine Department, with whom I'd been diving that morning, laughed at me when I showed concern, saying he couldn't wait to grab an underwater camera and head back out there.

It should be noted that Pete West owned a company that specialized in underwater shark filming on the Great Barrier Reef. Out of pride (and perhaps a residual touch of that centuries-old British-Australian rivalry), I refused to let myself be seen as afraid of the sharks after hearing his comments. I continued to dive between shoot schedules but spent much of my time underwater looking behind me for a tiger shark that never appeared.

Our location was Kao Tarota, in the far south, less than a mile from the Malaysian ocean border. The island itself was in a predominantly Muslim area. We soon came to realize that the local government considered itself separate from the federal government in Bangkok—déjà vu from the Marquesas. To further complicate things, the regional governor didn't have full power over the region. In fact, there was an uneasy informal truce between the Thai mafia and the local governor—in a sense, they shared power. This was never more evident than on the first day of shooting. The governor was due to pay us a visit, and it was explained to us by our location manager that the governor and his entourage would be accompanied by another gentleman and his entourage. In hushed tones, the location manager explained that this other gentleman was the head of the mafia and that we must show equal respect to both gentlemen and should address them in an equally deferential manner. Over and over, he reiterated how important this was. Sure enough, when the governor showed up he strode down the muddy jungle road followed by his government officials. Right next to him was the head of the mafia followed by his "business officials." It was an uneasy meeting. The governor and the mafia chief wore similar open-necked, short-sleeved baggy shirts. This being the first time I'd ever met the governor, I had no idea which one was the governor and which one was the mafia chief. Both smoked continually, smiled a lot, and were extremely overweight (a rare sight throughout Asia), and neither spoke English. I did what I do best in these situations: bowled them over with my boundless enthusiasm accompanied by lots of smiles and lots of bowing. It worked. Both offered their official blessings. It was time for filming to begin.

The contestants were told to walk through the Thai fishing village to board their colorful Thai longboats. As the contestants walked through the village, one of them immediately established his personality. Robb Zbacnik threw a skateboard on the ground and instead of walking like the others actually skated to the longboats.

Over the past decade of filming adventure television in remote lo-cales, I've witnessed countless culture clashes. But the look on the faces of the Thai children as Robb skated past was one of the great moments that I've experienced.

What followed was an opening different from any other in *Survivor* history. The longboats leaving the fishing village consisted of one boat of eight women and one boat of eight men. The television audience was being led to believe that the game would be between a tribe of men and a tribe of women. The castaways were driven to a small, beautiful is-land, where they met Jeff Probst for the first time. After brief interaction with the groups, Jeff said, "So the natural assumption is that we have a tribe of men and a tribe of women," to which both groups smiled and nodded.

I love watching the show's plot take an unexpected twist, so Jeff's next line stands out as one of the show's most memorable moments. "You should never make assumptions in the game of *Survivor*," he said. "Here's how it is going to work. I am going to choose two team captains. In Thai society, which honors the elderly, the two oldest among you will become those captains. Jeff called forward Jan Gentry and Jake Billingsley, both of whom were in their fifties. Schoolyard style, they would pick teams, alternating between men and women. Jake, whose tribe was called Sook Jai, chose a team of young, fit, attractive players. Jan, seemingly absentminded and not catching on, chose the older, slower, seasoned players for her Chuay Gahn tribe.

The game had begun. The choices sent shock waves throughout the production. We had analyzed the scenario a hundred times but had never considered that anyone would be crazy enough to choose all the older, unfit, and slower players. We felt certain, given the physical na-ture of the challenges, that Jan's team would be decimated. Not only would it be painful to watch, it would make for somewhat pathetic tele-vision.

We were wrong. The first challenge was a paddling race in heavy, wooden longboats. Each tribe circumnavigated an island, stopping to

solve puzzles along the way. Not only
did Jan's older tribe nearly win, but
they outpaddled Jake's younger tribe.
The only reason Jan's tribe lost was because Ghandia couldn't solve a puzzle
quickly enough. From that day forward,
Jan's tribe won almost every challenge.

The wise choice
isn't always
the obvious choice.

Meanwhile, Thailand was proving to be one of the most relaxing
shoots in *Survivor* history. After the tribulations of *Survivor: Marquesas*,
with the continual uncertainty about whether every day would be our
last day of filming due to the government or some local permit problems, we relished the change of pace. The crew lived in a combination
of beach huts and tents in the jungle next to a white sand beach. The
sand sloped down to the ocean, where the surfers on the crew were
treated to a perfect surf beach, with a stunning left-handed break. Thus
was born "SURFvivor." Crew members would finish their shifts and
grab surfboards that had been quickly shipped out from California, the
Gold Coast of Australia, and South Africa. Many of the crew actually
took cameras out into the water and shot some amazing footage of the
crew recreating on the waves. This was edited into a now-legendary
short film that is continually shown at every *Survivor* wrap party. Set to
classic sixties California surf music, SURFvivor has become a part of
Survivor history.

On that note, one of the greatest memories of my life was watching
my now nine-year-old son James being taught to surf by the head of the
Challenges Department, John Kirhoffer. In fact, one day John, James,
and I got up on our boards on the same wave. I looked across at James,
who smiled and yelled out in his little Malibu voice, "Party wave!" as
the three of us surfed in toward the beach.

The ghosts of the Marquesas were exorcised during those six exhilarating weeks. Thailand (and SURFvivor) proved the perfect tonic. Re-

freshed and rejuvenated, my personal bandwidth restored, I realized that I was becoming somewhat bored. I knew I was in the mood once again to Jump In to a new endeavor—something entirely unique and mind-blowing. Only I had no idea what that would be.

Once again, I balanced *Survivor* and *Eco-Challenge*. No sooner had *Survivor: Thailand* ended than I had the job of immediately finding a new *Eco-Challenge* location. This time I needed to scout for *Eco* in Fiji.

I long ago learned that when it comes to doing business in foreign lands, the blunt American technique of getting straight to the point doesn't get the job done. People from other cultures place a great value on getting to know a person on a social level before talking business. No matter whether the locale is a cattle rancher's home in the Australian Outback or a bistro in the heart of Paris, interpersonal relationships matter. It's all about looking people in the eye, finding out what makes them tick, and sharing my own stories so they can see what makes me tick. Some of my most memorable conversations have been those with total strangers, bonding before doing business.

Fiji was an extreme case in point. What I remember most from that scout was a special day spent with my oldest son, James, who accompanied me on the Fiji reconnaissance. I was viewed as the *Eco-Challenge* chief and James as the chief's son. There was no way I could do business there if I didn't show the proper respect. James naturally sat next to me at the meeting with the chief, and our delegation was completely formal. Lisa Hennessy, Scott Flavelle, Amanda Harrell, Kevin Hodder, and I sat with the warriors of the village inside a traditional Fijian long-house. Our two groups were separated by about ten meters. The barrier between us was a large, ornately carved kava bowl. Kava is made from grinding the roots of a pepper plant with saliva. More water and more saliva are then added, resulting in a drink that numbs your mouth and tastes like spicy dirt. One by one, the warriors offered us the kava bowl. Of course, I drank from it and showed no disgust at how bad it tasted.

When it was given to my son James, all the tribe warriors began to laugh, acknowledging that they were simply being courteous and that kids don't drink kava. James has traveled with me from the Outback of Australia to the high Atlas Mountains of Morocco to the windswept peaks of Argentina's Patagonia region and to Borneo for his first *Survivor*, then back to the Outback of Australia for his second *Survivor*, on to Africa for his Masai experience, then to the Marquesas, where he learned to scuba dive at age 8, and finally to Thailand, where he learned to surf and catch pythons. Now he was sitting before Fijian warriors in a cannibal village that tourists had never been to before and was confidently unaware of the warriors' laughs. He took the kava bowl and downed it in one gulp. As a group, we endured five rounds of the awful kava root before we received the blessing of the chief to continue our exploration of their lands.

We proceeded to board a raft made of twenty-foot lengths of bamboo lashed together with vines; ten-foot bamboo poles were used to propel the raft forward with the current. The heavens opened up as we began our journey, and the rain was so thick we could hardly see fifty yards ahead. The brown water of the quickly rising jungle river was pretty rough. Five hours later we arrived at an even more remote village. James and I entered the village together, both of us soaked to the skin. James was greeted with squeals of delight, as he was the first white child they'd ever seen. Soon he was surrounded by fifty ebony-skinned Fijian kids, who gently grabbed his arms and stroked his cheeks. I know that James's previous experience with indigenous people around the world caused him to do nothing but simply smile and enjoy it— whereas I'm sure kids who had never left American cities would have been scared to death and believed they were about to be thrown in a pot and boiled for dinner.

The weather cleared. A helicopter came to pick us up. James and I flew back to our hotel, exhausted and looking forward to getting out of our wet, smelly clothes, but glad for one more surreal father-and-son afternoon.

Fiji's darker, more dangerous side made itself known to the athletes of *Eco-Challenge* when the race was held later that year. They thought they would be racing through a tropical paradise—which they were—but the jungles of Fiji are dense and extremely difficult to navigate. There are also strange and almost diabolical forms of life, which I myself was not expecting the athletes to encounter—but which would change forever my feelings toward *Eco-Challenge*. In fact, because of Fiji, *Eco-Challenge* is now currently on hiatus. I made the decision to halt production until the time is right to begin again with a new passion and energy, and perhaps even with an entirely new way in which to conduct the race.

The first notable near-disaster during the race occurred when two American teams made a map-reading error. Producer Kevin Hodder and I saw them from a helicopter as we flew down by a valley off the racecourse. We were surprised to see that these two of the four teams were wading upstream in the totally wrong direction. We told the pilot to do a one-eighty, with the intention of using hand signals as we hovered to indicate that they should reverse their course to get back on track, knowing that were they to continue on their present course, the river would soon diminish to little more than a trickle. If they continued pushing on through the heavily jungled hillside, they would eventually discover that the top of the hillside yielded to sheer cliffs falling a thousand feet below them. If those cliffs were approached by an unsuspecting team at night, there was a high probability that they would walk over the edge.

With this in mind, Kevin and I had the helicopter turned around. But by then the two teams had vanished into the jungle. We spent an exhausting, frustrating hour until our fuel tank was almost dry, flying up and down that river valley, hoping to see them or attract their attention—but to no avail. As a last-ditch effort, we tried to use the helicopter as a large, visual signaling device by flying in the direction of a spot directly above where we believed them to be. To accomplish this we instructed the pilot to execute a series of abrupt stops and 180-degree turns, then fly straight forward in the correct direction. This, of course, was not an accepted or known helicopter signaling method, but we were desperate to do anything to suggest to these teams that they had gone the wrong way. Back and forth we flew, not knowing that they could hear us all the while but were unable to see our unorthodox signaling method because of the thick jungle canopy.

When we arrived back at base camp to refuel, we immediately alerted the *Eco-Challenge* technical director and renowned mountain guide Scott Flavelle of what we had just seen. His assessment was that he would expect anybody who reached the jungled hillside and the end of the river to realize their error and turn around. But then again, he couldn't believe that anybody could make an error of that magnitude and be traveling in their direction at all.

For thirty long hours, we had no news of that team. They eventually showed up at the correct checkpoint—not only did they go up the heavily jungled hillside at night, they also found a way down the sheer cliffs, got back on course, and proceeded as if nothing had happened. During those thirty hours, Kevin and I grew increasingly concerned as each hour passed. Although we had another fifty teams progressing on the racecourse, at every available opportunity we would fly that helicopter over the valley in the vain hope of sighting the eight missing Eco-Challengers. I have never discussed this with the press, but during those thirty hours I felt certain that somebody was going to die. I wished I'd never heard of *Eco-Challenge*.

Level heads will prevail.

Even when the teams stumbled safely into a checkpoint, my relief was short-lived. An emergency call had been relayed to Kevin and me from Scott Flavelle, telling us that a racer, FBI agent Cindy Coppola, had been severely bitten on the knee while wading waist-deep in a dark jungle river. In excruciating pain, her entire leg was swelling fast. Her heart rate was through the roof, and she was having trouble breathing. The only positive in this scenario was that her teammates were experienced military personnel, and calmly handled the emergency radio call with cool professionalism. They were worried but knew that panicking would not help rescue their delirious teammate. Their location was somewhere beneath thirty feet of jungle canopy, which meant that there would be no way for us to get a visual on their location. The global positioning system that the team was carrying and that was allowed to be used only in case of emergency was of no use unless it had a direct line of sight to the satellites orbiting the planet. The jungle canopy made that line of sight nonexistent. Our only hope was to fly our helicopter into the general area and have the pilot radio us when we sounded closest and farthest away. While Kevin and I were searching in our helicopter, the other *Eco-Challenge* helicopters carrying the medical rescue team joined us. Once we knew we at least were hovering near the right hillside, we instructed the team to pop their emergency orange smoke canister, knowing that as the smoke drifted up through the thick canopy of trees below, we could locate the team. The trees were so tall that we could barely see the orange smoke as it wafted through the treetops—but see it we did. The next stage was for a rescue medic to be lowered on a rope through the jungle canopy to the woman who was steadily worsening below. He made it just in time; she was winched to safety and survived. It was later determined that she had been bitten by a six-foot-long, fat, freshwater eel. As only *Eco-Challenge* athletes would do, her three remaining teammates refused to be winched out with her, preferring to continue to suffer the course to the finish, eels or no eels.

It was after that *Eco-Challenge* had finished—in fact, about two weeks later, while I was in the Amazon filming *Survivor 6* on the Rio Negro—that I got my worst news about *Eco-Challenge: Fiji*. Alexander Freitas, a member of a Brazilian team who had traveled with his teammates to Australia for a short vacation after Fiji, had become hospitalized in Sydney with strange, flulike symptoms. These steadily worsened. Alexander slipped into a coma of unknown tropical origin. I considered the irony that I was sitting in the Amazon jungle of Brazil, knowing that a Brazilian man who actually lived a short flight away in São Paulo was totally unconscious as result of something that had occurred while we'd been in Fiji together. It was later determined that Alexander had ingested a rat worm as a result of eating uncooked river shrimp as a means of sustenance while racing in *Eco-Challenge*. The rat worm had traveled from his stomach up to the brain, where it had burrowed in and shut down his body. It was only months later that Alexander finally woke up in a Brazilian hospital, having been flown home—possibly to die—to his native Brazil to be with his family. The fact that he eventually regained consciousness and began to recover did not actually make me feel any better about the risks of *Eco-Challenge*. I'd always thought it would be someone falling off a cliff or being drowned in Class IV rapids or trampled by a horse that would constitute our worst accidents. Who could believe it would turn out to be eating a tiny river shrimp?

That's when I made the decision to shut *Eco* down. Not for good, necessarily, but until I felt right about staging such a competition again.

I still don't know when or if I will produce another *Eco-Challenge*. The best and brightest in the world of adventure keep reminding me that *Eco-Challenge* is not a reality show, but a bona fide adventure on the scale of climbing Mount Everest or rafting the Zambezi or crossing the Sahara by camel. Humans have always sought out adventures; they seem to have a need to do so, and the types of people who tackle the extreme adventures understand the inherent risks. Nevertheless, they go for it. In fact, the year after the worst Everest disaster in history—the May 1996 tragedy that resulted in Jon Krakauer's book *Into Thin Air*—more people attempted to scale Everest than ever before.

This quest for adventure and the understanding of its risks are probably why I never heard a word of complaint from Alexander's teammates or family, or from any other *Eco-Challenge* athlete who has suffered sickness or injury. Though the race is still on hold, I've realized again the value that *Eco-Challenge* provides to the adventure-seeking world. I haven't given up the idea that another *Eco-Challenge* may be in my future.

I am, however, glad to have had the chance to step back from *Eco* for a while, to get mentally refreshed about this one-of-a-kind adventure. It wasn't getting stale, but it needed to be reinvented in a way that reflects the changing shape of adventure and television.

Chapter Sixteen

It's a Jungle Out There

The biggest danger to newcomers who sign up to compete in *Survivor* is that, after watching a few seasons of the show on TV, they incorrectly assume that it's as safe as the Jungle Cruise at Disneyland. They have no idea how real the dangers can be. The Amazon region contains so many dangers that I wanted the survivors for *Amazon* to be absolutely aware of what they would be facing. Ghandia's cobra incident in Thailand had been an example of the reality of these tropical jungles, but this setting was definitely even more perilous. I couldn't allow the survivors' own complacency to put them in serious or life-threatening danger. They had to remain aware that even though the oppressively thick jungle made it impossible to really see the threats, they were there all the same. In the Amazon so many things could kill you— the smallest spider hiding beneath a leaf, the stealthily silent jaguars whose paw prints we often saw at first light just outside our camp, or worst of all, giant anacondas, known to invisibly approach unsuspecting people via the bottom of small, inky-black streams and attack suddenly before a person even realized what was happening.

The Amazon required me to invent a clever way to remind our newest survivor tribes to never let down their guard. I decided that a little shock therapy might do the trick. *Survivor: Amazon* was shot in one of the most remote locations we had ever chosen. It required everyone to fly overnight from Miami through the Brazilian city of São Paulo and then onward by smaller plane to the remote river town of Manaus, located on the Rio Negro, thousands of miles deep into the Amazon jungle. As if this wasn't isolated enough, we then boarded a small boat and took it upriver for a few hours farther into the depths of the jungle. Here, in the most unlikely of places, was the Ariau Amazon Towers hotel, comprising ten cylindrical wooden buildings perched precariously atop fifty-foot-high poles so that even with the enormous depth fluctuations of the Amazon, the buildings would always remain above water. In the dry season those buildings stand the full fifty feet above the last remnants of the muddy, shallow river, looking like spaceships perched a thousand miles from anywhere, but in the rainy season the river rises so much that you can literally drive a boat right up to the lobby.

Immediately upon arriving at the Ariau, the newest crop of survivors staggered onto the wooden gangways, bleary-eyed, exhausted, and disoriented from their journey, and wondered "What the hell is this weird place doing here?" It was then that I hit them hard with my "shock therapy."

Before they had even unpacked their duffel bags, I gave them a quick "welcome to the Amazon" speech and then shuffled them into five or six waiting canoes. A local jungle guide paddled each canoe into a dark, forbidding inlet of the Rio Negro. The survivors were instructed to sit perfectly still in case the canoe tipped and they fell into the water. This was not water you wanted to fall into in the bright sunlight, let alone in the pitch-black of night—between the piranhas, the anacondas, and the caiman, they wouldn't last long. Sixteen wide-eyed city slickers sat as motionless as statues, fearing to even breathe too heavily lest the canoe become unstable. It was probably the most terrifying canoe trip of their lives. They sat like deer in the headlights as the guides shone their flashlights onto the surface of the river. Hundreds of red eyes stared back, some from as close as a couple of feet away. There were caiman everywhere. As the survivors paddled back to the Ariau after that shock therapy indoctrination, they were told stories of the natives, the spiders, the fire ants, and everything else previously unimaginable. They had gained a real understanding of the hazards of the Amazon.

When they returned to the Ariau, the survivors had gone from a state of bleary-eyed malaise to jumping out of their skins if so much as a leaf brushed past their bare leg. They were shown to an open dormitory where they would sleep in hammocks covered with mosquito net. I think each of them lay awake all night imagining that every sound they heard was some exotic creature coming to kill them. Heidi Strobel, a twenty-something teacher from Missouri, was so shaken that the next day she seriously considered going home. I worried initially that I had pushed them too hard too soon and started to second-guess myself, but after a few hours of talking with me, Heidi settled down and decided to stay. In fact, she went on to do very well in the game.

The Amazon experience really got into all of our souls. As far as the eye could see was thick, green jungle, which creates more than one-third of the earth's oxygen. Within that jungle are thousands of species that aren't even documented, as well as the more obvious, such as the brilliantly colored parrots alighting on every other tree you looked at. I remember sitting in the air-conditioned restaurant one lunchtime, simply glad for a respite from the engulfing humidity outside. Nearby was crew member Mike Murray, one of our cameramen. He heard a radio call about a jaguar that was swimming across an inlet of the Negro near the hotel. Grabbing his camera, Mike sprinted to commandeer a boat. He followed the swimming feline with the boat and was rewarded for his troubles when he captured the most incredible footage of that wild Amazonian jaguar swimming about two hundred meters before exiting the water. The gorgeous wild cat turned to stare directly into Mike's camera before running off into the jungle.

When people who are adventurous have an adventure immersion experience—in which they really live on the floor of the jungle, in the mountains, or in the desert—they eventually connect with their surroundings and become confident. They begin to feel as if they are a part of their environment. Such was the case with the *Amazon* survivors.

About a month into the game, a few of those survivors who were initially scared to go anywhere near the water took part in a boat-rowing challenge in an inlet of the Rio Negro where there were certain to be piranha and caiman. Despite all safety preparations, two of the boats actually accidentally sank during the challenge! But instead of the survivors fearfully swimming directly to the nearest shore, they carried on by swimming the entire race, ignoring whatever lived in that water. When I asked Jenna Morasca, a twenty-four-year-old swimsuit model (who had definitely looked like a deer in the headlights on the first night) why she had braved the dangerous creatures, she shrugged and said that they had lived in that jungle long enough to learn that in the bright sunlight the caiman were highly unlikely to attack, and that unless you were bleeding, the piranhas were unlikely to bother you. What a difference from that first night! These citified North Americans had quickly become comfortable in the most hostile jungle on earth. Jenna went on to become the third woman to win the million-dollar prize. It seemed appropriate for a woman to win the *Survivor* that was thematically based on the mythical Amazon women!

Keep your intended outcome in mind.

I'm asked quite frequently what it takes to win *Survivor*. There are loads of theories out there. Some people think the key is developing great alliances. Others think it's being as Machiavellian as possible. I believe the great players have one attribute in common: flexibility—and those who embody a trait I have come to call "flexible action" are most likely to win. This same trait is likewise required for success in both business and life in general.

The ability to keep your intended outcome in mind, while constantly analyzing whether your actions of that day are taking you *closer to* or *further from* that intended outcome, is critical to success. Too many people think they can make it by setting a goal and taking action, but they ultimately fail because they didn't have the awareness to recognize whether their actions were actually helping or hurting them. However, even that awareness is not enough. You need to have the courage to use that awareness that your plan is not working to drastically change your strategies and actions in order to make the plan work. And you may need to do this every week or even every day. This is what I mean by flexible action. You must pay attention and constantly make adjustments because, just as when you are driving a car, if you fall asleep at the wheel, you will crash. Another analogy is that of an airplane taking off in New York and heading for Los Angeles. The pilot sets a course to fly, but if the pilot does not constantly adjust for wind and weather variations, that plane will never arrive in Los Angeles. The pilot must continuously adjust for real-world variables in order to reach the destination.

Whether you are competing in *Survivor* or merely employing a Jump In philosophy in your business or personal life, you must always take flexible action. By its very nature, Jumping In means that at least half of what you think is right will go wrong. You must remain aware of what you are getting back as the result of your actions and, equally important, have the courage to take new and different action as needed.

Two people can experience the same situation but perceive it in totally different ways. A funny example of this occurred when Leslie Moonves visited the Ariau Amazon Towers. In the summer of 2003, six months after *Survivor: Amazon*, Les planned to take his annual "boys' summer trip." The "boys" were himself; Tom Freston, co-president of Viacom; Brian Grazer, president of Imagine Films and the producer behind such hits as *Splash, Backdraft, A Beautiful Mind*, and *8 Mile*; Jim Wiatt, chairman of William Morris; and their sons. After hearing about *Survivor: Amazon* and that the Ariau Amazon Towers was the best accommodation the series had ever had, Les decided the hotel would be a great place for their summer adventure. So they flew in a Gulfstream 5 private jet to Rio de Janeiro and on to the Amazon, where they booked accommodations at the Ariau.

A couple of weeks after he returned home from this trip I called Les about the upcoming *Survivor: Pearl Islands* series and casually but earnestly asked, "You must have had a great time at Ariau, huh?"

He replied, "You know, I've been meaning to call you about the trip."

I said, "It's okay, Leslie, you don't need to thank me. I'm just glad you got to experience the Ariau Towers. Isn't it a great place to stay?"

"Now I know that you are out of your mind," he answered. "That was the worst hotel I've ever stayed in. There are crazy monkeys, bugs, and snakes everywhere. I can't believe you had the crew stay in a place like that."

To that I replied, "Leslie, that is honestly by far the best accommodation the crew has ever had, and they are only hoping I can find something as good for them in the Pearl Islands." He was still laughing out loud as he hung up the phone. I'm sure he wished he'd slept in the G5.

> **Seize every opportunity as it presents itself.**

I personally love wild places and have become used to living half the year in beautifully hostile jungles—it has almost become second nature. So I was surprised when the Amazon really crawled into my soul, and I actually went through a spiritual awakening there. I will never forget the local Indians with their mystical movements through the jungle or the crimson and turquoise parrots flitting from tree to tree. I especially recall the shocking pink Amazonian dolphins, the color of their bodies contrasting sharply with the black waters of the Rio Negro as they surfaced and jumped. The Amazon was beautiful, but it was also the most ferociously wild place I have ever visited. Crew members were bitten by pirhanas when it became necessary to film in the Rio Negro; a black jaguar circled the survivors' camp each night; man-eating anacondas, some thirty feet long and colored an insidious olive green that blended perfectly with the jungle, slithered through the production compound; the favorite sleeping place for a band of twenty enormous crocodiles was on the beach near the crew bar. Of all these predators, one vicious species in particular caught my attention: ants. The ants of the Amazon are easily overlooked, but they are numerous and ruthless, cousins to Africa's legendary army ants. Their colonies numbered in the millions. It was fascinating to watch them swarm over other live insects or the carcass of a dead animal, picking it clean within a matter of hours.

They reminded me of the swarms of people living in the urban jungle—everyone crammed into cities and fighting for a place. Just like ants, people on the whole are industrious but will also pick your bones clean, given half a chance. I started to think about how to use the setting of an urban jungle for a new show. I wanted my next franchise to continue to deal with my study of social psychology through reality TV, and I thought that there must be a way to deal with the competitive brutalities of our daily lives in cities, which can be every bit as harsh as living in a jungle.

I've been fortunate that two of my longest-running franchises had focused on nature in the raw and how people interact with it. Nature strips away the veneer we show one another every day, at which point people become who they really are. The result is an incredible human drama set against a majestic natural backdrop. The ants were a reminder that nature in the raw, down to its smallest element, would eat you. If you lay down on the Amazon floor and fell asleep, you would get eaten, either by those ants or by something else.

I began to think about how people operate within the same food-chain situation in cities as they do in jungles. I wondered how I could use a TV show to illustrate my belief that only those who Jump In make it—the others get eaten.

It was clear that my new show would need to be about people wanting the American dream, wanting to get rich, wanting recognition. It would need to focus on aspiring moguls looking to be hired and mentored by a true leader of industry.

I decided to produce a televised interview for the dream job of a lifetime. But this would be no ordinary job interview. Following the success of reality-TV weekly elimination contests that had begun with my *Survivor* series, my new show would be a fifteen-week brutal test. The résumés and interviews would not get you the job; they would merely get you to the start of the contest. Sixteen highly qualified candidates would undergo a series of exhausting weekly business tasks, which would clearly demonstrate whether they had the Jump In mentality required to become a mogul.

As I was wondering about how to produce weekly tasks that would test the participants, I thought back to my Parachute Regiment training and some unusual exercises I was forced to go through in order to determine my level of resourcefulness under pressure. Although my training obviously revolved around weapons and tactics, the Parachute Regiment also wanted its leaders to think outside the box, and had highly unusual methods of teaching us to think and behave in that manner. One Friday evening at five, just as I was about to leave the barracks for a much-needed weekend rest, I was called to meet my platoon commander. He took away my unit insignia, along with my money and ID. I was given a mission. I had to find a way to make it from our base in western England to a commando base hundreds of miles away in Northern Scotland by the following Sunday. I made it there but not without stowing away on a train, hitching some rides, and even convincing a restaurant to feed me for free. I thought outside the box and knew that failure was not an option if I wanted to remain in that unit.

Another time, I was given an even more impossible task. Once again I was stripped of my insignia, identification, and money, and this time I was ordered to travel the two hundred miles to the center of London to get the signature of the conductor of that evening's orchestra concert at Covent Garden. This, by far, was one of the most demanding tasks I could ever have imagined. In addition to having to travel a great distance without any resources, I knew absolutely nothing about opera. I had never been to the opera house and I had only a few hours to accomplish this or fail. It was a bizarre task.

I began by hitching a ride on a truck. That was the easy part, but it got me only to the outskirts of London. It was now the height of the rush hour and no one would pick up a hitchhiker at that time in a bustling metropolis. If I'd had money, the practical way to travel into the heart of the city would have

You can achieve anything once you fully commit.

been by bus or the underground. But I was penniless. I stood around and considered trying to run to the opera, even though it was more than twenty-five miles away. Assuming I could find the way, I knew I could make it if I ran, but the risk of getting lost or being late was huge. I had to succeed. I decided to do something audacious. I hailed a cab, got in, and told the driver, "Look, you're gonna hate me, but I have no money. If you give me your name and address, I promise to send you the fare when I get back to my base. But right now I absolutely must get to the Covent Garden opera." The taxi driver looked at me like I was from Mars.

"You don't look like you're dressed for the opera," he said, suspiciously eyeing my boots and jeans. But after some serious convincing, he finally comprehended my earnest need to succeed and drove me to Covent Garden. As I sat in the back of that cab I realized two things: One, I would never have found my way to the opera in time if I'd gone on foot, and two, you can accomplish amazing things if you put aside your fear of rejection and Jump In. It was highly embarrassing to get in that cab and plead for a free ride, but I did it. After that, I knew I was capable of doing anything I set my mind to.

I arrived at Covent Garden, located in the heart of London, armed with newfound confidence after my taxi success. I talked my way backstage, then to the conductor's dressing room. But when I met with him face-to-face, I discovered that he was Italian! He was also extremely suspicious of my motives, but after wearing him down with much broken English, I got him to sign. Then I convinced another cabdriver to give me a ride out of London, and I made it back to base overnight. I, of course, mailed the cab fares, plus a healthy tip, to each of the cab-drivers.

All of my regimental mates were subjected to similar offbeat adventures. For instance, Simon Clegg, who went on to become the chairman of the British Olympic Association, and was awarded the Order of the British Empire (O.B.E.), was told he must make his way to London overnight and return by 8 A.M. with a copy of that morning's *Times*. Not only did that require getting the paper hot off the press, Simon was also told he must get the newspaper signed by William Rees-Mogg (now Lord Rees-Mogg), the editor in chief. Simon, of course, found a way to succeed.

Another example was the soldier ordered to travel to Heathrow Airport and return by morning with that day's Concorde menu (it changed daily), signed by the plane's captain.

The point of the exercises was simple: Be resourceful. Get results. Do what it takes. Most of my fellow paratroopers who went through those tests went on to succeed in life, too.

These unusual military training tasks were the inspiration for the tasks in my new business-world show. I wanted this TV show to uncover who truly had it and who didn't. You never know when hiring someone whether the person is the sort of resourceful go-getter who helps a company. You don't even know the person at all. This new TV show would allow the mogul doing the hiring to cut through the veneer of résumés and interviews and find the candidate who was truly the best of the best.

I also knew that this would make a great TV show because viewers in the U.S. thoroughly relate to a group of candidates pursuing the American dream. I was living, breathing, and eating this new idea. I'd even played around with a couple of names—"The Protégé" or "The Apprentice" (taken from "The Sorcerer's Apprentice," with the mogul as the sorcerer).

In my excitement I picked up my satellite phone and called Conrad Riggs from the jungle. He is my long-standing business manager and one of the best deal makers in the entire entertainment industry. I'm sure he was surprised to hear me call from the Amazon and expected an update on *Survivor.* I'm sure he was even more surprised when he heard the excitement in my voice. "I've got a new idea," I told

> **Never pitch ideas over the phone.**

him. He was extremely intrigued and pleaded with me to explain it over the phone, but as much as I wanted to blurt it out and get feedback, I resisted. I wanted him to get equally excited and to start thinking about what kind of deal we could negotiate. I knew how much better I am at pitching ideas face-to-face, so I resisted the urge.

It all goes back to the "lean-in" factor. If I pitch an idea and people respond by widening their eyes and leaning in to hear more, I know it's a good idea. Their pupils widen because they're interested. In response to bad ideas, people lean back, as if distancing themselves emotionally and physically. You can see their eyes glaze over. Face-to-face contact is critical in a pitch. Never pitch over the phone. I had to see whether or not Conrad would lean in. "I'll only tell you after the holidays, face-to-face," I said.

I continued developing the idea in my head as filming for *Survivor: Amazon* came to an end. Then I went to England with the children for a much-needed recharge of my batteries and to see my father for the holidays. But the apprentice idea never left my mind.

It wasn't until January that Conrad and I sat down at Geoffrey's restaurant in Malibu, where I pitched him my entire vision for "The Sorcerer's Apprentice." I even had a mogul in mind: Donald Trump.

Conrad leaned in so much he almost fell into his entrée. "That's the best idea I ever heard," he said. Conrad is nothing if not calculatingly and brilliantly candid. It was Conrad who had kept my spirits up by telling me that *Survivor* would work, even as every network was passing on it. I hoped he was right again. It had been worth waiting for a face-to-face moment, reaffirming my belief that you should never pitch over the phone.

We fine-tuned my idea for several weeks, during which time it became clear that my instincts about the mogul were correct. Donald Trump is not just a billionaire, he's a brand name, an easily recognizable figure whom every American knows. It became clear that my first big pitch would be to him, and I remained focused on this. I needed him to commit.

My meeting with The Donald at Trump Wollman Rink in May 2002 had been a positive experience, and I was thrilled, and a little nervous, about pitching him the show. Still, I didn't want to just throw out a one-line concept, hoping he would be interested. I wanted to have my pitch perfectly rehearsed. Trump would give me one shot, one opportunity. I could not afford to falter. I worked tirelessly to perfect the pitch.

In mid-February I traveled to New York on *Survivor* business. My plan was to set up a meeting with Trump for the end of that trip, by which time I'd be ready to pitch him. Since I would be in New York for several days, I would use the time beforehand to rehearse my thoughts so that I would be thoroughly prepared if we met.

I called his office to set up the meeting during the car ride from LaGuardia into Manhattan. Much to my surprise, his executive assistant, Norma Foerderer, immediately put Trump himself on the phone. "How are you doing, my man? I see your *Survivor* ratings are still on top. Isn't it great being number one? Where are you?" he asked.

I told him I was in the car, on my way into the city.

"Come right here right now," Donald said. "You'll be here in twenty minutes. Come straight up. Tell the doorman you're here to see me." Click. He was gone. The pitch was on. It was today. After my initial stunned realization that it was now or never, I smiled, knowing that it was for the best. Either I knew the project from top to bottom and believed in it or I didn't. It was time to Jump In again.

Taking a meeting with Donald Trump is an amazing experience. He's a serious multitasker, with laserlike focus and retention. He can automatically recall names, times, places, and deals from years ago. He is definitely an intimidating presence.

But I mustered my courage as I sat before him and pitched the show that would become *The Apprentice*. I delivered a clear, concise, and energetic outline of the entire series, its educational value, its TV drama, and its commercial potential. Forty-five minutes after sitting down, we shook hands on the deal that Donald Trump would host the show. That's how Trump does business. He acts on instinct. He is decisive, and he bets on people he believes have the ability to deliver. He told me to see Norma and tell her to have his agent at William Morris finalize the agreement.

Norma got Donald's agent on the phone. I was in a great mood; it had been a great afternoon. That was all about to change.

When I spoke on the phone with the agent, rather than focus on discussing the making of a business deal, the first thing he said was, "I wish you would have called me first. As Trump's agent, I should be hearing these ideas before him."

I was furious at his insistence that he had to hear an idea that Donald was already sold on. Totally exhausted from giving my all in pitching to Donald, I knew that pitching the agent over the phone now would be a huge mistake. Still, I mustered my energy reserves and repeated the idea to him anyway. As I concluded, I knew I had again pitched it fantastically, but there was a pause on the other end of the phone.

"I don't think that'll work," the agent said.

I was horrified and angry. This shortsighted man could effectively kill my new show. He was about to scuttle my entire afternoon of success. I had to think fast. I had to take the offensive. I had to win. The next few minutes would make or break whether *The Apprentice* would have Donald Trump as its mogul. "You're an agent, a deal maker, and you're telling me, the guy who brought *Survivor* to TV, that this won't work. How would you possibly know better than me? Better than Donald? You're wrong, and I'm now going to call Jim Wiatt, chairman of William Morris, and tell him you're wrong, and that your shortsightedness is about to cost William Morris a huge commission."

I wasn't bluffing. I immediately called Jim Wiatt and told him about the agent. I'd known Jim for quite some time and had even taken my children to a dinner with him while on vacation in Hawaii the summer before. He was a wonderful guy with a great sense of value. Jim Wiatt had terrific vision and calling him would at least buy me some time to think, as opposed to watching the entire deal disappear down the toilet with one quick flush. He knew that I had the ability to deliver great television and would not want a potentially lucrative piece of business for William Morris to evaporate because an agent had dismissed the idea in a few short minutes. Jim assured me not to worry. He would look into it personally. Then I mustered up the courage to walk back into Trump's office and tell him what had happened. I really did not know Trump and had no idea how he'd react to this news. It was obvious that this trepidation by his agent might give Trump cause to reconsider. It was gut-wrenching.

I took a deep breath and knocked on Donald's open office door. Once again sitting in front of him, I explained the entire William Morris mess and assured Donald of several things: that his agent was totally wrong and lacked vision, that I felt Trump himself was instinctually right and had great vision, that Jim Wiatt was supportive and was personally looking into it, and finally, that Mark Burnett knew exactly what he was doing and the show would be a hit.

I needn't have worried. Donald was everything I had heard he was. He simply laughed and shrugged it off. "My gut tells me this is gonna work. We're gonna do it. Simply propose a fair deal and we're in business." Right there and then I proposed a deal making Trump not just the on-camera host but also a partner in the profits of the show. We shook hands. We would do *The Apprentice* together.

Since that time, Donald Trump has often mentioned in the press that he does not necessarily listen to his agent. He subsequently left William Morris for Creative Artists Agency (CAA).

. . .

Conrad Riggs worked night and day negotiating the formal *Apprentice* contract. It took only two weeks for the contract to be formally agreed upon, then signed by Donald Trump. This is an unheard-of speed for a big deal like this, but it proved once again that Trump is an instinctual deal maker and a man who believes in jumping in.

Once the contract was signed, we had to sell our show to the networks. Donald told me that ABC had wanted to do a reality show with him for a long time, even going so far as to pitch him an *Osbournes*-style program requiring Trump to allow cameras into his personal life. They wanted Trump at work making deals and even at home, covering everything from his life, with the stunning Melania Knauss to watching him brush his legendary hair each morning. Trump had refused to do the show, even though ABC had offered him a huge fee, and the president of ABC, Lloyd Braun himself, had personally pitched Donald. Donald insisted that I pitch ABC first, knowing that they would jump at the chance and make my job of selling our franchise all the easier.

Coincidentally, ABC had also once agreed, in writing, to buy *Survivor* before CBS got involved. But they subsequently backed out because they chose to do *Who Wants to Be a Millionaire?* instead (which came back to haunt them when *Survivor* achieved such great ratings on CBS).

On March 5, 2003, I called Lloyd Braun at ABC, telling him I wanted to pitch the show. When he asked what it was about, I replied that I wouldn't tell him the idea over the phone. *(Never pitch over the phone!)* I subsequently met with and pitched the show to Lloyd and Susan Lyne (Lloyd's co-president), Duncan Gray (a new programmer who'd just joined ABC from London), and Andrea Wang (ABC's long-standing head of reality programming). My opening line was guaranteed to stun them: "I have exclusive rights to a reality show starring Donald Trump."

I thought Lloyd was going to fall off his chair. His jaw dropped. He started to tell me that he had personally been pursuing Donald for a show. I told Lloyd that I was fully aware of that, and that was why Donald and I had decided to come to ABC first. Lloyd flat out told me he wanted the show. I asked him to wait till he heard the entire idea.

As I pitched the show, the lean-in factor was forty-five degrees. I concluded by informing them that I was going to pitch other networks. Lloyd asked that we give ABC an exclusive negotiation period, which I politely declined, explaining that that would remove any leverage Conrad and I would have to secure a fair market price for this incredible new show.

I reminded ABC that they had heard it first. Therefore, the faster they put an offer on the table, the better the chance they had. Duncan Gray subsequently told Conrad that *The Apprentice* was the best idea he had ever heard. I knew that both Lloyd and Susan Lyne had wanted to buy *The Apprentice*, but because ABC was owned by Disney, they had to obtain corporate approval from above. They must have been two of the most frustrated network presidents ever because while NBC's Jeff Zucker and CBS's Leslie Moonves could call their own shots, Lloyd and Susan had their deal-making hands tied by the Disney hierarchy. Sure enough, when ABC came back they offered us only six episodes, instead of the thirteen we needed, and just two-thirds of the licensing fee I'd set as the base price. It was a risky strategy and could only mean that Disney believed the other networks would pass on this opportunity, which would leave ABC in a position to lowball us. Their strategy proved wrong. I knew Lloyd and Susan were very frustrated, and liked them both enormously, and knew that I'd work with them both someday, but probably not while they remained at ABC.

As I had warned ABC at that first meeting, I did go ahead and pitch both NBC and CBS. They both thought it was a brilliant idea, and each agreed to the thirteen-episode commitment and to the seven-figure licensing fee. It was a stalemate. It all came down to negotiating the best ratings bonuses—a fair share of advertising revenue linked to ratings success. I am always willing to make my biggest profits in success and to share in the risk with the network. It was these bonuses that would settle who got *The Apprentice*.

CBS had been my home for six successful seasons of *Survivor*. It would certainly provide me a level of comfort to have the network buy *The Apprentice,* but I made it clear that it was a jump ball. The best bid in the fastest time would win the show. CBS

Determination alone may close the deal.

was open to ratings bonuses and, although they negotiated fairly, they also made it clear that there was a ceiling to how much they would pay in success-based bonuses.

Jeff Zucker, the head of NBC Entertainment, also wanted the show and wanted to be in business with Mark Burnett Productions. And he wanted it fast. He invited Conrad and me to a second meeting at his Burbank office. As Zucker closed the door behind us, his words were simple: "I want this show. You're not leaving this building until we make a deal."

Zucker agreed to all of our terms and, in fact, a better ratings bonus structure than the CBS-imposed ceiling. The deal was fair, and we accepted. *The Apprentice* had been won by NBC.

We now had the funding. It was time to focus on beginning production. The first big questions were where we should have the candidates live and where we should build the boardroom so that it did not unduly hamper the day-to-day operations of Trump's empire while he played his part in the show. The locations obviously had to be in Manhattan. They needed to work for us as well as for Trump. This is where I found out what it's like to live in the Trump world. It's like living in a fantasyland. Everywhere you go with him, people wave and call his name. You get into his helicopter, and it's furnished better than some of the places I've lived. Getting on his private jet meant never having to go through security. Sometimes we'd just be hanging out, and he'd get the urge to call someone famous like George Steinbrenner, owner of the New York Yankees. Of course, everyone takes his calls; he's Donald Trump. Donald was used to making his business life totally productive. When I suggested that we move the show to a spot downtown because there was no available space in midtown Manhattan, he balked. Traveling downtown to an affordable location may have made sense for the costs of production, but it made no sense at all when you considered the inconvenience to Trump.

I was struggling about what to do over our location, knowing all the while that Donald would resent the hassle of leaving his opulent Trump Tower offices to travel through crazy Manhattan traffic to get to a downtown set, costing him valuable business time. Having the luxury of living and working in his own high-rise building, he solved both our problems.

"I have an empty floor in my building," he said, referring to Trump Tower. "I'll provide it for you at a reasonable cost. That way I just take the elevator from my apartment to my office and onto your set. It makes everything more productive." It was a win-win deal: We paid a reasonable price; Donald made money on an empty floor. And best of all, getting him to and (equally important) *keeping him on* the set now became way easier.

It was an elegant solution, but it came with significant hurdles. The empty floor was actually zoned for business use and had to be rezoned for temporary residential purposes. This meant the entire floor had to be altered to suit living codes, which meant, for instance, that a bedroom could be no more than fifty feet from an open window (which is why we clustered the bedrooms so close together). The outlets and plumbing were also to code, which meant the installation of sprinklers, some of which turned out to be too low for us to use with some of our cameras. Sheetrock needed to be used instead of the sort of fake walls found on a traditional television set. However, by the time we were done, that apartment was truly a home—a home with a television studio lighting grid on the ceiling, but still a home. Even Donald Trump's personal couch was used in the kitchen.

Putting the candidates' living suite in Trump Tower benefited the show in a way neither Donald nor I had realized when he made the offer. Whereas Donald had committed to working an hour each day during the filming of *The Apprentice,* his being so close to the set meant that he got way more involved and ended up working sometimes five or six hours per day—a huge benefit to the quality of the show!

The Apprentice was due to begin filming on September 14, 2003. Meanwhile, I was back in New York during April and May of that year filming a new show of mine called *The Restaurant,* about life inside the chaotic world of the restaurant business. I was also preparing for the *Survivor: Amazon* finale. It was to be our second time broadcasting from Trump Wollman Rink in Central Park. The *Marquesas* finale there had been a huge success, and we therefore decided to do it all over again. But this time it became a nightmare.

The entire set was built, at a huge cost, on Wollman Rink. We had rehearsed all week long in preparation for a big Sunday night finale. But then, just as before, the weather started closing in. Rain, we could deal with. Fifty-plus-mile-an-hour winds were another issue. We huddled all day Saturday, planning ways to secure the set and checking and rechecking weather predictions. But it was hopeless; the storm was going to be bigger than we had imagined, and to ensure safety we had to make the toughest of all decisions. So at seven o'clock the morning of the day we were to air, during a conference call with the network brass and the senior production staff, it was decided that we'd move the show to the David Letterman stage at the Ed Sullivan Theater. We went into immediate crisis mode and secured Dave's approval to be on his turf. There were conditions to that approval: No one was to look into his dressing room, and no one was to touch his desk. We covered his desk with fabric and wood; it emerged without a scratch. As for the dressing room issue, no one admitted to having looked inside.

Things were logistically so tight for this show that the crew was still putting trees on the set as the audience was brought in and as the taped portion of the broadcast started. It was the first (and so far only) time that the survivors were on the set for their "orientation" fitting while the audience was there.

Meanwhile, in the control room in the basement, it was clear that the place was designed for one purpose and one purpose only: David Letterman's show. It was touch and go right up to air.

At the last moment we realized that the pretaped spectacular entrance of Jeff Probst, arriving in Manhattan by helicopter and then transferring to a New York City taxi for a drive into Central Park, would no longer work. We had to reshoot Jeff arriving at the Ed Sullivan Theater. Time was tight, and the taped portion of the episode that showed the survivors still in the Amazon was already airing. We were only an hour away from needing to watch Jeff walk into the theater. I knew what to do. I grabbed Jay Bienstock, my co-executive producer, who was just sitting down in the audience to enjoy the show with his parents. His work was done, and the live show was not his responsibility. I explained to Jay, "In less than one hour the audience will watch Jeff arrive in Central Park, then notice that *in fact* we are in the Ed Sullivan Theater!"

Jay laughed and said, "Get me a Steadicam operator and Jeff."

We then all traipsed outside into the wind and rain, and shot Jeff exiting the subway at 53rd Street, crossing Broadway, and entering the theater. Jay then grabbed the tape and edited the sequence himself on an old machine in the Letterman studio. Half an hour later, Jay was sitting back next to his parents in the audience, watching along with America as Jeff (supposedly live) walked across the busy Manhattan intersection and into the theater. I remember looking across at Jay and locking eyes as we both smiled knowingly at the insanity and seat-of-the-pants way we made television. It's all part of the Mark Burnett Productions' Jump In philosophy. Jay has been around since the first Discovery Channel *Eco-Challenge*, when he worked for me as an editor. He lives and breathes our "don't bring me problems, just provide me solutions" way of operating. That night in New York City much of America watched as Jenna Morasca became the winner of the sixth *Survivor*. No one but us, however, was any the wiser that half an hour earlier we had no transition shot of Jeff's arrival. Thanks to Jay's professionalism and poise, it all worked out perfectly—it always does.

Just another day in the life of *Survivor!*

I had dealt with six seasons of *Survivor*, always worried that our big secret would leak out. But secrecy is more manageable on an island in the middle of nowhere. It is much harder on an island like Manhattan. So how on earth to keep the vital secrecy of *The Apprentice* intact? The answer was obvious. Hide in plain sight. You can't easily impress New Yorkers. They're cynical and busy, always in a rush—the opposite of Californians. I realized that you can't impress them with a camera crew. Even if they wanted to know what we were filming, they wouldn't ask. In New York, we could shoot without people even stopping to watch. You can't do that anywhere else in the world. We learned quickly that nobody bothered us or cared about what we were doing or who we were. Even when Donald Trump would step out of his limo to deliver a task to the candidates, it would make only a slight impact on the busy Manhattan streets, whereas in Los Angeles traffic would come to a grinding halt. Our secret was never in jeopardy.

I knew that in a serious hiring situation the CEO wouldn't be the only person in attendance. And who would believe a billionaire wouldn't have top executives to bounce ideas off of? It felt natural to have two other characters in the boardroom with Trump, which was vitally important to me. I had learned one fundamental truth in my short career: If something doesn't feel natural, it won't work in reality television. I told Trump this, mentioning that it allowed him to have conversations with other people in the boardroom. He immediately agreed. I let him pick the two people he wanted in the room with him, and he made a brilliant choice: one woman, one man; one older, one younger.

Although I instigated this extra element, even I didn't realize the enormous value of Caroline Kepcher and George Ross, who added much-needed drama to the show, especially when Donald sent people out of the boardroom. What would he have done without them? He would have had to sit alone twiddling his thumbs and waiting for a mo-

ment to call the apprentices back in. In addition to the boardroom situations, would viewers have believed that Donald Trump would spend
his time following the would-be apprentices around the city as they
met their challenges? If he went out on the streets for every challenge,
it would lessen his influence and authenticity. Clearly a billionaire like
Trump is too busy to chase his apprentices around all day long.

My Jump In philosophy came through once again. My instinct told
me that having Caroline and George on the show would work, but in
looking back, I see that it wasn't just a wonderful production enhance-
ment, it was an absolute necessity. Caroline and George turned out to
be iconic figures, having become celebrities in their own right. Caroline
even wrote a successful book for aspiring female executives based upon
her *Apprentice* experiences.

As for the players on *The Apprentice*, I set out looking for a cast
equally composed of eight people who had earned their money without
formal college educations and eight highly educated people with
MBAs. Having both types was important to me, because I needed a reason for America to root for each team. This was an age-old dividing
line: the haves and the have nots. I myself didn't go to college. I went
into the Parachute Regiment at seventeen, giving up the opportunity
for college. I had sufficiently good high school grades but my family
could not afford college. I had done well despite the lack of a business
school education, and I always liked to beat highly educated competitors. This, I decided, was an ideal creative way to captivate America
into rooting for one team or another.

I hired a young guy to head casting for *The Apprentice*. Rob La
Plante came highly recommended by NBC. As soon as I met him, I
liked him, and we spent a couple of hours that first day really talking
through my vision for the show and the kind of people we would need
in order to make this a hit. Rob suggested that in addition to soliciting
applications primarily by using commercials on NBC and NBC.com,
we approach and target business schools and chambers of commerce.
That proved to be a wonderful tool for getting the word out.

Casting *The Apprentice* was completely different from any type of casting I'd yet experienced. There were shocking levels of intellect and résumés of staggering depth to consider. Normally, part of the process is to weed out the wannabe actors and musicians who are hoping to get on the show and have instant careers. That was not a problem with *The Apprentice.* The applicants were inspirational because of their successes and were very polished. However, that proved to be a problem. All these people had spent countless hours learning how to interview for a job. They'd been rigorously trained to put their best foot forward. What I needed for the show, however, was to see the real person, someone with many facets. So the interviews became a little like peeling an onion layer by layer, trying to uncover what lies beneath. The ones who made the show did so because they were capable of revealing parts of their background they might not otherwise reveal during a professional business interview—for example, the time Omarosa lifted her shirt and showed us the six-inch stab wound in her abdomen!

Unfortunately, although we found hundreds of wonderfully talented and charismatic people who were perfect for the cast, we could find only *two* people without a college education who I truly believed could do well. I realized instinctively that the two teams needed to be evenly matched and that the audience had to be impressed by the business savvy of both teams. They would clearly have different ways of looking at the same problem, but both views needed to be brilliant and inspiring. If I had a bunch of high school graduates who were far outclassed by the MBAs, it could make my show into a joke. I had thousands of wonderful college-educated candidates who fit my bill, but only two high school grads whom I believed in. The problem was that I had told NBC that the show's theme would be about exploring this dynamic. When I revealed to NBC executives that I was having a huge problem living up to this, they became concerned and summoned me to Burbank to discuss the "Big Problem," as they referred to it. Now remember, this was my first NBC show. Here's where I jumped in again.

As I drove to NBC, I took a call from a journalist who interviewed me about my *Survivor: Amazon* series and in particular how well the women had done against the men. Here was another journalist questioning whether *Survivor 7* (*Pearl Islands*) could possibly be as good as *Survivor: Amazon* because the men-versus-women theme had given the series such an easy-to-root-for creative through line of drama. As I explained that I was certain that *Pearl Islands* would do well based on the casting tapes I was seeing and its pirate theme, a lightbulb lit up in my head. Bingo! *The Apprentice* would shift focus to the "glass ceiling" concept, and pit women against men. This was another age-old business conflict. Women believe that they are held back, underpaid, and treated unfairly. But given a level playing field, women universally feel that they could dominate. Here was a perfect way to test the theory.

I arrived in Burbank to meet a roomful of various NBC department heads. I pitched the "battle of the sexes" as if I had been contemplating it all along. They loved it; "Big Problem" solved; we moved on to other creative subjects, such as promotions and advertising.

I had no idea whether the men-versus-women angle would really work, but I jumped in and made NBC happy. Less confident—or maybe more mentally stable—people would have discussed the pros and cons of the idea, then had it analyzed before asking NBC for permission to go with this new theme. Not me. Jeff Zucker expects show runners who can be decisive and lead from the front, show runners who can make him feel it was worth paying big bucks for big results. If I had gone into NBC unsure and asking Zucker's permission or, worse yet, that of his executives, he would have become nervous.

Like me, NBC had no idea whether my women-versus-men idea would work, but at least we had a plan, we had a direction, and we were already walking in that direction. I was leading from the front. Zucker often told me that he expected to have bought a leader in me. That's what I had to make sure he continually got.

We now continued our casting with this new theme in mind and instantly things fell into place. Rob LaPlante found one of the smartest, most charismatic, and dynamic casts ever for a reality show. This was going to be one hell of a contest. And if the experience of *Survivor* held true, this sure-to-be-hard-fought contest would translate into an incredible TV show.

But long before I would get to watch *The Apprentice* cast in action I had to produce *Survivor: Pearl Islands* in Panama. The freight train that was my year just kept on moving.

Chapter Seventeen

Panama Nights

B andwidth" is a twenty-first-century term. In this digital world, bandwidth is a measure of how much information can be sent and received. In my world, bandwidth refers to how much work I can take on at any given moment. I constantly try to expand my bandwidth, taking on as much work as possible to achieve maximum results. Hey, we only live once! I achieve this by delegating, no matter how enormous the task.

Although I had been working long hours finalizing details for the upcoming shooting of the first *Apprentice* series and handling the enormous complications and amount of work that came along with it, I still had managed to focus attention on my next big shoots: *Survivor 7* and *Survivor 8*. The schedule would be extremely tight. First I would shoot *Survivor 7* in Panama, then fly back to Manhattan to shoot *The Apprentice,* then fly back to a still-unnamed location to shoot *Survivor 8*.

Expand your bandwidth.

Yes, my bandwidth was truly being tested. Sometimes it seems as though I've bitten off more than I can chew, but I just keep on chewing. The two Panama *Survivors* (yes, two!) would become some of the most-watched and beloved series in the franchise's history, as well as being good case studies in bandwidth.

Every summer the networks produce an extravaganza called the Up Fronts. These are elaborate introductions of the fall shows to advertisers, journalists, and affiliates. The Up Fronts are where most of the commercial time for the year is sold, and it's extremely important for the networks that they appear innovative, successful, and, above all, entertaining. At the 2001 Up Fronts at Carnegie Hall, for instance, I was brought onstage with Jeff Probst to introduce *Survivor 2*. Leslie Moonves surprised me by having Gloria Gaynor come out and sing her hit song "I Will Survive" to Jeff and me, in front of this enormous crowd of people. "Amazing" is the only word to describe this.

During the summer of 2003, I once again attended the Up Fronts, this time mere days before flying to Panama to shoot *Survivor 7*. Donald Trump, who conducted his Miss Universe Pageant there, made several phone calls to the government to allow us the sort of access and privacy we needed—although there were still problems: Panama's navy did a bait and switch on us when it came to acting as our security. They originally agreed, but when the time came they gave the production a laundry list of things they wanted. Permits were required for everything from filming to use of watercraft, but important people would mysteriously disappear when it came time to sign those permits, then they would reappear just in time to receive a "donation."

Survivor 7 would be titled *Pearl Islands* and have a pirate theme, based on the legends of pirates like Sir Henry Morgan and Sir Frances Drake, who was considered a privateer by the British but something much worse by the people of Panama. He plundered and burned the Panama coast with such ferocity that to this day Panamanian parents tell their children that if they don't behave, "El Drago"—Drake—will come get them.

Once I finished *Pearl Islands,* I would head right back to New York City to begin shooting the first *Apprentice,* and then mere days after wrapping that, I would need to head *somewhere* to start on *Survivor 8*. However, *Survivor 8* didn't even have a location, let alone a theme yet, and it was only six short months away. All this was manageable within my bandwidth but only if I hurriedly figured out where the hell we'd shoot *Survivor 8* so we could at least start preplanning where to ship our fifty containers of gear immediately after we wrapped *Pearl Islands*. This was going to be a risky few months, and although I was an expert at jumping in, I needed a quick fix to find my new location and theme.

That fix came from the unlikeliest of places. In the week before the Up Fronts, Leslie Moonves called me and tossed a strongly worded suggestion my way. "You've been talking about bringing back your old *Survivor* favorites for an all-star show since Africa. That was two years ago. Let's do it this year. I want you to announce it at the Up Fronts," he said.

This wasn't a suggestion; it was an order. Leslie clearly had done his math and figured CBS could use the attraction of the all-stars to bring in major advertising revenue—especially if he announced it at the Up Fronts.

However, I was torn. On the one hand, this gave me an instant theme that would probably work, but it sounded like we were "jumping the shark." (This term describes the last-ditch stunt that signals the end of a franchise. It originated in the waning days of the TV sitcom *Happy Days*. Desperate for ratings, the producers concocted an outrageous episode that featured Fonzie jumping a pool of sharks on his motorcycle. *Happy Days* was canceled soon after.)

Also, I wondered whether America would embrace this idea, which was vastly different from our core show. *Survivor* had worked based on the concept of sixteen strangers building a world. Not only would the all-stars know each other, but most of them had become friends.

I tossed and turned all night following Les's call. I knew his primary focus was the next month's advertising sales, but I also knew he believed strongly in the future of the *Survivor* franchise. Why would he ask me to jump the shark so soon? I woke up early and called Les on his cell phone. In answer to my concerns he said, "Mark, if you believe that all-stars will be seen as jumping the shark, don't do it. However, I believe that it will reignite a new, higher level of excitement in the franchise and will carry us to *Survivor 16*."

I said I'd think it through and call him back. I took a walk in Central Park and went over and over the scenario in my mind. I realized that I was overanalyzing the situation and that I had to simply follow my gut. Leslie had been completely right about putting *Survivor 2* on Thursdays up against *Friends,* and even though I was afraid back then, I still remembered the excitement and the way that my instinct had told me to go with it. Here again, I was a little afraid, but for some reason just "felt" it was the right choice. I called Leslie back and told him I would announce the all-stars at Carnegie Hall later that day. Having jumped in, I tried to supress my nerves as I waited backstage for my turn to go on, hoping the audience would react favorably.

If there was any doubt in my mind about whether the time was right for *Survivor: All-Stars* they were quickly allayed when I took center stage at Carnegie Hall later that afternoon. This time Destiny's Child came onstage, singing "Survivor." Once again, it was exhilarating but so weird to be sung to on that stage. Only in America could this happen to a working-class boy. We then brought out Sue Hawk, Richard Hatch, Jerri Manthey, Tina Wesson, and Rudy Boesch to join Jeff Probst and me on the stage. The cheers were thunderous and got bigger with each survivor who joined us. The cheers for Rudy reached a crescendo. The place simply erupted for the crusty old Navy SEAL. Afterward, Richard Hatch, who still doesn't comprehend that he is one of the show's all-time villains, couldn't understand why the inspirational Rudy got bigger cheers. When I announced that they would all be coming back for another *Survivor,* this time with an all-star cast of the show's greatest players, Carnegie Hall once again erupted in massive cheers and a standing ovation. Les had been right again. The time was now. I had no doubt in my mind that we had our biggest hit on our hands. Another bonus was that I could do something I had never done before: I could stage back-to-back *Survivor* series on the same islands.

Both *Survivor: Pearl Islands* and *Survivor 8* could be shot in Panama because *All-Stars* did not need a fresh, marketable location. The fact that the show consisted of returning favorites was theme enough. But in reality, even though reusing the location would save me an enormous amount of preparation for *Survivor 8*, there was still a lot of work to do before we could fulfill the public's high expectations. And I had to produce both *Survivor 7* and the first *Apprentice* before the all-stars even set foot on a *Survivor* island for the second time.

Before I knew it, I was flying to Panama, the cheers from Carnegie Hall still ringing in my head, to film what I intended to be a deliberately disorienting *Survivor 7*. This, the seventh group of castaways, had seen the show on television so many times that they thought they knew how the game was played. They underestimated me. *Survivor* would never be predictable. As I had done in Thailand and the Amazon, I was going to reinvent the game again. But this time I planned to add two highly unexpected new twists to the game: First, I would surprise the survivors by forcing them to begin the game with just the clothes on their backs, like real castaways, and second, I would add the ultimate twist: allowing someone who had been voted off to be voted back into the game to try all over again.

I chose Panama as the location for *Survivor 7* (and, subsequently, *Survivor 8*) because Central America was still relatively safe in terms of world events. I found this to be utterly ironic, because two decades ago Central America was the last place in the world one thought of in terms of political stability. A further irony was that I had been headed for Central America back in 1982, when I first came to America, but had chosen to stay in Los Angeles at my mother's urging. Well, Mom, I finally got to go to Central America. This time she would be proud of the circumstances.

The first hint that Panama would be physically challenging came during the location scout. We flew to the Pearl Islands and found an island with an old well—an old pirate well, as it turned out—that had a piece of wood lying across the wooden top. As we bent forward to examine the well, that piece of wood started moving. It was a boa constrictor! And that's not all. During the next twenty minutes, every piece of wood in the jungle around us seemed to move. There were more boas in this area than we could have imagined.

The snakes—which included the large and lethal bushmaster—

were a minor obstacle compared to the complex weather systems en-
veloping Panama. The *Survivor* Marine Department, headed by Lance
Julian, who has also worked on feature films including Kevin Costner's
Waterworld back in the '90s and *Master and Commander* starring Rus-
sell Crowe in 2002, was destined to play a huge role in the production.
The pirate theme meant that *Pearl Islands* would be a completely
ocean-based, waterborne *Survivor*. Because Panama is so narrow, bridg-
ing two oceans, the weather systems are violent and fast. (Lance once
figured that we had fifteen minutes' warning at most before a major
storm.) In Panama, it rains all the time. The reason the Panama Canal
works is that, despite the fact that every time those lock gates are released millions of gallons of water are released into the ocean, enormous quantities of rainfall soon replenish the locks.

An interesting side note about the Panama Canal is that entire valleys were flooded during its construction, creating enormous lakes. At
the time, all the wildlife in that area made its way to the top of the highest peaks, which became islands in the midst of those flooded valleys.
These species have remained in this pristine state atop their own little
islands for more than a century and are part of the Smithsonian Con-
servation and Research Center. I once flew by helicopter from one side
of Panama to the other—from the Pacific Ocean to the Atlantic—and
looked down on these green islands in the middle of the world's most
vital waterway. It's incredible.

In the minds of myself and my crew, *Survivor 7* and *Survivor 8* in
Panama were not two distinctly separate productions but one single,
continuous production, albeit separated bang in the middle by my first
urban island production in Manhattan, with Donald Trump. Having
both versions of *Survivor* in Panama allowed us to operate from the
same hotel on the island of Contadora (most crew members even got
the same hotel room twice), and meant that we were actually saved
from the logistical nightmare of shipping more than fifty oceangoing
containers somewhere else in the world.

Both Panama *Survivor* series were without a doubt two of the most logistically challenging productions we have ever worked on. To begin with, all crew and equipment had to be transported to the Pearl Islands by boat—some twenty-three miles over completely exposed, unprotected ocean water. A large southwest swell, two to three knots of current, a seventeen-foot rise and fall of the tide, and heavy thunderstorms made for interesting days on the water. It seemed like every day on the ocean we were subject to intense weather, and numerous resupply trips were canceled or delayed as the result of storm systems that originated in the northern Amazon and intensified as they headed west, eventually hitting Panama with heavy rains and forty-knot winds. Lance's team treated the weather with the greatest of respect, and organized real-time Doppler weather radar, hourly satellite images, and independent weather assessment from Commanders Weather to enable us to make practical operational decisions.

Once the ships arrived at the Pearl Islands, the challenges involved with filming an entirely water-based production grew really apparent. Not a single location—whether it be the Tribal Council, Ponderosa, Tribe Camps, Challenges, or Rewards—could be accessed by road. Given this, the Marine Department crewed up with fifty-five vessels, and 118 personnel in order to service production needs twenty-four hours a day, seven days a week for thirty-nine days, in whatever weather conditions nature threw at us. It was as if we were producing a waterborne Operation Desert Storm. And despite the experience and diligence of the Marine Department, we still endured a substantial amount of downtime due to an unlikely source: needlefish!

The needlefish problem wasn't discovered until we turned on the running lights during a nighttime ferry. Running at night requires that all vessels have the appropriate navigation lights in order to ensure the safe navigation of vessels during nighttime and periods of reduced visibility. Ironically, the very lights that were required to keep us safe were what placed our crews and vessels in harm's way. Attracted by the navigation lights on the boats, the needlefish in the area would chase the vessels, thinking that they were about to get an easy meal. Coming almost completely out of the water and skimming the surface with only their tails to propel themselves, the fish would get a rude awakening once they found themselves impaled on the side of a twenty-four-foot inflatable boat.

More often than not, the beak of the fish would break off, effectively plugging the hole, thus enabling the boat to continue operating until it got back to base and could be repaired. Despite outfitting the boats with protective rubber skirts, fish continued to puncture the boats throughout the show's production. Fortunately, none of our crew was ever hit by one of these flying fish, because if a needlefish could pierce a thick rubber boat think of the damage it could do to a human!

Although we spent many of our *Survivor* days tooling around at night in small boats, we never got used to Panama's violent weather. Often we'd be coming back from the Tribal Council, which was on a separate island, and there would be so many independent storm systems that at times lightning was striking the ocean all around us. One night we experienced the worst storm ever. I honestly was wondering if I was going to get back to the hotel alive. Jeff Probst later told me it was the first time he ever really worried for the safety of the castaways. Jeff actually made a radio call to the camera crews at the tribal beaches to make sure they'd all made it back safely from the Tribal Council. That night was casting director Lynne Spillman's first-ever trip to a *Survivor* location. It might be the last time she comes.

I was often told by the numerous feature film veterans on the crew that making movies was way easier than this twenty-four-hour-a-day reality stuff!

The *Survivor: Amazon* production was the start of a trend whereby the crew stayed in hotels—rustic hotels, but still hotels, with flushing toilets and occasional hot water in the showers. Our days of living in tent cities were over. In Panama we found the Hotel Contadora. It was the sort of resort that had probably been stylish a few decades back, but was now slightly run-down. There were seven pods of rooms with a mess hall in the center, which always made it easy to find people if you were looking for them.

My room was large, and it even had a kitchen and a separate dining room that I turned into a conference room. I kept my refrigerator well stocked with beer and candy, so when I called a meeting of the producers and department heads, they would all come over and we'd have a few beers and sort out the issues of the day. Those meetings always underscored for me how far we'd come with *Survivor*. Meetings used to take hours, but now we knew how to do our job so well that we were able to conduct them in shorthand. We were basically a championship team that knew the playbook inside and out.

James and Cameron also came for a visit, continuing the naturalist studies they had begun in Thailand. Cameron especially loved the pirate theme and constantly walked around the Tribal Council wearing the pirate sword and musket that the Art Department had given him. James, on the other hand, focused on scuba diving. He even commandeered a new toy that the company had purchased. It was an underwater scooter to help our underwater filming teams get to more spots faster. It was very James Bond, and James Burnett became quite the expert. The one thing both kids got addicted to was fishing with big lures off the back of the boat as we returned from every challenge and Tribal Council. The biggest fish of the trip was caught by six-year-old Cameron. It was a large mahimahi, and he and James proudly presented it to Simon, our caterer, to cook for the crew. It was a wonderful sight to watch my two little boys carrying the sautéed mahimahi from table to table and, as they regarded it, feeding the crew.

The Contadora Hotel had a large, run-down zoo on its property. Because I hate to see animals locked up, I don't like zoos—not even good zoos. So I tried to avoid the Contadora's zoo. But my youngest son, Cameron, certainly visited the zoo.

One day, he came to me, tears streaming down his face, and said, "Daddy, there's a deer in a rabbit cage." It was finally enough to get me over there. Sure enough, there was a type of miniature deer crammed into a tiny "hutch." It wasn't a full-grown deer, but it looked so sad and so scared that we let it out. That day we came up with the idea to re-build that zoo to make it more appropriate for the animals. It became the production within the production. One of my favorite employees, Lissa Ruben, whom we had first hired for *Survivor: Africa,* was a staunch environmentalist. She took on the management role for the zoo project in her spare time. The Art Department got to work, and we even flew in a zoo designer from Australia. This project became an im-portant labor of love for all of us, and we were overjoyed as we wit-nessed the animals becoming happier.

Meanwhile, sixteen other people had a lot more on their minds than redesigning a zoo. The Pearl Islands were a brutal *Survivor* envi-ronment, with nonstop rain and some of the toughest game playing, as well as some of the most lovable and *hated* characters ever seen. Two of *Survivor's* most memorable characters were introduced on the Pearl Islands. One was Rupert Boneham, the other was Johnny Fair-play. Rupert's audition tape will go down as one of the best in *Sur-vivor* history. He was in a small pond with his pet alligator, acting like a crazed mountain man. His smile and presence were there for all to see. I knew I wanted him from the moment I saw him, and I couldn't wait to see how that lovable giant would play the game. He reminded me of someone straight out of the Harry Potter stories, a small child stuck inside Hagrid's body. Rupert really was an endearing modern-day pirate.

Johnny Fairplay, on the other hand, was discovered by Lynne Spill-man at a gas station bus stop at Venice Beach. His offbeat look in-trigued her, so she gave him her card and suggested that he apply for the show. I knew that he would make a perfect antagonist to Rupert's protagonist, and we cast him immediately. When, late in the filming, he told the ultimate sympathy lie—that his grandmother had died—I was not at all surprised. It was typical Johnny.

And the twists introduced in *Survivor: Pearl Islands* really worked.

My ploy to return an already voted-out player to the game worked. I called it the Outcast Challenge. Furthermore, much to the surprise of the two dwindling tribes, I marched out a third tribe at the Immunity Challenge on day 18. This tribe consisted of the first six survivors who had been brutally voted out and never expected to be seen again. If the outcasts could beat both tribes, they would have the privilege of voting back in one of their brethren. The outcasts were totally energized at the prospect of payback, and they won the challenge convincingly. Later that night, at a special Tribal Council, the outcasts voted Lil Morris, the scout troop leader, back into the game. She worked hard, playing the game with all her heart and soul, and eventually she made it to the final two, winning the second-place $100,000. The first-place, million-dollar winner—making it four women and three men who had now won *Survivor*—was Sandra Diaz-Twine, an army wife of Puerto Rican ancestry from Washington state. Sandra had been brash and blunt, and had played the game in an honest, blue-collar way. She deserved to win. The money would completely change her family's life, and I couldn't have been happier signing her check.

It had been a perfect summer in the Pearl Islands: wonderful characters, great drama, and lovely family time with the kids. It seemed to fly by. Before I knew it, I was leaving the Pearl Islands on a small plane. Typically, I had always been sad to leave behind beautiful *Survivor* locations (except the Marquesas!) because I knew I might never return. But this time it was different. I knew I'd be back to shoot *All-Stars* in only three months, and I couldn't wait. But wait I'd have to, because rather than relax or spend time in the office, I was heading to New York City, where we were only a week away from shooting the first season of *The Apprentice*.

Like the first *Survivor, The Apprentice* was an unknown entity. Creating the first episode of any new reality show is a wild and wacky ride because you *think* you have it right and you *hope* you have it right, but in the back of your mind you are praying that you *are* right, and that the show simply makes sense.

Day one of *The Apprentice* was September 15, 2003. The first big moment came when the candidates met Donald Trump in the boardroom and heard how the contest was going to work. As I watched the filming on a monitor in the control room and saw Donald divide the teams into men versus women, I knew we had a great show on our hands. The energy was fantastic. Donald delivered great, funny lines that were not scripted—they just came to him. He is not only a smart man, he is also quick-witted, and that's a large part of the success of the show.

As the pressure of the game intensified during the next few months, the characters that we believed would be great, based upon the casting interviews, flourished beyond our wildest dreams. Who can forget the antics of Sam Solovey? First he attempted to sell lemonade for $1,000 per glass, during a later task he curled up in a fetal position on the floor, and finally, upon being fired, he stared at Donald Trump like a madman. But that was only the beginning. Omarosa Manigault-Stallworth's name became indelibly impressed on the minds of viewers when she fought with Ereka Vetrini over her belief that she had been racially targeted and when she claimed that a small piece of plaster had injured her during one of the challenges—although she was later given a clean bill of health by a doctor. This culminated in the unforgettable scene where, much to the displeasure of her teammates, she sat out the task that required teams to renovate an apartment, only to go outside and join a game of street basketball while on camera! As if this wasn't enough, Omarosa returned to the series for the finale, as a member of Kwame Jackson's team, and was caught lying on camera. In the end, this was probably what cost Kwame the job with Donald Trump.

Other standout apprentices were Amy Henry, who was continually traded from team to team because she was so damn good; Troy McClain, the lovable country guy from Idaho; Nick Warnock, the New Jersey copier salesman who seemed to fall for Amy; and, of course, the ultimate winner, Bill Rancic, who went on to work for Donald Trump as his apprentice in Chicago, overseeing construction of Trump's newest high-rise in the Windy City.

But all this was to be revealed to America much later. *The Apprentice* finished filming in late October 2003, but its premier broadcast was not until January 2004, and Bill's win would not be divulged until the live finale in May. In the interim, as soon as I'd wrapped shooting on *The Apprentice*, I left New York and headed straight back to Panama to shoot *Survivor: All-Stars*, for which the Pearl Islands would be the backdrop. All the big names from *Survivor*'s past would duke it out one final time.

Memories came flooding back as our small plane landed on the tiny Contadora runway. I was especially glad to land because the pilot had let James and Cameron take turns at the controls. Surprisingly, they flew the plane smoothly. When I asked them why it was so easy, they told me that it was because it was like playing video games! As the plane taxied to a halt beside our hotel, I saw the smiling face of Lissa Ruben greeting me. She had had only a short break, and therefore had spent almost the entire year in Panama, far from her native Kenya. The first thing she did was provide an update on our zoo, which we inspected before heading for our rooms. It was in great shape, with enlarged cages and greenery everywhere. I had no way of knowing how the animals really felt, but Lissa, our own Doctor Dolittle, assured Cameron they were loving their constantly expanding home. Much to Cameron's delight, the zoo project would be completed by the time we finished *All-Stars* and left Contadora for the last time. I had not seen him so happy since he managed to hold onto his Buzz Lightyear backpack when giving the rest of his toys to the Masai kids two years earlier.

Returning to Panama was truly like coming home. I even moved back into the same hotel room I'd had previously. This was the first time that any of us on the *Survivor* crew had returned to shoot in the same place again. Everything was so familiar: the jetty we had built for Pearl Islands, the dive shack where all our scuba gear was still housed, and, of course, the smiling staff, who seemed so happy to see us all again.

I had thought *All-Stars* would be an intriguing way to play the game, and the show would get some of *Survivor*'s best-ever ratings, but while we were filming, a feeling of general weariness enveloped the production. To begin with, the castaways had played the game before. Typically, people are begging to be on the show, but to actually get agreements with the all-stars, lengthy and exhausting contract negotiations had been necessary. It was really good training for me—a lesson in working with celebrities. The toughest was Sue Hawk, because she had a gig on the TV Guide channel. I thought things would get easier once the game began, but the castaways' initial happiness about being in Panama and enjoying another dose of fame quickly disappeared as the harsh realities of playing the game kicked in. I think every one of them was questioning whether they had lost their minds to volunteer to do this all over again. To make matters worse, it rained every day. There were snakes all over the place. There was no fire on which to cook hot meals. By the third day, memories of their previous long-term experiences on the show began working their way into the minds of the castaways, who clearly recalled the fatigue and hunger of day thirty-nine. That was when their resolve began to weaken.

The castaways responded in two ways. First, they engaged in petty retribution—for example, voting off previous winner Tina Wesson. Her only crime was that she'd been smart enough to play the game well in Australia. Then the castaways stooped to a new low by voting off their own personal favorite, Rudy Boesch. Despite his curmudgeonly demeanor, Rudy is extremely well liked. Voting him off made little sense.

Soon after, Jenna Morasca became the first previous winner to quit the game. She had an intuition that her mother's cancer was worsening, and she wanted to go home. At the time, even I wondered if it was a way to rationalize Jenna's desire to leave the game. But less than a week after she arrived home in Pittsburgh, her mother died. Thank God, Jenna was by her side. It was one of the most moving episodes of *Survivor* ever.

Shortly after Jenna went home, another previous winner, Richard Hatch, bit the dust. His departure was followed by the second person to quit *All-Stars*. This time it was Susan Hawk. There had been an unfortunate moment when, the day before he was voted out, Richard had brushed his naked body up against her while attempting to pass her on a narrow balance beam. What had looked innocuous to most observers was for Susan a very negative experience. After speaking with her about it, I completely understood. Richard felt terrible as well and made it clear that he would have been much more careful had he realized how distressing this would be. It was an awful moment when she quit the show, and it was hard to watch. This also, I think, marked the point at which the castaways realized it was time to stop griping and start playing the game properly. Rob Mariano's march to the final two was a result of that mentality.

I was initially concerned that *All-Stars* would become boring. Unlike in previous seasons, the castaways all knew each other well. I was afraid they might play the game too lightly, treating it as a social occasion. I needn't have worried. My fears had blinded me to one major element: The fact that they all knew each other meant that these "friends" took the normal, run-of-the mill *Survivor* betrayals very much to heart. It's one thing to backstab a stranger, but something entirely different when you do it to a friend.

This became obvious when Rob and the doe-eyed Amber Brkich began a fairly serious relationship in the middle of the game. There had been minor flirtations on the show before, but theirs was the first true *Survivor* romance. It would play a huge part in the outcome of the game. At one point Rob asked Lex van den Berghe to use his influence to save Amber from being voted out. Lex complied. But Rob repaid him by voting Lex out at the next Tribal Council. In a normal game, that betrayal would have been taken hard. But on *All-Stars*, it was as if Rob had really stuck a dagger in Lex's back. Kathy O'Brien, a warmhearted woman from Vermont, took that vote almost as badly as Lex. She cried her eyes out. As it turned out, the lovers Rob and Amber were the final two. But Lex got his revenge. In an angry and emotional final Tribal Council, he cast a vote that ensured that Amber was awarded the million-dollar prize.

In my opinion, Rob had played the game better than anyone—perhaps more shrewdly than it had ever been played before. But he lost, not because he had viciously trampled over friend and enemy alike on his march to the final two, but because he failed to realize that it is impossible to win if you don't show compassion while eliminating the competition. The final Tribal Council punctuated the most riveting, dramatic *Survivor* series ever. And to think that in the first few weeks I had been worried about the lack of drama. Boy, was I wrong!

By the time we wrapped *All-Stars*, everyone in the crew was ready to get out of Panama as soon as possible. The emotional toll that the game had taken on the survivors seemed to spill over onto the crew, many of whom had spent seven months away from home. However, one uplifting event happened just before we all flew home. I had received a rough cut of the first episode of *The Apprentice* and decided to show it to the toughest critics in the world: the *Survivor* producing team. The team that produced *The Apprentice* was led by Jay Bienstock, who had previously produced *Survivor*. I sat with bated breath as the twenty or so *Survivor* producers watched the entire ninety-minute opening episode of *The Apprentice*. As they watched the show, I watched them, seeking honest, unfiltered reactions.

To my relief, they were all totally engaged in the drama, laughing and cringing at all the right moments. Then, as David Gould, the venture capitalist, became the first-ever candidate fired and the credits rolled, the entire *Survivor* producing team applauded loudly.

Jeff Probst came to me as they all headed out of my room and made a beeline toward the bar. "You've got a winner, Mark," he said.

I could only hope that Jeff was right. I would find out in three short weeks, once the holidays were over and *The Apprentice* premiered on NBC on January 8, 2004.

Chapter Eighteen

Reinvention

One thing that I have learned through the years is that no matter how much I achieve or how solid my track record might be, there is no such thing as guaranteed success. I must continue reinventing my shows and reinventing myself, thinking up fresh shows and new business strategies. This generally means a great deal of hard work. Sometimes it leads to wonderful successes, and sometimes not. Either way, Newton's law of physics—a body in motion stays in motion, but a body at rest stays at rest—applies. If I don't keep pushing forward, always forward, disregarding risk and seeing only results, whatever potential I have will wither.

A body in motion stays in motion.

The business free-for-all that defined 2004 exemplifies this.

At the end of 2003 I convinced the WB network to buy a pilot of my first-ever sitcom, *Commando Nanny*. Despite my past successes, I still needed to prove that I could deliver quality programs in areas other than reality TV. I had high hopes for the series and was committed to doing as I always do, bringing in the best possible people to get the job done right. But *Commando Nanny* was snakebit from the start. Its rise and eventual fall even have the feel of a reality show for TV producers, complete with offbeat tasks, high-level meetings, and quirks of fate. What made this roller-coaster ride all the more emotional was that *Commando Nanny* was based on my life story—a fictionalized tale of my beginnings in America, my seemingly crazy jump from commando to nanny in twenty-four hours. This story is key to what I stand for. To say that I cared deeply about its fate was an understatement.

Enjoy the highs.

When New Year's 2004 rolled around, I was immersed in *Commando Nanny* logistics, preparing for *Contender* pitches, and overseeing *Survivor: All-Stars* editing. My focus for the first week of 2004, however, was *The Apprentice*. Donald Trump and I seemed to be joined at the hip as we conducted a whirlwind series of interviews. It's amazing how the press can raise you up when you succeed, then take you down just as fast if you stumble. The best thing to do is enjoy the ride while it's fun and not wait for it to end. I enjoyed every minute of having both shows, *All-Stars* and *The Apprentice,* making headlines, and being hailed as a true player in the entertainment industry. In a blur of fast-paced, back-to-back appearances, Trump and I appeared on the *Today* show with Katie and Matt, CNN with Paula Zahn, *The O'Reilly Factor,* and even *Larry King Live,* not to mention interviews with numerous print journalists and cable outlets. Although a little overwhelming, it was the best way to launch a new show. Everyone wanted to see Trump, which was great, but they all asked the same questions.

"Does America *really* want to see a show about business?" they would ask. "Does America *really* want to watch a show hosted by Donald Trump?"

They all knew that my *Survivor* success had bought me the chance to put this show on air, but would it really work? Times like this truly test the Jump In philosophy. I had to simply believe in our production quality, our casting, and, most important, our storytelling. Working under me was the best team in the business. We'd been together for years. The new show looked terrific.

Even so, I'd be lying to say I wasn't scared. Donald, on the other hand, simply smiled. Time after time, when faced with those tough questions, he simply turned to me and said, "Mark Burnett is the best reality producer in the world, the show is the best, it is educational, and it will be a hit!"

> **Any sign of weakness in a leader will be magnified by naysayers.**

Trump has supreme confidence. When he commits to an idea, he commits fully. A true leader, he knows that any sign of weakness will be magnified by naysayers. Whether leading men into battle, playing sports, or making business decisions, leaders need to choose their course and stay positive at all times—no matter what. Trump exemplifies this.

As usual, Donald Trump was right about the show. *The Apprentice* premiered in the first week of January 2004. The ratings were phenomenal, and they grew larger with each passing week that the show aired. Shortly after *The Apprentice* took America by storm, *Survivor: All-Stars* premiered on CBS, with a lead-in from Super Bowl XXXVIII, and was instantly kicking.

I was living a producer's dream. Thursday nights (the most lucrative night on television) became a showcase for my programs, with *Survivor: All-Stars* airing on CBS from eight to nine o'clock and *The Apprentice* on NBC from nine to ten o'clock. The only downside for me was when Jeff Zucker supersized *The Apprentice* so that it overlapped with the last fifteen minutes of *Survivor*. Viewers had to choose between the two. Obviously, I understand gamesmanship and competitiveness, but this was a no-win for me. I wanted both my shows to succeed. However, legally I was in no position to complain. The lesson from this situation, and from other data collected, was that reality-show viewers tend to be loyal to reality shows, and scripted-show viewers tend to be loyal to scripted shows. Therefore, putting a reality show on directly opposite another reality show simply erodes the ratings of both. This was proven again when *The Apprentice* was moved twice and ended up against *American Idol*. Both suffered. *Survivor* does well against the NBC comedies, and *The Apprentice* holds its own against the CBS juggernaut *CSI*. Subsequently, when I renegotiated for future seasons of *The Apprentice*, I got a clause preventing it from being broadcast against *Survivor*.

When I look back at the beginning of 2004, I remember a time of nonstop accolades—a validation for the years of struggle and near catastrophes. Shortly after *The Apprentice* premiered, I won my fourth People's Choice Award in as many years, for *Survivor: Pearl Islands*. Then *Time* magazine gave me the great honor of naming me to its list of the world's 100 most influential people. The British press made fun of the fact that I, a TV producer, was listed ahead of British Prime Minister Tony Blair. I also received the Brandon Tartikoff Legacy Award for contributions to television. At the time, I couldn't help but think how proud my mother would have been if she'd lived to see that day. I kept remembering her telling me I could do anything I wanted to do with my life, just so long as I believed in myself and worked hard. It's amazing how far people can go in life when they've been showered with unconditional love and told they are believed in. Positive reinforcement—it's an important lesson for every parent.

In late January 2004, I flew back to London for my dad's eightieth birthday. While in London, I planned a series of casting meetings for *Commando Nanny* with Carol Dudley, our U.K. casting director (the lead actor would be British, of course). Two crucial events happened there—one a great celebration, the other a clumsy act of fate. Both symbolized all that was to come for *Commando Nanny*.

My dad is Scottish by birth, born on the same day as that great Scottish poet, Robert Burns. There is an annual tradition in Scotland known as Burns Night, which involves celebrating the poet's legacy in a most traditional, if slightly outrageous, fashion. I planned a surprise for my dad to coincide with that. First, we arranged for him to be dressed in a full kilt, complete with a sheathed dagger. My relatives, family friends, and I then gathered with my dad in a riverside country pub to celebrate. As we sat down, the haunting tones of a Scottish bagpipe could be heard outside the room. The piper entered, as is tradition on Burns Night, while a ceremonial haggis was presented to my dad— another Burns Night tradition. After that, Dad knew just what to do. Pulling out his dagger, he recited all eight stanzas of Burns's poem *"Address to a Haggis,"* then sliced open the cooked sheep stomach on the plate before him, revealing the vegetables and spices that had been baked inside. As anyone who has ever celebrated Burns Night knows, the instant the patriarch stabs the haggis, the party begins. And what a party it was. Think *Braveheart* meets line dancing.

The next day at lunch, I met with casting director Carol Dudley at the Connaught, one of London's poshest hotels. As we discussed casting, a waiter marched across the room to deliver her soup. Somehow he tripped, dropping the entire tureen of thick green pea soup straight into Carol's purse! Instead of getting mad, however, Carol simply reached down and picked up the purse with two fingers. "Take it," she ordered the waiter, "and bring it back clean." She then turned to me and continued our meeting as if nothing had happened.

Of course, another bowl of soup was soon brought, and we finished our lunch an hour later. When the waiter brought the check, he also returned Carol's expensive leather purse, spotlessly clean and looking good as new!

During my four-day stay in London, I interviewed several actors to play the part of me (which is a strange experience, by the way). Though many were good, none seemed quite right.

On February 16, Carol Dudley called to recommend a young actor named Owain Yeoman for the lead. I loved his audition and called his agent immediately to sign him for the show. The agent was at ICM, a guy named Dar Rollins. "I'm sorry," he told me, "but Owain's unavailable. There's another project he really wants to do."

I hung up, quite disappointed. But I don't understand "no," so I called right back. Somehow—and this was a strange turn of events—

the agent's line was still connected to mine. When I picked up the phone, I listened in shock as the agent spoke with Owain on another line, convincing him not to take the lead in *Commando Nanny*, despite the fact that Owain really wanted the part! I was horrified. But in some ways it was a blessing because I learned a lot. I am now continually suspicious about whether actors—or indeed producers and directors—with agents *ever* get the true story about what they are offered. Whenever possible, I always talk directly to the talent. Not about the financial aspect of the deal—that's the agent's *proper* job function—but, instead, about the creative idea, and whether or not the actor really likes it. I don't need an agent trying to explain my vision, *secondhand*, to anybody.

Meanwhile, Jeffrey Katzenberg and I were fine-tuning the premise of *The Contender*, preparing to pitch it to all four networks. We had spent months making sure that our innovative program would not just make for great television but appeal to male and female viewers of all ages as well. I was confident that not only would it have the same dynamic impact on television as *Survivor* and *The Apprentice*, it would revolutionize reality programming altogether.

The Contender would be the first prime-time TV show to actually launch a business. Unlike *Survivor* and *The Apprentice*, where the characters discovered don't actually provide any business value to the production company, the boxers would enter into promotional contracts with us. Once the TV series ended, we would continue to benefit the boxers and our business partners by staging pay-for-view matches featuring our new stars. Just think if Omarosa and Erika were boxers—can you imagine how much income could be generated by broadcasting their rematch?

The Contender was smart business and was a crucial step for me. Although I had continually reinvented *Survivor* to keep it fresh and compelling, and would do the same for *The Apprentice*, I wanted to raise the stakes with *The Contender*. I totally believed in the boxing show's underlying values. It was about dreams and hope—two of the most powerful human motivators—and about underdogs striving to realize their potential. It was a real-life *Rocky* story, with Sly Stallone, the man who'd created *Rocky*, mentoring these young boxers out of obscurity and into the big time. It would hit viewers with the same sort of emotional wallop as when they watched the Olympics.

Television, as you have seen by now, is primarily about creating entertainment. But make no mistake, it is also a bottom-line business. And as happens every so often in any industry, there comes a time for a new business model—a new paradigm for how the money gets distributed. With *The Contender*, Jeffrey and I wanted to initiate such a change. Our mission was to reinvent the nature of television financial deals.

As producers, doing all the heavy lifting and giving our souls to invent, craft, and deliver a hit series to NBC, we wanted to share in the potentially huge financial upside of success. Typically, successful producers will negotiate substantial ratings bonuses. This allows the producers to share in the TV networks' higher advertising revenue created by increased ratings. Top producers can receive a financial bonus based upon this. Jeffrey and I wanted to go a step further.

The plan we developed came out of the success I had been having with product placement within my shows. Instead of limiting on-air sponsor product exposure to commercials, *Survivor* had always included sponsor products within the drama. This was how I originally convinced Leslie Moonves to take a risk on me and on *Survivor*. That had worked year after year and had generated substantial income over and above the traditional cost of commercials. The public (despite early network concerns) had accepted this organic and seamless integration. It made sense and was humorous to see the value the starving survivors placed upon one shared can of soda or a communal bag of potato chips. The public loved the irony and the humor. *The Apprentice* went further by actually building the drama around the products. It worked beautifully. In fact, the integrity of *The Apprentice* benefited by having major brands become the business challenge for the candidates. Procter & Gamble, for instance, allowed *Apprentice* 2 teams to design a marketing scheme to launch their new product known as Vanilla Crest. The winning team was clever enough to hire New York Mets star Mike Piazza to be the pitchman. It became one of the most successful marketing campaigns in P&G history and was a great business arrangement for *The Apprentice*—a true win-win situation.

Conrad Riggs had suggested that Jeffrey and I make a deal that omitted the usual bonus for big ratings. Instead, we wanted to control a third of all the commercials within the series. This would allow us to design a marketing approach that combined both the product placement and the commercials used to *support* that product placement. For their part, the network would receive a fair price for the commercials they provided to us. We would profit from the resale of the commercials based upon their "increased value" when combined with guaranteed product placement. Conrad's idea was genius. It was also a revolutionary reinvention of the relationship among TV producers, the TV networks, and their key sponsors. If we could pull it off, this would again be a huge win-win. Sponsors had long wanted to assist in designing their placement and to effectively partner with the producers. Such a thing had never before happened in the history of network television. We wanted to redefine the old system, whereby producers and sponsors were kept as separate as church and state.

Contender was good to go. We knew our dramatic arcs, we had our major star in Sly, and we knew the business deal we wanted. Confident of success, Jeffrey, Conrad, and I scheduled meetings. Our plan was to pitch all four major networks in only two days, but not to engage in any actual negotiations until all four had heard the same pitch. That way we could be totally fair to everyone when—as we knew it would—*The Contender* negotiations became contentious. We set an expensive, but reasonable, floor price for the minimum bid.

It was time to sell our show.

Meanwhile, on *Commando Nanny* . . .

On February 20, I went to a taping of *Everybody Loves Raymond*, where I watched Gary Halverson and Lisa Helfrich-Jackson in action.

Both of these talented people had agreed to work on *Commando Nanny*. As I watched them, I was very impressed. Even though I didn't yet have a lead actor, I did have a great script, a great director, and a great producer.

On February 27, I taped an interview for the WB Up Fronts. If all went well, *Commando Nanny* would be a bright spot in their fall lineup.

Jeffrey and I pitched *The Contender* to Fox and CBS on the third Tuesday in February, and to NBC and ABC the following morning. Jeffrey and I had pitched together only once before. It was the night I first met Sly, but we knew even then that we clicked. Jeffrey was my kind of guy. Even though he was a giant in the industry, he was always willing to do the actual pitching. In fact, Jeffrey was the first person I'd met who was actually better at pitching an idea than I was!

Together, we set the networks on fire. All four agreed to the floor price. The negotiations intensified, and as they did, ABC and Fox fell by the wayside, resulting in a repeat of what happened with *The Apprentice* with only CBS and NBC seriously negotiating on the commercials.

It was a tough time for me. *The Apprentice*, my new, huge success, was at NBC. But I had been at CBS with *Survivor* for so long and had weathered so many battles with them that I leaned toward Leslie Moonves. When I realized how I truly felt about this, I did the smartest thing I could do: I took myself out of the negotiations, leaving them to Jeffrey and Conrad. There was too much at stake. Jeffrey was too experienced to get emotionally involved, and Conrad always took a very Zen approach. It's worth noting that Conrad previously worked at Disney while Jeffrey was president there. Conrad surprised us both one night over dinner, telling us that he took the job at Disney only because he believed in Jeffrey Katzenberg and that after Jeffrey left Disney, Conrad went out on his own.

Conrad and Jeffrey finalized the nitty-gritty of the deal. It all came down to the price we'd pay for commercials. Eventually, NBC won a hard-fought battle. However, both NBC and CBS had seen the wisdom of our new business approach. By allowing us to enter into this kind of arrangement, both networks knew that they would be servicing the long-term relationship with their sponsors in the most effective way possible. NBC would later tell us that in addition to this being smart business, they were happy that such an arrangement would make Jeffrey and me even more motivated to see *The Contender* succeed. We would throw every ounce of our talent into making a one-of-a-kind show of very high quality. That's partly why they agreed to the deal.

They were right. Jeffrey and I weren't just filming a television show, we were the custodians of an entire sport. Despite the more personal tone of the show, *The Contender* had to be filmed on the same epic scale as *Survivor*. To succeed as a pure sport, combined with its inherent emotional drama, it also needed authentic boxing touchstones. From the training regimens to the boxing gym itself, and even including simple elements such as the clothing our boxers wore and the places they fought, we wanted to tap into the public's subconscious memories of the sport of boxing.

For instance, all the great fights in recent history seemed to have taken place in Las Vegas. So Jeffrey and I realized it was vital to stage our finale there. Our first choice was Caesars Palace, the most storied boxing casino in town. However, Caesars' boxing dominance had recently been challenged by the Mandalay Bay Casino, which had made a name for itself by building a huge boxing auditorium and hosting several highly publicized title fights. One such fight was the super welterweight title bout between the champion, Sugar Shane Mosley, and Winky Wright. We all attended and watched Wright defeat Mosley to take the undisputed crown. The next day I decided to test my marketing theories and ask fifty people at random in a Las Vegas mall to identify the super welterweight champion. *None knew.* This confirmed my excitement at the opportunity before us. In the old days of Muhammad Ali or, even more recently, Sugar Ray Leonard, everyone in the country heard about it when they won. It was common knowledge. But today, boxing—outside of the negative interest generated around Mike Tyson—had become so diminished that nobody but serious fans really knew who any champions were. To help boxing regain its stature we intended to create inspiring characters in *The Contender*, characters who were not only great boxers, but whom people really cared about. Reality TV was the perfect way to reignite the fire under boxing. And we alone would be the ones to reignite it.

While Mandalay Bay had focused on boxing, Caesars had taken a similar gamble in the area of pure entertainment, building a special auditorium for Celine Dion. Her Cirque du Soleil–inspired revue was an overwhelming success, reestablishing Caesars as one of Las Vegas's premier hotels. However, Caesars had all but lost its share of the lucrative fight industry because of Mandalay Bay's success. We proposed a once-in-a-lifetime chance to Caesars: *The Contender* would exclusively stage not only our finale there at Caesars Palace, but every subsequent Nevada fight that we promoted. The word came back right away: Caesars was very interested.

I flew to Las Vegas on March 2 to make a deal. I had two other bits of business to attend to while I was there, as well. First, I was producing a show there called *The Casino*, which detailed life behind the scenes at the Golden Nugget. The owners were two young guys who had grown up in Vegas, made a fortune starting up an Internet travel site, then bought the Nugget from MGM. The idea of filming two rookie casino owners had seemed like a great idea, and Tim Poster and Tom Breitling had agreed to let us send camera crews to record their trials. But they grew wary of the cameras almost as soon as filming began. They started holding sensitive business meetings behind closed doors, forbidding the cameras to enter. The very meetings we needed—the juicy, sensitive business problems—were off-limits to my crews. My first stop when I flew to Las Vegas was to meet with Tim and Tom. I quickly realized they weren't going to back down, and that they were, in fact, way more concerned with running their multimillion-dollar business than in giving us the total access that to me had always been a crucial part of the project. In retrospect, it was probably unavoidable that once the cameras started rolling, they became more sensitive to the downside of letting every business challenge play out in public. I was unhappy, but I totally understood the pressures they were under, having borrowed $200 million and having only a *temporary* gaming license.

It was time for "Plan B."

We had planned half the show's story lines to be about the casino's employees and guests. With less access to Tim and Tom, we had to beef up this aspect of the show. (The show went on to do just all right in the United States, but the more risqué, unedited versions, which were sold to foreign markets, easily won their time slots.)

Next, I made my way to Caesars Palace. I was with my girlfriend, Roma Downey. She was every bit the angel she played on TV. I had liked her very much from the start, and things had just begun to turn romantic when we flew to Las Vegas. In addition to my meetings, I planned to take Roma to an Elton John concert while we were there. A car from Caesars had picked us up at the airport, taken us to my meeting at the Nugget, then brought us back to Caesars for my meeting about *The Contender* boxing facility. The casino's management had been kind enough to offer us a suite during our stay. After our car dropped us off at the hotel, we were taken up in a private elevator to a luxurious floor. The hallways were tiled in marble, and the views out the windows were spectacular. The concierge led us down a hallway, past a room featuring a grand piano. "Where's our suite?" I asked, in awe of all I saw.

"You're in it," came the reply.

I was stunned. The place was beyond massive. There was a theater room, a sunken dining room, a bar, a desk bigger than half a basketball court, and a Jacuzzi so large I could swim laps in it. When we finally arrived in the sitting area, there was a bottle of Dom Perignon on ice, a platter of chocolate-covered strawberries, and an envelope containing two front-row tickets to Elton John's show. When Vegas wants to make an impression, it knows how to do it. So even though I had gotten nowhere with Tim and Tom, at least I was guaranteed a great night in town.

The concert was terrific. It was a night I will never forget. The next day began with tragedy, when I learned that a Navy SEAL friend named Scott Helvenston had been killed the day before and then had his burned body dragged through the streets in Fallujah. Later in the day, Caesars came to an agreement to provide an arena for *The Contender.* NBC's faith in my and Jeffrey's abilities to go to great lengths for the show was proving to be justified.

We then took the deal making one step further, into a realm never before seen in television. Jeffrey and I realized that the classic equipment in the boxing world was made by Everlast. As we were doing production designs, that name kept jumping out at us. Almost a hundred years old, Everlast makes gloves, speed bags, heavy bags, headgear, T-shirts, and almost everything else a boxer might need to climb into the ring—including parts of the ring itself! By accident and through necessity, Everlast was getting massive product placement on *The Contender.* There was no way around it. Everlast means boxing. Having our boxers wear another company's products would brand us as neophytes. Clearly, Everlast products had to be on the show.

Typically, companies pay millions for that kind of exposure. But Everlast was not a Fortune 500 company. It lacked the wherewithal to pay for product placement the way PepsiCo, Home Depot, or equivalent heavy-hitters could afford to do. What Jeffrey and I needed to do was find a way to keep Everlast in the show, yet somehow realize a profit.

Jeffrey, drawing on his decades in the movie business, remembered the story about George Lucas taking stock warrants on Hasbro in return for letting the company have exclusive rights to Star Wars toys. Lucas made money only if the toys sold. It was a fair deal for both parties. "We should get stock warrants on Everlast," Jeffrey said out of the blue one day. "Get on it."

At this point, Everlast had no idea that we preferred to use its equipment on the show. My job was to inform Everlast that we would accept its equipment for use on the show, *but not unless* we received those stock positions. If I did not get this deal done, we would need to quickly find another equipment manufacturer. It was critical to Jeffrey and me that we share in the enormous financial gain any equipment supplier would receive from our TV exposure. We *wanted* Everlast, but

I believed deep down that Everlast *needed* us more. Getting the deal done was a matter of making sure the company realized that.

Time was short. We needed the equipment to be delivered to the gym for the start of *The Contender* shoot within eight weeks. Furthermore, I was leaving in just three days, flying halfway around the world to Vanuatu to begin producing *Survivor 9*.

I tracked down George Horowitz, CEO of Everlast. On the one day in my schedule that I had open, he would be in Colorado seeing accounts. The only solution was to fly to Denver and meet him at the airport as he was waiting for his plane out to New York. Unfortunately, there were no scheduled flights that allowed me to intercept him. I decided to Jump In. I booked a private jet and flew from Santa Monica to Denver early in the morning, where I caught up with George at the airport. In a two-hour lunch meeting, we agreed to a three-year deal whereby Jeffrey and I acquired five percent of Everlast for each of the first three seasons of *The Contender*. At the end of those three years, we would own a position in fifteen percent of the company's stock. We were doing in a reality series what had never been done before: taking a major position in a widely known public company. Instead of just selling product placement for the benefit of another company's brand or product, realizing an up-front payment but not sharing in the money that would result, we were now financially motivated to ensure that Everlast achieved maximum results.

It was a smart move for Everlast, having Sugar Ray Leonard, DreamWorks, Stallone, and me in a business relationship with them. And it was great for our venture to be breaking new ground so early. It was Katzenberg's idea, and I had executed it. We were a strong team. I felt as if nothing stood between us and *Contender*'s success.

So I was floored when I received a call from Jeff Wald, our fifth partner and the person who had originally brought the idea of a boxing business to Jeffrey Katzenberg, telling us that Fox planned to do a boxing show similar to ours. Fox had been the first network we pitched. Unwilling to agree to our revolutionary terms, they instead ripped off our idea! Even though they knew that NBC would be airing our show, Fox rationalized that it could rush its version into production and air it ahead of us. If its show bombed, it would work for it anyway because it would taint the boxing show concept. If its show was a hit, then our show would suddenly become irrelevant. There's an old saying that goes something along the lines of "being second sucks." And even though it was less than ideal, Fox planned to make sure that Jeffrey Katzenberg and I would be second when it came to presenting a boxing reality show to the world.

Jeffrey and I, however, are both fighters. This is both ironic and fitting in light of *The Contender*. If our boxing show was going to be the huge hit we hoped it would be, there would have to be great fighting on the television screen by the boxers themselves, and great fighting behind the scenes by Jeffrey and me. We put on the gloves and stepped into the ring.

Our first order of business was getting another top-name boxer to join Sugar Ray Leonard on the show. Jeffrey and I immediately sought out Oscar de la Hoya—"the Golden Boy"—and arranged a meeting at Mastro's Restaurant. Located on Canon Drive in the heart of Beverly Hills, Mastro's is probably the most exclusive steak house in the greater Los Angeles area. We ate in the private dining room with Oscar and his manager, Richard Schaeffer. Jeffrey and I pitched them the entire show in the hope that Oscar, with his well-known face, enormous boxing talent, and outgoing personality, would be a huge addition to the show. After listening to our pitch, he told us he would think about it.

A couple days later, Oscar and Richard Schaeffer called back to say they weren't interested in doing reality TV. I was disappointed, but wished them well. Oscar is in the waning days of his career, looking to make the transition into a new stage of his life. Obviously, he wants to make all the right moves. If reality TV didn't feel right to him, I certainly understood.

A couple weeks later, however, Jeffrey and I learned, to our complete shock, that Oscar had signed on to be the host of Fox's rip-off show, which was now being called *The Next Great Champ*. The company producing it would be the Dutch entity Endemol, the largest reality-show company in the world, known for making low-end, cheap programs.

Round one to Fox.

I was livid, but Jeffrey felt betrayed, which is worse. What really upset Jeffrey was that he'd been in the business for thirty years and he'd never before seen this sort of ruthless behavior. What Fox had done was not wrong in terms of pure legality, but I considered it highly immoral. Co-opting someone's idea, their lifeblood, was beyond the pale, in my opinion. Seeking to restore dignity to the proceedings, Jeffrey set up a meeting with his old friend, Peter Chernin, the number two man at Fox. There was a certain irony in this for me. It was Peter Chernin, after all, who, when we met in Sydney four years previously, had advised me how to expand my staff and delegate, thus growing my business. His advice had paid off. Because of it, here I was in a dispute with him over a show that, had I not taken his advice, I would not be an owner of.

The meeting took place over dinner, again at Mastro's. On one side of the table were Peter Chernin and Gail Berman, president of the entertainment division at Fox. Jeffrey and I sat on the other side. We were confident that once Peter heard all the factors involved, he would realize the right thing to do was to not rip us off.

Jeffrey hadn't gotten beyond the first two minutes of his explanation when Peter interrupted. "Who the hell do you guys think you are? You don't own boxing. You didn't invent it. You can't stop us from filming a boxing reality show."

"But we pitched you first; we gave you our entire creative plan. It was a fair bidding process—a jump ball—and you lost," Jeffrey replied.

Berman piped up, pointing out that the game wasn't played like that anymore. "The unscripted business is highly competitive. This is the way business is conducted now."

Jeffrey didn't say another word. A man of high integrity, Jeffrey told me quietly that we should just leave right then and there.

In fact, we finished our dinner. As we left, Jeffrey said the only reason he stayed was out of respect for me. He knew that I had another significant piece of business at Fox (*The Casino*) and wanted to make sure the two issues remained separate.

A week later, however, Peter Chernin ran into Jeffrey on the floor of the Staples Center just before the start of a Lakers game. "Hey, come on, Jeffrey," Peter said, "no hard feelings."

"That's fine, Peter," Jeffrey replied. "But sometime in the next few years, you may need something from me. When I refuse and you get upset, I'll be saying to you, 'Come on, Peter, no hard feelings.' I just hope you'll be taking it as well as I am."

Clearly, round two was a draw.

But I never had any doubt that it was a fight we were going to win. Nobody can rush headlong into an impossible production schedule and make an unscripted show worthy of prime-time television. It just can't be done. Quite frankly, Steven Spielberg could have made *Saving Private Ryan* in only twenty percent of the time that it actually took him, but it would never have been as good. The same holds true for reality television. The public has already seen very good shows, and has come to demand it. A half-assed show will come across sloppy and rushed, full of poorly conceived story lines. Jeffrey and I resolved to focus on making high-quality, polished stories, no matter what Fox was doing. The public, we were sure, wouldn't pay much attention to their show.

Or so we hoped. Only time would tell whether we were right.

Chapter Nineteen

Vanuatu

As hectic and challenging as they were proving to be, the first months of 2004 were my kind of fun. I had two top-ten shows dominating Thursday nights, *The Contender* was being prepped for a big summer shoot, and equally important, I'd been constantly checking in with my *Survivor* advance scouting team. They had finally discovered what sounded like a great location for *Survivor* 9.

I had sat my location scouts down way back in Panama, during the *Survivor: All-Stars* shoot, and warned them that keeping the franchise going would require a unique cast and an incredible location. I wanted someplace with intense island mystique: "Bali Hai" meets *King Kong* meets *Cast Away*. On top of that, I wanted a tribal culture to rival that of the Marquesas. I was asking a hell of a lot. But following the fantastic ratings of *All-Stars*, with its familiar and beloved characters, it was going to take a lot to keep the audience interested.

Luckily, my production team is the best. The search was on. Holly Wofford and Viki Cacciatore traveled the entire world in early 2004, looking for that epic and mysterious location. All the while, I had the more enjoyable—and easier—job of overseeing the phenomenally successful airings of both *Survivor: All-Stars* and the first season of *The Apprentice*. Tom Shelly and Jay Bienstock, respectively, were handling the microdetails of each, and had become friendly rivals as each show tried to outrate the other. It was fun to watch these two executive producers, who just eight years earlier had worked for me in middle management positions on the first Discovery Channel *Eco-Challenge*. From a wonderful niche cable show, they had risen to a point in their careers where they were now running the two top unscripted shows in the U.S. I couldn't have been prouder of their success.

The same held true on *The Contender*. Again, it was all made easier because *Contender* was being run by the extremely strong combination of Lisa Hennessy, who'd also worked alongside Tom and Jay on *Eco-Challenge* in 1996, and Bruce Beresford-Redman, who previously worked as supervising producer under both Tom and Jay on *Survivor*. It was gratifying to see Peter Chernin's advice on growing by delegation come true. I had surrounded myself with the best, and had kept them on my team for many years. They had all become great executives and had helped Mark Burnett Productions grow into a powerhouse.

In one of their weekly calls back to America from their world travels, Holly and Viki reported that they had recently left Mozambique and Madagascar in Africa and had just arrived in the South Pacific. What a great job they have, and what a great phone call I got. "We have found a location you will love for *Survivor 9*," Holly said as soon as I picked up the phone.

"Does it have everything I've asked for, or am I asking for too much?" was my reply.

"It's more."

I leaned in. "Where is it?"

"Vanuatu."

"Van a what?"

Holly laughed. "I've finally found somewhere you haven't heard of."

She described the island nation of Vanuatu, midway between Fiji and the east coast of Australia. Consisting of eighty-three islands, it's spread over the ocean in the shape of a "Y," each island surrounded by a tropical reef. Within these islands were more than a dozen active, fire-spewing volcanoes and a fierce tribal population steeped in black magic. The last known local act of cannibalism took place in 1972. The native tribes hadn't exactly rushed headlong into the modern age.

I immediately checked the Internet for the scouting photos they had just e-mailed. I realized that Holly and Viki were, in fact, *under-selling* me. My next questions to them were: Is this logistically feasible? And: Could we afford it?

Holly and Viki assured me that we could pull this off. The decision was made. Vanuatu was a go.

I was so happy to have found such a fantastic location. In the back of my mind, amid all the fun of early 2004, the issue of a poorly chosen *Survivor* location was the one thing that could create unneeded pressure and setbacks in what was shaping up to be an incredibly challenging year. I had continually Jumped In. The culmination of a ton of hard work, successful guesses, and a fair amount of luck had paid off. A *Survivor 9* location that would knock the socks off of America made me rest just a little easier.

Finally! During the first week of April, having given up on the fight to get Owain Yeoman to accept the job, *Commando Nanny*'s lead actor was chosen. His name was Philip Winchester. Rather than being British, he was an American actor who trained in London and does a perfect British accent. Not only that, veteran TV actor Gerald McRaney signed to play the role of the millionaire employer.

April 14 saw the first table read, which is where the cast members all sit around a long table and perform their lines. It went very well, and I left on an emotional high.

A week later, the *Commando Nanny* pilot was taped before a live audience. The laughter was loud and genuine. The WB was thrilled, and though they wouldn't commit yet, they appeared ready to give us the thumbs-up for their fall schedule. Life was good; my first sitcom seemed destined for success.

Then on April 29, writer Dave Flebotte asked to be released from his contract. He'd been offered the position as show runner on the more established *Will & Grace*, along with a two-year guaranteed contract that would pay him five times as much as he would earn on *Commando Nanny*, which still hadn't officially been picked up by the WB for the fall schedule. I released him. Dave had a young family and needed the financial security that *Will & Grace* could offer. Besides, you can't force an artist to create art. A disgruntled Dave Flebotte might have been so frustrated by staying that he would write bad scripts.

Now, however, the show couldn't go forward. I needed a new head writer, and fast. I began reading comedy spec scripts and meeting with comedy writers, familiarizing myself with the comedy process. I learned that when head writers are selected, they pick their own team of writers to work with. Soon after, the network selected Rachel Sweet, who had previously written for *George Lopez*, as our new head writer. I just hoped she was as good as Dave Flebotte.

During the first few weeks of May, I was in New York for *The Apprentice* and *Survivor: All-Star* finales. Again, all went well. We staged the *All-Stars* finale live at Madison Square Garden in New York City. It had been our biggest audience ever, with more than five thousand people in attendance. It was fitting for the *All-Stars*, one of our greatest television seasons, to take place at Madison Square Garden, one of the grandest locations we could find. America watched as a brutal final Tribal Council, characterized by hurt feelings and finger-pointing, led up to the crucial final vote. The prize, however, had to wait. In a moment unprecedented in television history, Boston Rob Mariano halted Jeff Probst as he was about to read the final votes. Rob then got down on one knee and proposed to Amber Brkich right there on camera. It was Rob's way of making sure that, win or lose, his love for Amber would be seen as real and not just part of a reality show. The crowd went silent, anxiously waiting for Amber's answer. They let out a collective roar of celebration when she accepted. Both sets of parents were in the audience, tears streaming down their faces. It was truly a wonderful moment. I can personally vouch that *Survivor*'s first real romance was more than just a reality show hookup. Rob and Amber are really, truly in love.

Jeff Probst, however, had the unenviable task of bringing everyone back from their euphoria to remind them that there was still business at hand. He had a million dollars to award. He did it in the masterful Jeff Probst way and everyone quickly settled down. One by one, the votes were read. Although Rob had been the mastermind who got both himself and Amber all the way to the final two, his ruthless way of getting there had cost him first place. The votes for Amber were actually votes against Rob. Either way, she became *Survivor*'s eighth millionaire, and the fifth woman to take the big prize.

But I wasn't finished. I had Jeff Probst surprise everybody by announcing one more Tribal Council. It would occur four days after Amber's victory and would be called America's Tribal Council.

I had decided that we would allow a second million dollars to be awarded. But this time, as a reward for eight seasons of loyal viewing, rather than the survivors, the viewers themselves would vote online for their favorite survivor. America's Tribal Council was set for Thursday, May 13, in New York City. Our crew for the live show would have no time off; instead, they would need to prepare a whole new stage at Chelsea Studios for a smaller, more intimate (but no less demanding) *All-Stars* second finale.

I was now busier than ever. This was shaping up to be a crazy week. As the *Survivor* crew was prepping this second *Survivor* finale, the *Apprentice* crew had an equally demanding job. On Monday, May 10, just seven hours after the celebration of Sunday's *Survivor* finale had ended, *Apprentice 2* would begin shooting. Fortunately, all three productions took place in New York City! Even I, someone who prides himself on Jumping In and just doing things that I'm only half sure of, have not yet figured out how to be in two places at once.

The start of any new season is typically nerve-racking, but I can always tell how a season will pan out from the first couple of hours of shooting. And from the first moment that Raj (wearing his red pants and bow tie) walked into Trump Tower, followed almost immediately by Bradford's brutal comment comparing Pamela to Cruella De Vil, I knew that *Apprentice 2* was going to be great.

Two days later, I was back on the set of *America's Tribal Council*. It was to be a celebration of eight incredible seasons of a show that had changed American television. Its culmination was to be the vote by American viewers for their favorite all-time survivor. But in the lead-up we decided to have some fun and present a few extra awards, including one for the worst villain (Johnny Fairplay), the sexiest survivor (Colby Donaldson), and the best moment (Rupert Boneham stealing the shoes on Pearl Island). It was a wonderful evening of live television, and as it drew to a close it was time to find out who was America's favorite survivor.

No one was surprised (but they were definitely overjoyed) when Rupert was awarded his million dollars. I was personally thrilled to sign the check, making Rupert our ninth *Survivor* millionaire. He is a genuinely great person and had entertained millions for two back-to-back seasons, earning every penny. That night he gave each of my sons, James and Cameron, crystal necklaces, which he had made with his own hands. They cherish them to this day. It was the end of an incredible week that included Rob and Amber's engagement, two million-dollar winners, seeing Raj begin *Apprentice 2,* and my first-ever Martha Stewart meeting (more on that later). I was a very happy camper.

Not even more *Commando Nanny* calamities could dilute my enthusiasm. Although, of course, calamity was becoming business as usual in my sitcom world. Lisa Helfrich-Jackson, as expected, had gone back to *Everybody Loves Raymond* once they announced that it would return for a final season. She was wonderful, and I would greatly miss her distinctive producing style. On May 25, I hired Faye Oshima Belyeu. She was a solid producer, and I looked forward to getting to know her.

As all this was happening, six thousand miles to the west, on the tiny island nation of Vanuatu, other major *Survivor* efforts were under way. The Tribal Council was being built, challenges were being readied, and fifty-five oceangoing containers were winding their way from storage in Port Klang, Malaysia, to Vanuatu. Our equipment had grown so large that we required an entire ship to move it all. We used to think that having ten containers of equipment sharing space on other people's ships made us an enormous production. Now we needed an entire ship to ourselves.

While the *Survivor* advance production team was working its fingers to the bone in Vanuatu, I began promoting *The Contender*. NBC had even flown Jeffrey Katzenberg, Sly Stallone, Sugar Ray Leonard, and me to New York City to appear at the network's 2004 Up Fronts presentation at Radio City Music Hall. I'd been aware of the crowd reactions to Sly a few times before, but nothing had prepared me for the response he generated as we walked the red carpet into the auditorium. The little bit of celebrity I'd attained because of my shows now highlighted the word "little." Sly Stallone and Sugar Ray Leonard were American folk heroes.

During the ceremony that followed, *The Contender* was introduced by Jeff Zucker, who showed a three-minute presentation clip that received thunderous applause. Afterward, one of my biggest fears about my boxing show was calmed. At least a hundred women had individually come up to me during the afterparty and explained, one after another, that they thought they would have no interest in a boxing drama—but having seen the way we would tell the stories of these young boxers fighting to improve the lives of their families, and how their hopes and dreams were on the line, they had been converted. I left that party on cloud nine, and knew that Jeffrey Katzenberg's idea for a boxing show, told in my unscripted drama style, would work.

One side note about *The Contender* was the series of nonstop licensing meetings in final preparation for the necessary legal requirement of obtaining my boxing promoter license. I had entered a whole new world in which a reality show would not just feature ordinary people. The "ordinary people" on *The Contender* would be professional athletes. The legal requirements were onerous and time-consuming.

That was the hard part. The fun part was constructing the fighters' new world. I helped to design the boxing arena and gymnasium above which our sixteen *Contender* hopefuls would live. Designing the gym was great fun, and the Everlast equipment that I had secured on my one-day private jet trip to Denver a few months earlier was now complementing our state-of-the-art facility. In the center of the gym we placed two side-by-side boxing rings, using the biggest American flag I'd ever seen as a backdrop. Behind the flag were enormous windows, allowing light to filter through Old Glory, giving the boxing rings a majestic glow. This gym would be the absolute best training facility our *Contender* hopefuls would have ever used. In addition, their living quarters were luxurious. I wanted these sixteen disadvantaged young men to get a taste of the high life that could be theirs simply by doing well on our show.

I knew we had it right when Sugar Ray Leonard came to our gym for the first time. His eyes lit up immediately, and he flashed that big smile. His approval was all I needed.

In the blink of an eye, it seemed that I was touching down in Port-Vila, on the island of Efate, in the country of Vanuatu. Having spent so much time over the last six months rushing around on business, I had decided to combine family time with work time. Consequently, I had six people arriving with me that night. Roma; her eight-year-old daughter, Reilly; and my sons, James (now eleven) and Cameron (now seven). I even had my eighty-year-old father and his loving companion of the last few years, Jean, with me. It had been a long, twenty-hour trip, anticipating seeing Vanuatu's "islands of fire." We were not disappointed.

The first day of shooting was something my family will never forget. If ever I needed an epic movie style for the first episode of a *Survivor* series, it was now. This series would be following *All-Stars* and the audience's favorite son, Rupert. I knew that in order to shake America out of *All-Stars* fever, I had to outdo myself. I wanted my production team to conjure up images of Captain Cook in the audience's minds during the first day's *Survivor* marooning. I had described the scene that I wanted: A sailing ship would enter the bay. Then, hundreds of natives in canoes would paddle out to the wide-eyed survivors, their intentions unclear.

Vanuatu's wild-looking natives were more than happy to provide their traditional greeting for our sixteen unsuspecting Americans. Tradition dictates that visitors to the island should encounter an intimidating mixture of welcome and threat as they first set foot on the islands of fire. The tribes did not disappoint. Jeff Probst was paddled in a war canoe behind the initial wave of warrior-laden war canoes that confronted the survivors as they stood on the sailing ship's deck. Upon seeing Jeff, the survivors' initial fear subsided. They felt safer. Jeff explained that they were all guests on these mystical, remote islands, and that they must all honor tribal traditions. They might see things they wouldn't be comfortable with, but the chief had assured Jeff they would be safe and said that they should merely show respect.

What followed was a three-hour combination of both aggressive and friendly dancing, followed by a spectacle I will never forget. As the sun set and the tribal camp was lit only by fiery torches, things grew darker in many ways. A sacrifice had to take place to ensure that the island spirits would not be angry at these visitors. My family sat among the production crew in the shadows at the edge of the village, observing but not encroaching on the very real experience the survivors were undergoing. It was so colorful, so noisy, and so mystical that the children hardly moved an inch. I knew that my boys could handle what was to come, but I warned Roma that all this might be a bit much for young Reilly, who was making her first trip to a wild land. Roma sat Reilly on her lap, ready to hold her tight and cover her eyes if need arose.

As the drumbeats grew menacing, the Ambram people appeared in the village. Ambram is an island north of Efate, and its people are feared by all. Not only are they fierce warriors, but it is believed that they can kill people with their black magic. Even more haunting, four of the Ambrams who had entered the presence of the survivors weren't just ordinary Ambram. They were witch doctors. None of the other natives would even look at them, for fear of attracting a spell. Ambram witch doctors never show their faces, so all four were wearing large, birdlike masks. They separated the men and the women into distinct groups, which, as I'd guessed, provided just the reactions I had hoped for. The women in this tribal society were treated as subordinate to the men, but our *Survivor* women didn't appreciate being forced to sit on the ground beside all the native women while the *Survivor* men were given an almost honorary position beside Chief Mor Mor. Our men were even given ceremonial kava to drink. Although it tasted bitter and half of them spat it out, the fact that the *Survivor* women weren't even offered it greatly offended them. This provided some memorable television sound bites and caused immediate animosity among what had now become, by natural selection, the two *Survivor* tribes of men versus women. My son James turned to look at me as Chief Mor Mor gave the men kava. He was clearly remembering his big day in Fiji two years earlier when he had gone through a similar kava ceremony himself. (He later confided that although his kava had tasted equally as bad as the survivors', he hadn't spit it out, and he felt disappointed in a couple of the survivor men.)

Following the arrival of the Ambram witch doctors and Chief Mor Mor's kava ceremony, I knew the requisite animal sacrifice was coming. I used to be uncomfortable with these types of sacrifices. But I've learned through my years on *Eco-Challenge* and *Survivor* that many cultures practiced such rituals. While in their land, we had to honor their ancient ways. I was especially sensitive since we had failed to sacrifice an animal and daub its blood on a banyan tree before shooting the first *Survivor* in Borneo. Within days, that tree (for no apparent reason) had fallen and demolished our production set (luckily, killing nobody).

I leaned over and whispered in Roma's ear to be prepared to comfort Reilly and cover her eyes if things became gruesome. We had initially discussed taking her away, but Reilly pleaded to stay. Roma had correctly concluded that the fallout from my boys' giving Reilly a hard time for leaving early would make the rest of the young girl's trip unbearable. The Ambram then reentered the village clearing, this time followed by a group of warriors carrying a wild boar tethered to a pole by its feet.

Roma smiled at me, thinking that the pig was already dead, but her eyes almost popped out of her head as it craned its neck to look in our direction. Despite the horrified anticipation of all the survivors (men and women alike), the pig was killed with two swift, accurate club blows to the skull. It was over in an instant. Reilly was none the worse for witnessing this scene. Chief Mor Mor then took the pig's blood and smeared it on the faces of the male survivors. This further emphasized the gender division between the two tribes. It was the most dramatic first night of a *Survivor* series ever—part *National Geographic* and part *Heart of Darkness*. I doubt anyone in attendance will ever forget it. More important for me, the American audience would be so taken with the Captain Cook–style arrival of the new survivors on Vanuatu's islands of fire that they would quickly relinquish their attachment to their beloved Rupert and the rest of the all-stars.

During the course of the next thirty-nine days, the survivors would encounter tropical storms, an earthquake, and continual eruptions from the surrounding volcanoes. They would eventually be part of some of the biggest ratings in *Survivor* history. American viewers would be enthralled as they watched Chris Daugherty survive his initial embarrassment in the early challenges, going on to become the last male among a tribe made up entirely of women. Chris would survive week after week of precarious votes as Twila Tanner fought herself into the final two. It was one of our simplest yet most dramatic seasons. The game itself remained organic, with the human drama matching the incredible power of some of the most active volcanoes on earth that formed the backdrop. Holly and Viki had met my demand for a *King Kong* location, and Lynne Spillman had, as always, cast an incredible group of players. All of this was wrapped up in one of the most highly polished productions in history. Not only was *Survivor* alive after nine seasons, it was stronger than ever.

The same could not be said for *Commando Nanny*. All seemed to be going well through the summer of 2004. Then on August 11, just as Vanuatu was wrapping production in the South Pacific, and the day before *Commando Nanny*'s pilot was to be reshot, Philip Winchester broke his ankle. The pilot was put on hold for recasting. But guess who was available? Owain Yeoman! I called Dar Rollins at ICM, where we made nice in that phony Hollywood way, then struck a deal for Owain to join the show. We needed to wait two weeks for his work visa to be approved, so we set the end of August as a tentative time period for the reshoot.

Again, all seemed to be going smoothly. Then, unbelievably, on August 23, two days before the table read with the new cast, Gerald McRaney found out that he had a malignant tumor on his lung. The show was put on hiatus and the crew was laid off, as he underwent surgery. This was so much bad luck that I wondered whether this might be a message from above. All we could do was wait and hope that the irreplaceable McRaney would recover and be able to return to work. While everyone else was on hiatus, our new head writer, Rachel Sweet, continued to develop the scripts that would follow Dave Flebotte's pilot. I hoped they would be good.

The casting director of *The Contender* was Michelle McNulty, who had learned her craft by working on *Survivor* under Lynne Spillman. But even for someone accustomed to the arduous and sometimes surreal *Survivor* casting process, *The Contender* had been out of the ordinary. Michelle was extremely adept at spotting great characters, but she had no way to tell whether they were authentically great boxers. This was a problem: The only way for *Contender* to realize its full potential was to find the perfect combination of great boxers who were also characters whom America would buy into.

To ensure that these contenders were great boxers, I added Prentiss Byrd (former manager of the famous Thomas Hearns) to Michelle's casting team. Ironically, Hearns had suffered his biggest defeat at the hands of our cohost, Sugar Ray Leonard. Prentiss and Michelle formed a solid team, and from six thousand contender hopefuls, we selected the sixteen best.

In mid-August, these sixteen hopefuls walked into *The Contender* gym for the first time. One of the last to arrive was Ahmed Kaddour, a European champion of Arabic descent, whose nickname was Babyface. He was an extremely capable boxer. Having never been beaten, he fancied himself a future Hollywood star, walking into *The Contender* gym wearing a flashy outfit that included a flowered blazer, white shoes, and sunglasses. He looked like he had stepped out of a 1950s Sinatra movie. The boxers who had chosen to dress more conservatively for their big day erupted into catcalls and whistles. We caught it on camera as Anthony Bonsante, a single father of two from Minnesota, and as blue-collar as they come, whispered to the boxer next to him, "You know everybody wants to kick his butt!"

Again, I could tell in those first few moments that we were embarking on another dramatic production. In my preplanning I had realized that we needed to appeal to a female audience. My plan to achieve that was to rent eight single-family homes close to the gym so that the boxers with wives and children could spend part of their time during the competition with their families. I knew that this was an important creative decision because during my early discussions with Sylvester Stallone, he had told me that you can tell more about a fight from having the camera on the fighter's wife or girlfriend than you ever could by covering every angle of every single punch. I took this to heart. Having the boxer's families as part of the series was the best move I'd made on the entire *Contender*.

Fox aired its first episodes shortly after *The Contender* began filming on August 16, 2004. The ratings were so poor that Fox switched it to one of their sports channels after just a few weeks, effectively the same as canceling it. Fox would go on to parody *The Apprentice* in fall 2004 with a Richard Branson show, *The Rebel Billionaire*, which also flopped. There were certainly no tears shed for Fox. Gail Berman's comment that "this is the way the business is conducted now" clearly referred only to *her* approach to business deals, not *creative* success. The moral here is that originality will always win out over imitation.

> **Originality will win out over imitation.**

Meanwhile, at our *Contender* set in Pasadena, just one block off the freeway, you could see the lift this news gave our crew and the two teams of boxers. Fox had gotten its just deserts.

From the very beginning—and probably inspired by Steven Spielberg's comment that he considered *Survivor* and *The Apprentice* to be filmmaking rather than reality TV—I was determined that we would again take our storytelling to a whole new level with this boxing series. I discussed with Jeffrey Katzenberg that I wanted to really improve the music on *The Contender* and would ask the brilliant composers with whom I'd established longstanding relationships to provide a Hans Zimmer–type feel. Zimmer had written the music for *Driving Miss Daisy, The Thin Red Line,* and *Gladiator.* Jeffrey looked at me and said, "Why copy Hans Zimmer when we can have Hans Zimmer?"

"Jeffrey," I replied, "Hans Zimmer is never going to agree to work on a reality show and we could never afford him."

"*Gladiator* was a DreamWorks movie," said Jeffrey. "Hans is a good friend of mine. He's one of the most collaborative geniuses that I've ever worked with. He will love working on this *and* will make it affordable."

Of course, Jeffrey soon made it happen. One of the biggest thrills of my career was sitting in Hans Zimmer's Bavarian castle–themed studio with ten of my senior producers and composers, listening to one of the most heroic scores I'd ever heard. Thanks to Jeffrey (and, of course, Hans), we were now definitely on track for *The Contender* to look and sound like a major feature film.

Simultaneously, Conrad Riggs had been spearheading our sponsorship efforts in an effort to ensure that our hard-fought negotiation to control a third of all the commercials and accompanying product placement in our show was actualized and turned into profits. Conrad, Jeffrey, and I secured Toyota, Gatorade, Sierra Mist (both of the latter PepsiCo brands), and Home Depot. This was the first time a production company had made such deals on network television. The old financial model of television deals had been altered in favor of a more aggressive approach—one that allowed all three parties (NBC, sponsors, and ourselves) to benefit.

The almost two months of *Contender* filming were nonstop excitement. Not only did every three days culminate in some of the most exciting boxing action I'd ever seen, but my partners, Jeffrey, Sly, Ray, and Jeff Wald, invited some of their A-list celebrity friends. It was amazing to be sitting ringside next to such legends of film as Mel Gibson, Sharon Stone, James Caan, Burt Reynolds, Elliott Gould, and James Brolin, as well as some young and upcoming actors from NBC's dramas and soap operas, and stars from the world of music as diverse as Paul Stanley from Kiss, Steve Van Zandt from Springsteen's E Street Band and *The Sopranos*, and Wyclef Jean from the Fugees. The other four hundred audience members who packed our small auditorium within *The Contender* gym included every member of our production staff.

The energy of these fights was unlike anything I've ever experienced. *The Contender* soon became one of the hottest tickets in Hollywood. This energy translated directly onto the television screen, reminding me of the *Rocky* movies. But what really distinguished *The Contender* from any previous reality show was the heart and soul of these young fighters. They were not fighting for themselves, they were fighting for a better life for their families. The emotional triumphs and defeats were some of the most compelling moments in unscripted dramatic television.

It was all about the stakes. *Survivor* and *The Apprentice* were the pinnacle of reality television. But *The Contender*'s stakes were even higher because the boxers' losses would go on their all-important fight records. This was their chosen profession. Unlike the contestants on *The Apprentice* and *Survivor*, these boxers couldn't get voted out or fired and simply return to their jobs. Any loss directly affected how they made their living, and could greatly diminish their market value. They had all chosen to step up and take that risk for their first true opportunity at greatness. These high stakes made the television drama as good as it gets.

Meanwhile, in the soap opera that *Commando Nanny* had become, there was finally some good news. On September 30, Gerald McRaney had sufficiently recovered from his brave battle with cancer to return to work. I really like and respect Mac, and he is a fine actor and a great guy. Additionally, Roma and Mac are good friends, having worked together on *Touched by an Angel*. His experience, therefore, hit close to home, and it was such a great relief that he had survived. I knew that working would be the best tonic for him. With Mac back, it was all systems go. We did the table read for the reshoot with new cast members Owain Yeoman and Kristin Dattilo. All went well. Less than a week later, on October 5, in my absence and while I was away shooting *Apprentice 3*, my staff reshot the *Commando Nanny* pilot. There were hugs all around when they finished. Apparently, it was a great night, and a surprising improvement over the original pilot episode.

There was widespread euphoria the next day, and Rachael Harrell, who had been promoted earlier in the year from my assistant to manager of my scripted business, excitedly called me to say that she was about to sit down and listen to a table read for the follow-up episode. This was Rachel Sweet's first script for the show, and we had high hopes—but they were dashed.

Rachael Harrell called to tell me that, to everyone's surprise, the script lacked the funny, family tone of Dave Flebotte's pilot script. Instead, Rachel Sweet was sending the show in a dark, edgy direction that wasn't in keeping with the original pitch. The network was worried about this new direction and immediately spoke to her about future story lines. Rachel's explanation was both simple and nonnegotiable: It was clear that we needed to seek out other solutions. "That's how I write."

On October 7, the crew was laid off a third time. Tim Kelleher, Rachel Sweet's second-in-command, decided to step up in an attempt to save the floundering series. He created five new story lines, going back to the original family tone. I loved them.

On October 12, Tim, Rachael Harrell, and I met with the WB for Tim to pitch the new story lines. They were fantastic; Tim had totally delivered. He was exactly in line with what the network said it wanted. I was ecstatic. The WB, however, said that it wanted a few days to think everything over. It didn't sound good.

I headed back to New York to continue working on *Apprentice 3*. While still in New York, I got a call from David Janollari of the WB. Bad news. Although he loved Tim Kelleher's new outlines for the series, the network bean counter's analysis showed that we had run out of time and money. David canceled *Commando Nanny*. Ironically, the TV series chronicling my beginnings in America was canceled on October 18, 2004—twenty-two years to the day after I arrived.

I've had enough failures and middling efforts over the years that I can usually immediately forget about them and move on to something new, but my travails with *Commando Nanny* were heartbreaking. I so wanted it to succeed. I took it hard.

Chapter Twenty

Martha

Now here's that Martha Stewart story I promised. You readers have followed my improbable life story from the day I came to America, and you know how I've put the Jump In philosophy to the test time and again—coming to America, racing the Raid, organizing *Eco-Challenge*, entering the TV world, enduring the ordeals of *Survivor* and *The Apprentice* and *The Contender*, learning the ways of big business. Jump In is about seizing opportunities, even when those opportunities might not seem obvious. Such was the case when I first began thinking of partnering with Martha Stewart: the adventure/reality TV guy, a man at home in the jungle muck, working hand in hand with the spic-and-span woman the tabloids refer to as "the domestic diva." Talk about incongruity! But I saw a business opportunity there, and in I jumped.

It began during the hectic early days of 2004. I had always admired Martha, not only because she was the world's first self-made female billionaire, but also because she had tapped into something that greatly interested me: Martha had managed to take a daytime TV show with fairly small viewership and convince that handful of viewers to rush out and buy her products. This made her show, in my mind, the epitome of transactional television.

Her loyal viewers became loyal customers. As a result, her personal fortune skyrocketed. When she got tangled up in legal problems in recent years, what caught my attention most was that many people wrote her off. I saw things quite differently. I believed that the integrity of Martha Stewart would come through in the end. She would weather this storm, roll up her sleeves, and fight back. The women of the U.S., I believed, would rally around Martha and remain loyal customers. I couldn't understand why nobody else was seeing this.

I decided that I had to meet her. This wouldn't be easy. With her legal problems compounding her already packed business schedule, I knew that I would never get a meeting without a personal introduction. I started to ask around in Los Angeles for someone who knew her on a personal level and who might be willing to make a phone call on my behalf. That person turned out to be Wendy Goldberg, the wife of Leonard Goldberg, producer of decades of successful TV series such as *Hart to Hart*, *Fantasy Island*, *Starsky & Hutch*, and *Charlie's Angels*, the latter two of which he more recently produced as feature films. He is a bona fide Hollywood legend. I had met the Goldbergs at a Donald Trump affair in Beverly Hills, and they both told me that they enjoyed my work. Leonard had gone so far as to say that I wasn't in the reality business; I was in the dramatic storytelling business. Coming from him, this was a big compliment. With this in mind, I mustered up the courage to ask Wendy to call Martha for me. She immediately agreed. We joked about what her finder's fee would be if Martha and I ended up doing business together. We settled on a watch of her choosing from Hermes in Beverly Hills, and we shook hands on the deal.

Wendy made the call, and Martha agreed to see me. The day Martha had available in her calendar was May 11. This was smack in the middle of my two *Survivor* finales and the beginning of *The Apprentice 2* shoot, with all the publicity and logistical headaches they implied. It would be my busiest week in years, but I had an intuition that I should not pass up this opportunity. Despite the crazy schedule ahead, I agreed to meet on the eleventh.

There's something slightly intimidating about meeting Martha Stewart face-to-face—not just in a business way, but in a way I don't usually give much thought to: subtle color combinations. It was with this lack of thought that I started my day.

I was in Manhattan on the morning of May 11, dressing before heading downtown to meet Martha. I put on my typical business attire—today it happened to be a striped Paul Smith shirt combined with a checkered Paul Smith suit. I was comfortable in these clashing garments, and they were one of my only remaining connections to London style. It wasn't until I was in the lobby of Martha's office building and caught my own reflection that I started thinking, "Oh my God, Martha is going to have a coronary."

I stepped out of the elevator into her reception area and was quickly shown into the traditional, stylish Martha Stewart green conference room. It was perfection in detail and taste. My red and brown checks and stripes couldn't have clashed more. As I was wondering whether I should mention my clothes before she did, in walked the woman herself. She greeted me with a firm handshake.

Having recently seen Martha on every magazine cover and on every news show, I felt I was in the presence of a movie star. She *oozed* presence. After greeting me, her next line was, "What a fabulous outfit, I must get a picture with you." She then handed a camera to her CEO, Sharon Patrick, who laughingly took a couple of snapshots.

I liked her instantly. Over the next hour, I told her that I would love to find a way to become involved in her television world. Both she and Sharon were well informed about my accomplishments and seemed genuinely interested in doing something together. I was most impressed with Martha's total focus despite the enormous legal pressures she was under. She was living life in a goldfish bowl, but her business focus reminded me of that of Jeffrey Katzenberg and Donald Trump. I wanted to partner with another winner, and I knew Martha and I could do great things together. We agreed to meet again to try to figure out what to do together in the TV business. I had jumped in at my busiest time ever, simply as the result of a gut feeling. Having met her personally, I knew in my bones that I had done the right thing.

Over the next month, as my business took me back to Los Angeles, we spoke on the phone. By early July, the start of the *Survivor: Vanuatu* shoot was rapidly approaching, but I felt the need to meet with Martha once again to cement our relationship before flying off on location.

I flew back to New York City to attend a dinner with Martha, Sharon Patrick, and their lawyer, Larry Scheer. I waited for Martha in the bar area of the Chambers Hotel. She arrived before the others, and as she walked through the lobby bar, again I just knew that I should be in business with her. Everybody stopped, turned, and stared at her. Despite her legal woes, those stares weren't incriminating. They were full of awe. Martha simply has the same X factor as movie stars and rock stars.

We shook hands and the maître d' ushered us downstairs. Town is a four-star restaurant in the basement of the Chambers Hotel, and I had booked my favorite corner table. The fact that I even *had* a favorite corner table in a top New York restaurant was hilarious to me, because I was always aware of how close I had been back in England to ending up working in the same factory as my parents.

Escorting Martha to this table was a much bigger reminder of her celebrity. We were no longer in the private sanctum of her conference room, but out in public. All heads turned. I even heard a few whispers of "That's Martha Stewart and she's with Mark Burnett." The staff at Town always made me feel special, and I knew Martha would appreciate both their attention and the incredible food. If anybody is a food expert, it is Martha. We were seated, and we chatted over a glass of chardonnay while waiting for Sharon and Larry. Martha was totally relaxed, upbeat, and focused. This formidable woman showed no signs of fatigue from her relentless legal troubles.

I had decided to dress a little more conservatively that night and was wearing a simple black suit with an open-necked white shirt.

When Sharon arrived a few minutes later, she revealed the sly sense of humor that exists beneath the surface seriousness in Martha Stewart's company. Sharon approached the table wearing a specially designed pinstriped suit with a clashing striped man's shirt. She looked great. She shook my hand and announced, "I thought I'd come as Mark Burnett."

We all laughed. It was a magnificent dinner, with fine wine and lots of fun. I discovered that Martha loves adventure, and was even a little jealous of my upcoming trip to Vanuatu. She is my kind of person. We really clicked.

By the end of the evening, we had resolved that I would help Martha reinvent her syndicated television show, *Martha Stewart Living,* which had been removed from a number of stations as a result of her legal troubles. This was a wonderful opportunity for me to enter a whole new arena. Daytime syndication would be my new challenge. As I escorted Martha to her waiting car, she invited Roma and me to stay at Skylands, her famous estate in Maine. I had seen Skylands featured on her television show and knew that Roma would love it. Martha and I were becoming fast friends.

We were also becoming business partners. Of course, it was her legal troubles that presented the open door. They made her pause long enough to consider me as a valuable partner. She realized that associating with my brand as we worked side by side to reinvent her syndicated show would be smart business. We were betting that combining my creative vision with her powerful brand and transactional television expertise, adding our mutual vast experience with major sponsors to the mix, would pay off in a big way.

We both felt that the syndication marketplace had lost its luster. With the exception of the ever-present *Oprah,* the newer *Dr. Phil,* and the newest addition, *The Insider,* there was little in the way of innovative and exciting programming. A reinvented, vibrant, and accessible *Martha Stewart Living* daytime show would quickly be welcomed. Beyond simply gaining financially from the television show, I contended that her association with my brand would give Wall Street such confidence that her flagging stock would perk up at the mere announcement of our deal.

I thought it appropriate that I receive warrants for her company stock. These warrants allowed me to purchase shares (the number of which could grow to as many as 2.5 million) for the price at which her stock closed on the day prior to our deal becoming public. I acted fast and secured an agreement for both the syndicated show and an as-yet-unnamed reality show. My swift action resulted in her stock price being locked for my future purchase at the depressed price of $12.59. I believed that this company was totally undervalued. In the week following the formal public announcement of our alliance, the stock jumped to almost $18. My simple gut feeling that Martha's legal woes would be temporary and that her true value would be untarnished—even enhanced—as she made her comeback was proven right. I had Jumped In, and it had paid off again.

Later that summer, Roma and I took Martha up on her offer to visit Skylands. We flew to a small airfield near Mount Desert Island, the location of Skylands, where Martha lived most summer weekends. I knew it was a beautiful home from what I had seen on TV, but I had no idea how impressive it really was. Skylands had originally been the summer home of the Ford family—yes, as in *Edsel* Ford. Martha had purchased it a few years earlier. Although she had done some modernizing, installing certain conveniences and landscaping and furnishing in classic Martha style, she had maintained much of its original pristine condition. She had thrown *nothing* away when she bought the home fully furnished—even including the handwritten paper place settings for Ford family dinners and all of their books and memorabilia. Martha is a very savvy woman who understood that she had acquired a piece of American history. She lovingly restored the guesthouses, the horse stables, and the grounds to their original glory. Her attention to detail extends to having the groundskeepers lay gravel on all the driveways and walkways each spring, only to sweep it up again and store it each winter so that the ground can breathe and the gravel can be maintained.

If ever a person personifies perfection, it is Martha Stewart. She even makes sure that the quality of the many retail products sold by Kmart under her name is proven by daily use of them in her stately home, where all of the interior furnishings are in shades of gray and Martha's famous green. None looked out of place there. Her taste is exquisite.

After being welcomed, Roma and I were ushered upstairs and into a gorgeous guest suite, with a huge balcony overlooking the sea. We showered, and I threw on my khaki pants and an olive-green shirt. Roma, pretty as ever, dressed in a lovely orange and turquoise summer outfit. Roma looked good in anything, but this morning she looked particularly beautiful. It was great to be away from the production for a couple of days and get to know Martha better.

Roma and I couldn't help smiling as we traipsed downstairs and into a beautiful room where a perfectly laid table awaited us. Martha, her daughter Alexis, and Kevin Sharkey and Hannah Milman (two of Martha's key executives) were already there when we entered the breakfast room. With the biggest smile, Martha looked up from what she was doing and said, "Roma, I don't think I've ever quite seen that color combination in my home before. I must get my camera."

She proceeded to photograph Roma in her beautiful but rather bright outfit against a backdrop of Martha Stewart's subtle greens and grays. Only Martha could get away with this. She didn't look at this as something personal; she merely saw the interesting color combinations and contrasts and delivered the remark in a most unoffending way. Roma, as always, was her gracious self, and afterward we all sat down to the most delicious Martha Stewart breakfast.

The rest of the weekend was filled with delectable meals, great conversation, hiking in the nearby mountains, and even a boat trip to the mainland in Martha's famous picnic boat, which she piloted herself.

The Maine coastline is spectacular. We arrived at a small dock on the mainland, which left us about a mile-long leisurely walk into a small village. It was a pleasant day, and we enjoyed the stroll. I was particularly amused when villagers tending their gardens realized that the woman commenting on their plants was Martha Stewart. After the initial shock, they loved how knowledgeable and approachable she was. As we neared the village, a bus approached. Martha stuck her arm out to stop the bus, and we all climbed aboard.

This remarkable woman seemed to be on the cover of every newspaper on a daily basis. She was enduring the worst muckraking legal accusations imaginable, and yet her demeanor toward everybody was positive and cheerful. She fit into Maine village life like a hand in a glove.

On our last morning at Skylands, and just for fun, we watched a few of Martha's videos. One showed the *correct* way to fold a T-shirt. It reminded me of an origami technique and seemed confusing, but somehow I thought I understood it. So I stepped up and offered to try it. Roma, Alexis, Kevin, and Hannah all smiled expectantly at the mess I was about to make. I took off my shirt, crouched on the floor, and in fifteen seconds did it perfectly. I don't know how, but I did it. Martha loved it, and it was a hilarious ending to one of the best weekends Roma and I have ever spent. Also, I had become closer to Martha than I thought would be possible in such a short time.

After our weekend, a refreshed Roma and I flew back to Los Angeles so that I could finish up the final few days of *The Contender*. The series ended as well as it had begun, with exciting boxing action and a combination of heartbreaking defeats and heroic victories before the most energetically enthusiastic crowd I had ever seen. I loved making *The Contender,* and had not seen such honor since my days in the Parachute Regiment. These boxers were brave and full of integrity. All that remained after the fiercely competitive final few elimination bouts was to hold the finals "live" at Caesars Palace in Las Vegas. The winner would receive $1 million in purse money, with $250,000 going to the runner-up. These professional boxers whom we had rescued from obscurity had never been close to such a payday, and both of them deserved every penny.

In the week before she entered Alderson Federal Prison Camp, I again had dinner with Martha at Town. It was impossible to detect that she was only three days away from incarceration. I admired her more and more. We even visited the kitchen staff at Town, and she joked with them that she hoped tonight's food would be especially good because that privilege was only days away from disappearing. The next day I drove up to visit her television facility in Connecticut, where Martha gave me a personal tour before we taped some "sit down and chat" sessions on the *Martha Stewart Living* TV set in anticipation of selling the updated version. As before, she barely acknowledged what was in store for her, and even then it was only as she reassured her wonderfully articulate ninety-year-old mom that she'd be okay. Martha is so used to working hard that I think she regarded her impending ordeal simply as something she had to do. She would just roll up her sleeves, never complain, and get on with it. An old saying of British prime minister Benjamin Disraeli came to mind as I considered Martha's strength: "Never complain and never explain."

Never complain— never explain.

As I left Connecticut, during the last moments that I would see her before she went to prison, I promised Martha that I would visit her as often as I could during her five-month incarceration. My visits would be entirely social. It was illegal to discuss business with a prisoner, and in a way I was glad of that. I had come to truly enjoy spending social time with Martha, but because we were both fairly driven, conversation invariably turned to business. It would be nice to just chat without the slightest intention of discussing business.

It's probable that lots of people had made such promises to her, but as a new friend, I felt it was important that I make good on mine. I would go to see her in two weeks' time, on my way back home to Los

Angeles from my continued work on *Apprentice 3* in New York. However, the logistics of traveling to visit Martha in prison would be daunting. Her location in West Virginia is not exactly an airline hub. To get
there from New York, I would have to fly to Atlanta, then connect on a
second flight, backtracking to West Virginia. This would take an entire
day. Then I would have to spend the night, meet with Martha the next
day, and spend another night before flying back into Atlanta, then
home the following day. Three whole days for a three-hour meeting—it
didn't seem to be an efficient use of my time and, more important, I
would be trading time with my sons, James and Cameron, in order to
keep my word to Martha. I had to find a solution. The solution was
easy—it just cost money. But my time with my children is worth more
than money. As I did for the Everlast meeting, I rented a private jet to fly
me to West Virginia. I could leave New York early in the morning, see
Martha during morning visiting hours, then fly to California, getting
home to my boys by late afternoon.

A car picked me up in front of Trump International just after six.
Within a half hour I was at Teterboro Airport in New Jersey. The car
drove me straight out on the tarmac to the plane. We took off within
minutes of my arrival. By 8:30 the pilot had come back and announced that we were on our final approach to West Virginia's Green-
brier Valley Airport. I looked out the window and was amazed at how
beautiful the countryside was. The reds and yellows of fall contrasted
sharply with the rolling green hills. The autumn sun was warm on my
face as I stepped off the plane. I was struck by the odd thought that, as
usual, I was perfectly happy in such a beautiful outdoor environment,
but I doubted I'd be feeling so happy if I were forced to spend time
there, as Martha was.

My thoughts turned totally to her as I made the one-hour drive to
the prison. How was she doing? What was it like at Alderson? I had
read awful reports of violence and terror in the tabloids and could only
hope they were gross exaggerations.

My driver was an older local man who'd recently retired from dairy farming. He had an interesting accent and a friendly, rural disposition. As we drove through some of the most stunning fall foliage I have ever seen, we chatted. It didn't take him long to figure out why I was going to Alderson. Flying in on a private jet was a huge clue, and I wasn't about to lie. The driver made it perfectly clear that he and all the locals were thrilled to have Martha in their community, and that they believed she had gotten a raw deal. I chose to reveal nothing about Martha and simply be warm and polite. As we approached Alderson, it was obvious that he knew the drill, explaining to me that he would have to drop me off before the security gate and wouldn't be allowed to park and wait for me. He'd have to come back at a predetermined time. We agreed upon three hours later, at 1 P.M. He also told me that once I passed through the gates, I was on the "inside." I would not be able to leave and reenter, so I'd better make sure I had everything I needed. He stopped short of the ominous-looking security gate. As I got out, he said, "Make sure you tell Martha, sir, that we're all proud to have her here, and would be proud to have her or her family buy a house hereabouts. Yes, sir."

He was genuinely sweet, part of the heart and soul of our country. I assured him I would pass his message along. I entered through the guard gate and signed in at the visitor center. The guard who signed me in was jovial. As I struggled to write Martha's prisoner number on the form, he rattled off her digits, rapid-fire: "55170-054, Stewart, Martha. That's one I obviously know," he said with a huge, friendly laugh.

My first impression of life inside Alderson came from this guard, and my fears were somehow immediately calmed. He telephoned somebody to let Martha know I had arrived. I stepped away to gaze through the visiting-room windows at the inside of the prison. It was a beautiful old brick facility, built shortly after the turn of the century for suffragettes. I found this ironic. The very facility that had been built especially to house women who were imprisoned *because* they dared to protest for the right to vote now housed about one thousand women who, as convicted felons, would *never* again be allowed to vote. Martha would later tell me that this was one aspect of her punishment that saddened her almost as much as losing her privacy and freedom in this five months away from home. She cherished her right to vote. Personally, I don't understand why those who have paid their price to society and come back to begin life again cannot vote. It makes no sense.

The facility looked like a well-organized all-woman military academy. Manicured grounds separated the several beautiful brick buildings, and pairs of women walked along the pathways—they were not marching, but they were controlled. I again noticed the splendor of fall, the manicured green grass dotted with the reds, yellows, and oranges of fallen leaves, which had been raked into piles. Everything was shipshape—or should I say "prison shape." Clearly, the guards weren't out raking leaves. All in all, Alderson seemed as pleasant as you could hope for a prison. I searched the grounds for a view of Martha, my excitement growing. Then I saw her. She looked similar to the way she had looked at Skylands: tennis shoes, khaki pants, and a green workshirt.

As Martha entered the visitor center, all the prisoners and their families stared, and a few people whispered, "Look, it's Martha."

The guard with the sense of humor changed his tone to serious. "We'll have none of that here. Settle down and mind your own business."

Another good sign. This place was run tightly. I knew she would be safe.

Martha came over and gave me a hug. She invited me outside to walk in the small visitors' garden. It had become a beautiful fall day, and we pulled up a couple of chairs and sat in the sun, careful to sit with our backs to the hillside across the way. "Paparazzi," she explained. Even here, Martha couldn't escape her fishbowl life.

After reassuring me that she was doing fine, we chatted over the next three hours about prison life, families, travel, and the fall colors. It was a pleasure simply to converse. Martha explained to me that she had been tasked later that day with cleaning the floor-waxing machine, a job that most people would loathe. Martha, however, relishes this sort of work and had asked the prison guards for paraffin, turpentine, and other necessary items in anticipation of getting the job done. She is unafraid of hard work, and enjoys problem solving. I am confident that this powerful side of her personality will combine with my Jump In philosophy to make for some dynamic business ventures in the years to come.

I returned to New York a few weeks later to meet with several of Martha Stewart's board members. In the months prior to her incarceration, her company had begun to beef up its board. Two of its newest members came from the media industry. One, Charles Koppelman, had built an empire in music publishing, and had worked with Billy Joel, Barbra Streisand and, most recently, Michael Jackson. He is a very astute businessman who recognizes the long-term solid value of Martha's company. Charles and I got along well, sharing similar visions of how to add to Martha's value. The other board member was a top-notch executive named Susan Lyne—yes, Susan Lyne, the former head of ABC, who prior to that had been a major player in the publishing industry.

I had gotten to know Susan well through various Hollywood functions, and also through pitching her *The Apprentice* and *The Contender*. She had realized that both shows would do well but, as with Lloyd Braun, her copresident at ABC, her hands were tied by the Disney corporate structure and she couldn't bid for them. It is worth noting that it was Susan, who, prior to resigning from ABC, had given the greenlight to *Desperate Housewives*. This has turned around the fortunes of ABC, leaving Fox firmly in last place among the big four networks.

Working with Susan and Charles was a pleasure. I was not surprised when it was reported in the news in mid-November that Susan Lyne had replaced Sharon Patrick as Martha Stewart's new CEO. Sharon had served Martha well, but clearly the board thought it was time for a change in anticipation of Martha's return to the company in 2005. I couldn't think of a more experienced, more qualified, and more dynamic new leader than Susan Lyne. It was with this added bonus that I contemplated Martha's return and the exciting business we could do together.

Epilogue

I often find myself looking back over the last twenty years, totally amazed at all that has come to pass. I arrived in America as a naïve kid looking for military work in Nicaragua, but did a "one-eighty," and following my intuition took a job as a nanny in Beverly Hills. A few years later I was pursuing the American dream. I may only have been selling T-shirts on Venice Beach, but it was my own thriving business.

Then a decade ago, I "jumped in" and got into entertainment, a business I knew nothing about. I certainly did not know how to swim. I was frantically trying to wrangle financing for the first *Eco-Challenge*, working out of a small bedroom office. But the key was that I was passionate about what I was trying to create back then. I followed my instinct. I believed. Nothing has changed since those beginnings of *Eco-Challenge*, except the scale. I am just as passionate about what I am trying to create now as I was in those early days. I continually take risks and I always try to reinvent to keep things fresh.

That's the key.

For instance, I'm thrilled with how *Apprentice 3* is shaping up. It has a different theme from our two previous seasons. Twice now we focused on the question of the glass ceiling in business, and watched men and women duke it out in the boardroom. But for *Apprentice 3* we had over one million applicants downloading the application from NBC.com, which made it possible to try to fulfill my original promise to NBC. Surely, from this enormous number, we could find nine highly successful entrepreneurs who have only high school educations, to compete against nine highly educated college graduates who now were successful business executives. Find them we did.

Apprentice 3 is *Book Smart* versus *Street Smart*. Both groups had about the same average age and about the same high IQ. The big difference was that the high school grads earned an average of $300,000, which was *three times* that of the college grads. Both groups believed they would kick the others' butt. The game was on.

The next *Survivor* will be *Survivor: Palau*, set on a small island nation in Micronesia. It is truly the most beautiful location we have ever filmed at. The water is literally turquoise and the hundreds of islands that make up this little country are pristine. I had heard of the incredible undersea life that Palau had to offer but what I saw and what we filmed surpassed even my wildest expectations.

Once again I have reinvented the classic game of *Survivor* and this time the entire experience starts in a way viewers have never seen before. The survivors themselves didn't know what to think and were completely off balance for days. I have always believed that the key to getting at people's true emotions is through peeling away the fake veneer that we all use as a protective device. New, uncertain and confusing situations cause us to immediately get real. *Survivor: Palau* took them there instantly and the immediate ensuing drama was raw. It will be a great series.

I've also continued to re-invent our business models. I am committed to never doing business deals in a traditional way simply because that's how *"it's always been done."* Part of this innovative business approach has been the acquisition of stock warrants in both Everlast and Martha Stewart Omnimedia. I'm also thrilled about the ongoing process of owning a portion of the TV commercials and integrating the products of those companies that sponsor my shows.

I've come a long way since my initial television sponsorship deals, which were designed as an absolute "necessity" for *Eco-Challenge* to *even* survive. Those early days of learning to integrate sponsors into a television show had become successful, partly through my naïveté and partly through pure tenacity. It was this "in the trenches," hands-on experience of mine that convinced Leslie Moonves to take the initial risk on *Survivor*. It was these early deals, using clever product placements to add value to advertisers, which ended up making *Survivor* far more profitable for CBS. What initially started on *Eco-Challenge* as a way to scrape by had now come full circle. Sponsorship sales are now an integral part of my business plan.

What do the next few years hold for Mark Burnett Productions?

The first week of December 2004 was a great indicator of the direction in which my company and I are now headed. It began when Jeffrey Katzenberg and I flew to Madagascar aboard the DreamWorks jet. Jeffrey was going there in preparation for his next animated film, *Madagascar,* to be released in the summer of 2005, while I was researching future *Survivor* locations. More than ten years after the Red Island had taught me the valuable lessons that would one day lead to my success, I was returning. I had come so far as a businessman and father in those years. The significance of coming back to this special place one more time was not lost on me.

Next we flew to New York. On the same day, in different parts of the city, both of us made important announcements. Jeffrey held a press conference to tell of DreamWorks's phenomenal corporate earnings for 2004, while I appeared before the press with Jeff Zucker and Susan Lyne in Martha Stewart's west side corporate offices to announce her new syndicated daytime show, which will air on NBC starting in the fall of 2005. It was an incredible day and the Martha Stewart Omnimedia stock price rose to $26.66—the highest it had been since January 2001. This reinforced that my gut feeling about being in business with Martha had been right.

But I wasn't through. As night fell over Manhattan, Jeffrey and I flew by helicopter to Athens, New York, where Steven Spielberg and

Tom Cruise were filming *War of the Worlds* with a cast of more than one thousand. Also there, producing the movie for Steven, was Kathleen Kennedy, one of the most successful movie producers in history. Everyone there was so inclusive, even taking the time to show me how the shots were planned and executed. It was a lesson in filmmaking from two ultimate geniuses of the business. Believe me, I was like a kid in a candy store. I know I must make a movie.

When I look ahead, I see us as successful in syndicated TV through my business with Martha. I also see us in the music business through my CBS show, where we are going to search for a rock superstar to become the new lead singer of the Australian rock band INXS. And movies have to be on my horizon. That day with the "triple black" Firebird, when I met Steven Spielberg for the very first time, inspired me so much that I know that I *have* to make a movie. It scares me, but I have to try. But most of all, I am thankful for the opportunities I've had and the friends I've made along the way. Who'd have thought it?

Ten years from now I'll be looking back again, hopefully amazed at another decade of risk-taking and bold business adventures. As I've mentioned already, Jump In is more than a business philosophy, it's a mindset. Life is too short to be timid. The key to my continued success is to not let the scale to which my company has grown, cause me to become too analytical. Too cautious. Taking risks has worked for me and I promise to keep "Jumping In."

So if you have an idea, a passion, a belief. Go ahead, Jump In. What're you waiting for?

ABOUT THE AUTHOR

Emmy Award-winning television producer MARK BURNETT was recently featured in *Time* magazine's "Time 100" list of the most influential people in the world today; named on the "Top 101 Most Powerful People in Entertainment" list by *Entertainment Weekly;* and garnered the #1 position on *TV Guide*'s "Most Valuable Players" list. He has produced three *Apprentice*s, ten *Survivor*s, nine *Eco-Challenge*s, and will soon premiere his new series, *The Contender*

ABOUT THE TYPE

This book was set in Arepo. Recently designed, Arepo has a strong calligraphic influence. It's designer, Sumner Stone, studied calligraphy and mathematics in college, but decided to make a career in type. His calligraphic skills led him to Hallmark and ultimately to Adobe Systems, where he was director of type developement and head of a team that would make new digital versions of the classic typefaces for the computer revolution. The name *Arepo* is part of a magic palindrome found as grafitti in ancient Rome.